11 Plus Non-Verbal Ability Workbook

A workbook teaching both the 2D and 3D techniques required for both CEM and GL exams.

Author: Christine R. Draper and Phillip R. Draper

The answers are available separately or at: http://www.achieve2day.co.uk/workbooks

Published: achieve2day, Slough, 2016

ISBN: 978-1-909986-32-9

# INDEX

# CHAPTER 1: SHAPES AND FILLS

NVR simply consists of shapes that move and change.

Shapes can have straight sides,

e.g.:

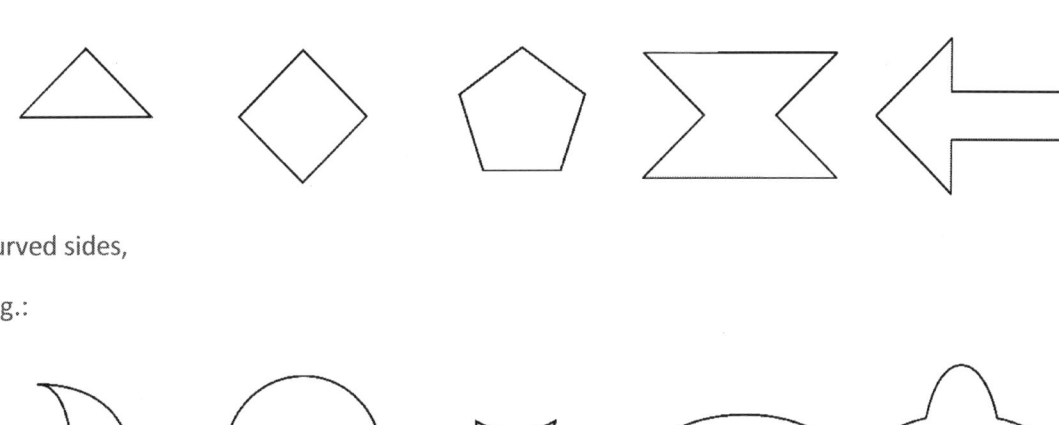

curved sides,

e.g.:

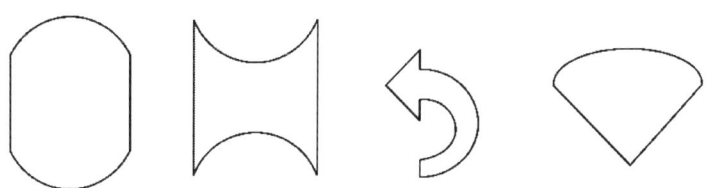

or both:

e.g.:

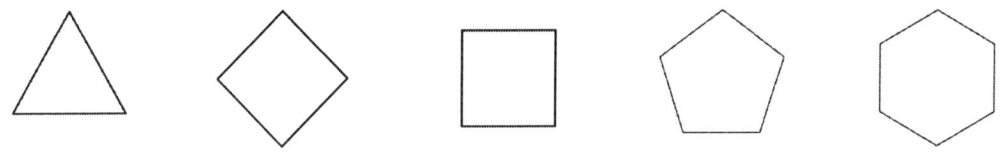

Shapes with straight sides can be regular – i.e. all sides having the same length

e.g.:

or irregular e.g.:

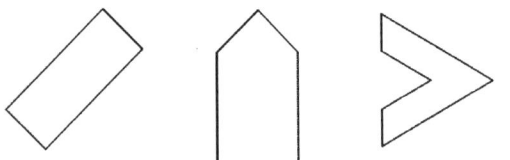

Shapes can have different types of fills.

Such as:          lines,          dotted          block          or liquid fills.

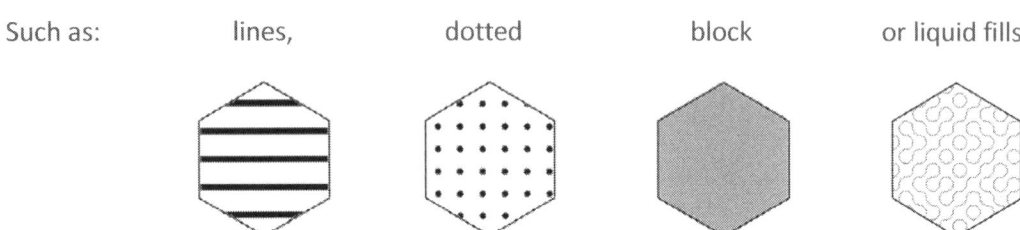

These fills can be different shades, from light to dark.  e.g.:

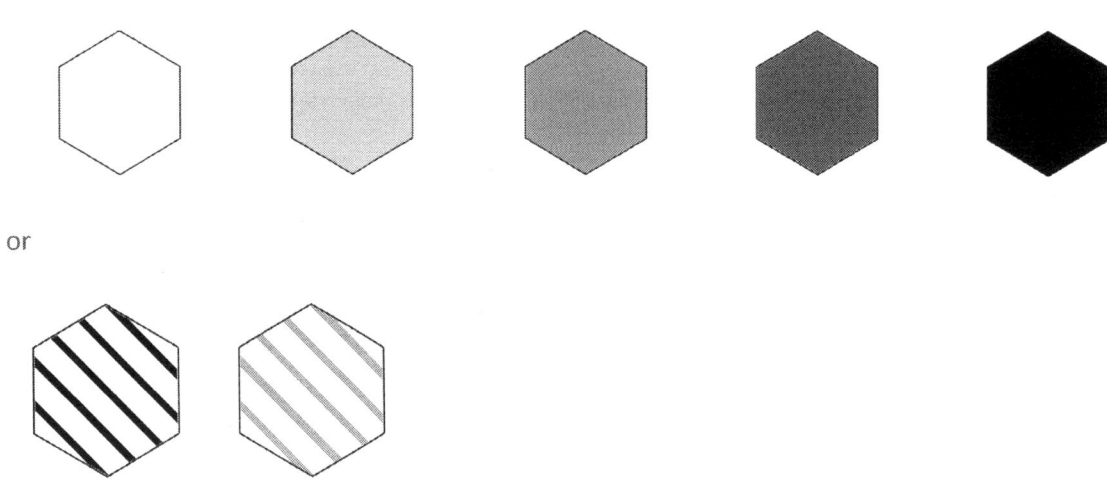

or

Far apart or close together.

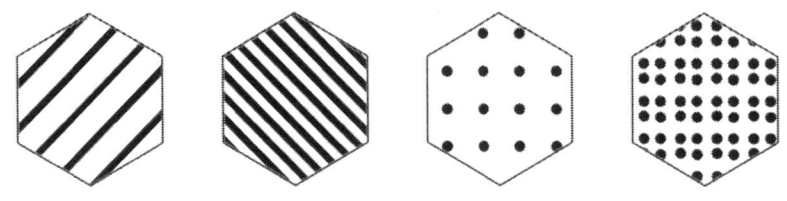

Practice questions

In the questions below choose all that apply.

1.  Which shapes have curved sides?

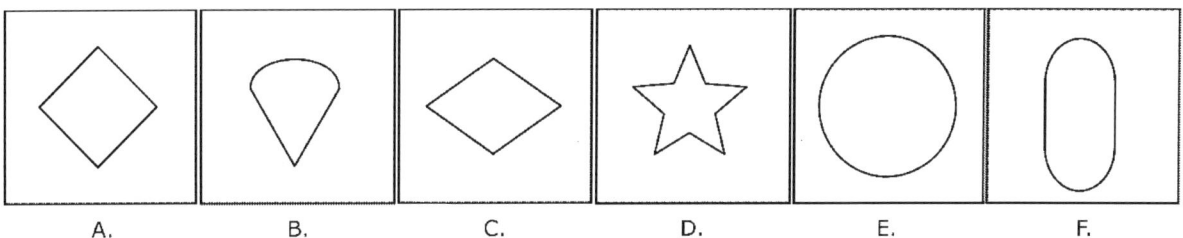

A.  B.  C.  D.  E.  F.

2.  Which of these shapes are not regular?

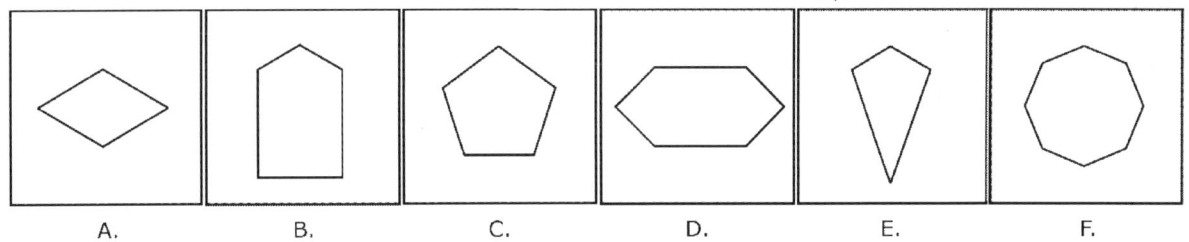

A.  B.  C.  D.  E.  F.

3.  Which of these shapes have similar fills?

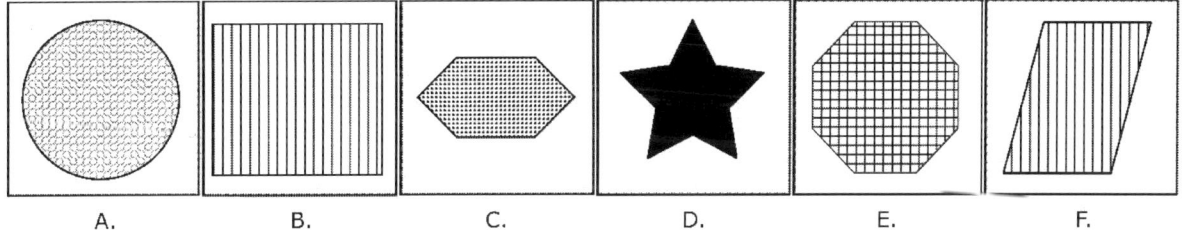

A.  B.  C.  D.  E.  F.

4.  Which of these shapes have six sides?

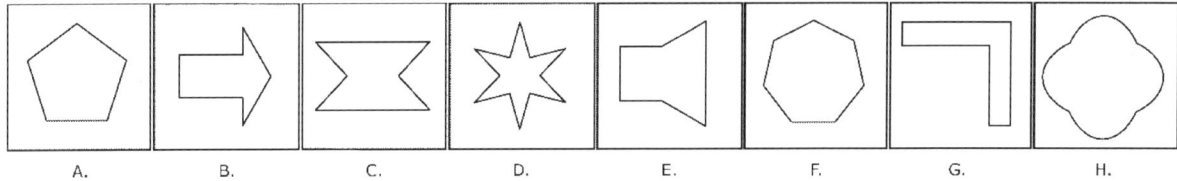

A.  B.  C.  D.  E.  F.  G.  H.

# EXERCISE 1
Which is the odd one out?

1.

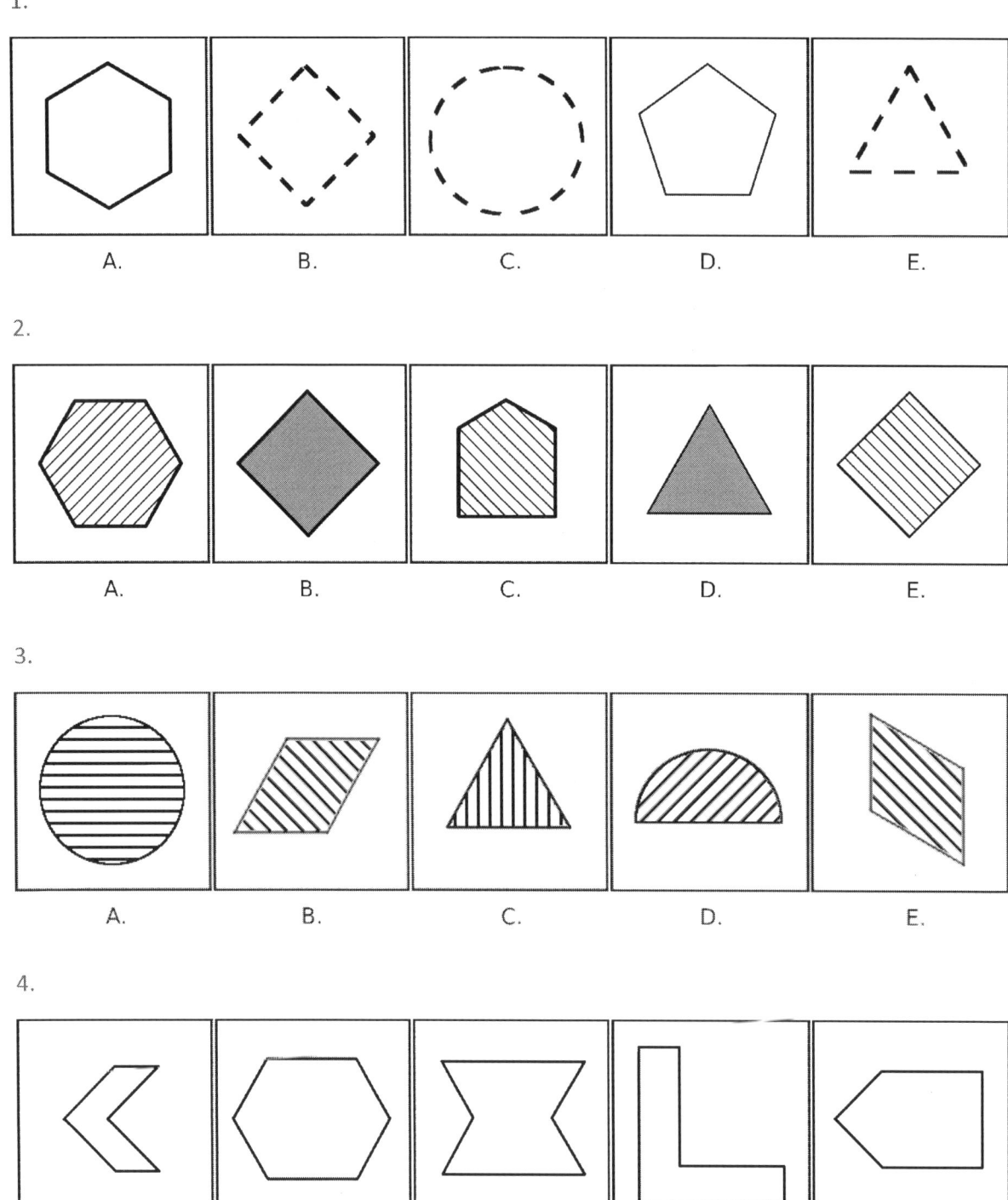

2.

3.

4.

A.          B.          C.          D.          E.

5.

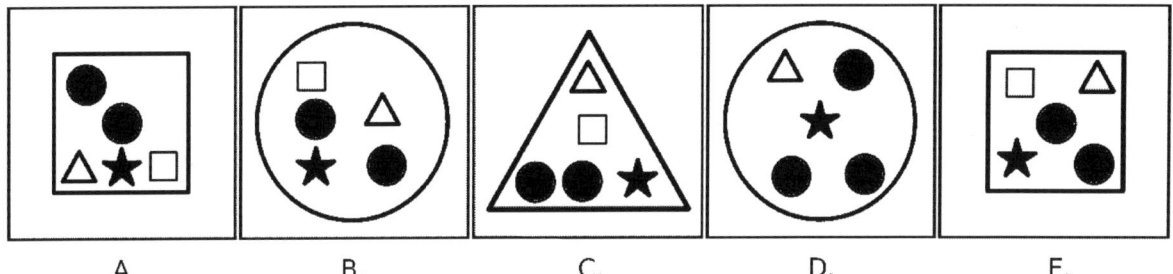

A.        B.        C.        D.        E.

6.

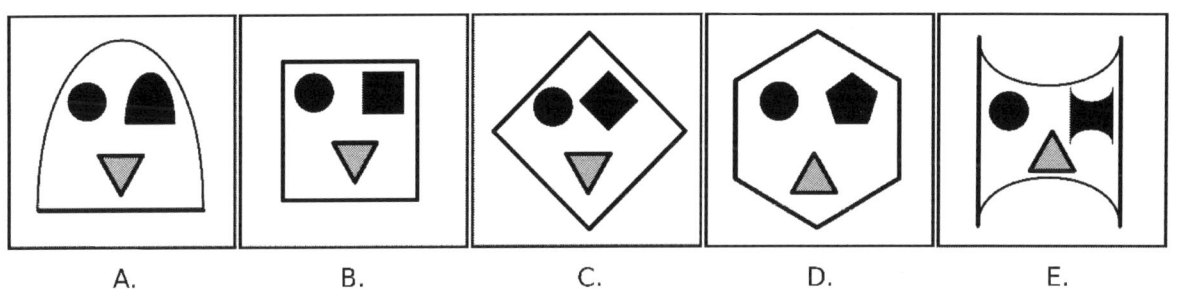

A.        B.        C.        D.        E.

What figure is missing from the series below?

7.

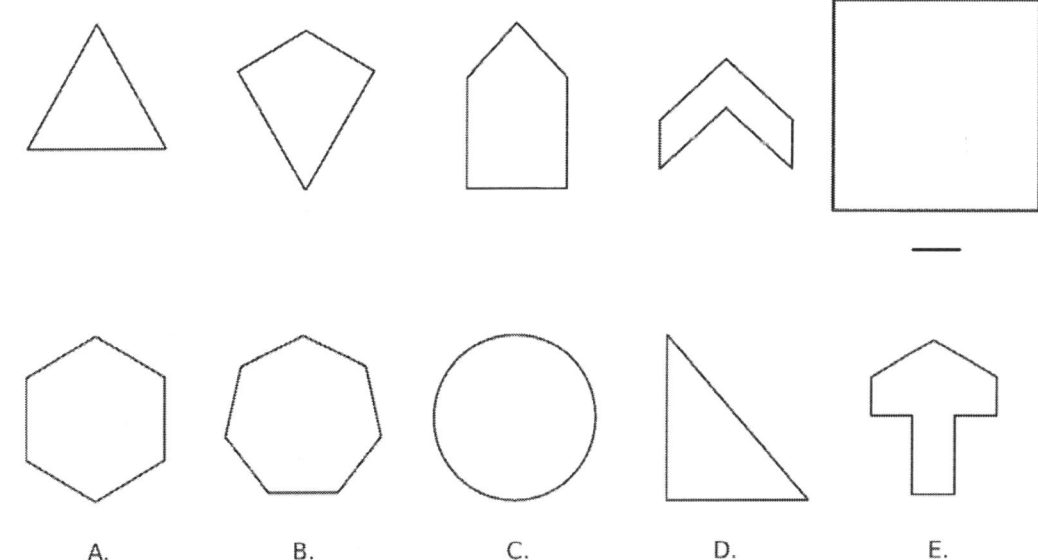

A.        B.        C.        D.        E.

8.

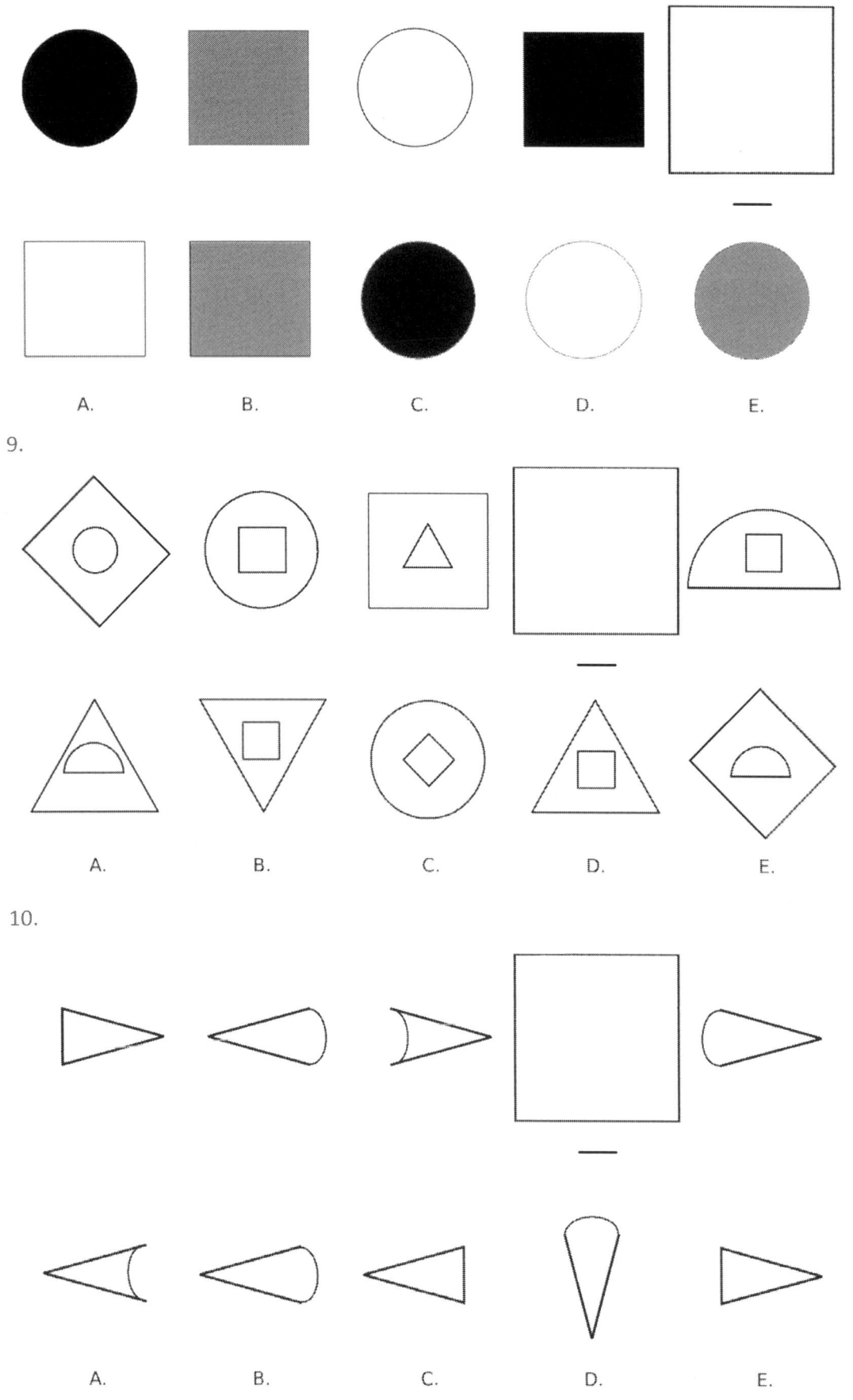

A.　　B.　　C.　　D.　　E.

9.

A.　　B.　　C.　　D.　　E.

10.

A.　　B.　　C.　　D.　　E.

# CHAPTER 2: LINES

Shapes can be drawn with different lines.

Lines can be:

Thick ▬▬▬▬▬ or thin, ——————

Solid, —————— dashed ━ ━ ━ ━ or dotted. •••••••••••••

Black —————— or grey ▬▬▬▬▬

## PRACTICE QUESTIONS.

In the questions below choose all that apply.

1: Which shapes have curved lines?

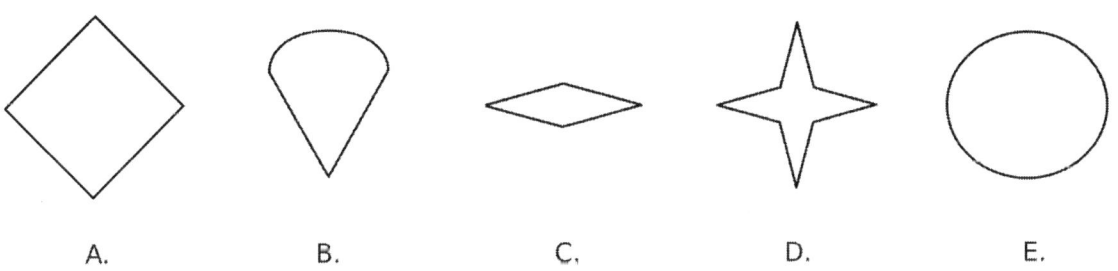

|       |       |       |       |       |
|-------|-------|-------|-------|-------|
| A.    | B.    | C,    | D.    | E.    |

2: Which have four lines?

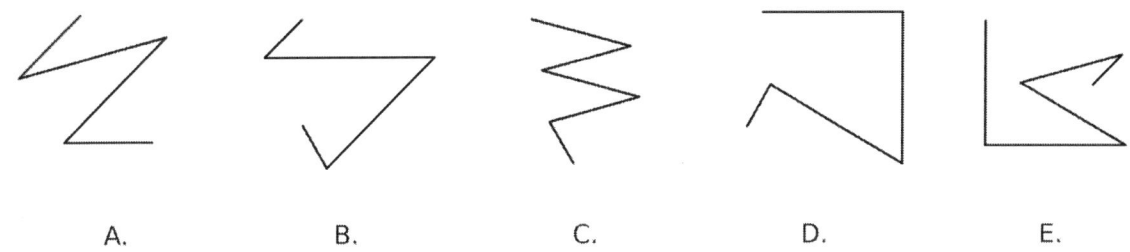

|       |       |       |       |       |
|-------|-------|-------|-------|-------|
| A.    | B.    | C.    | D.    | E.    |

3:  Which have dotted lines?

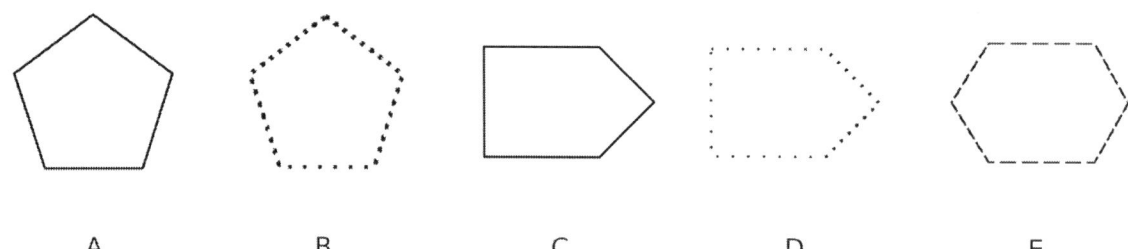

| A. | B. | C. | D. | E. |

4: Which have two thick lines?

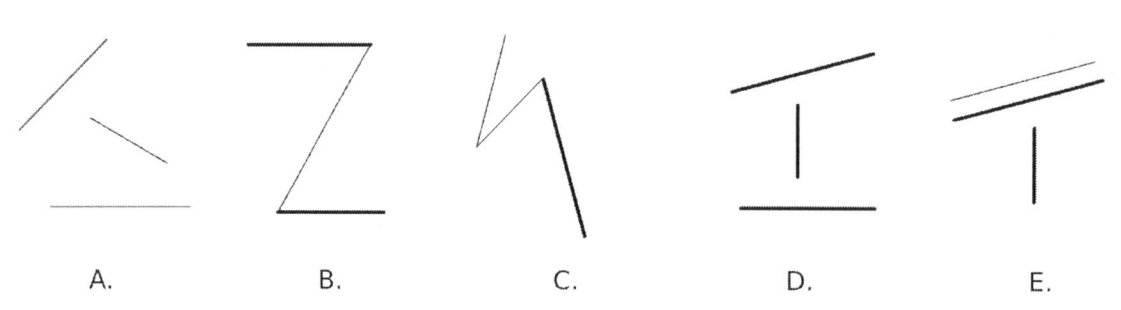

| A. | B. | C. | D. | E. |

## EXERCISE 2:
Which is the odd one out?

1.

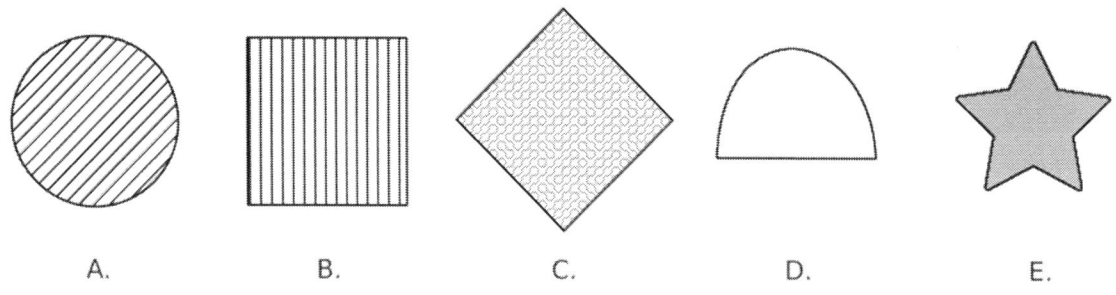

| A. | B. | C. | D. | E. |

2.

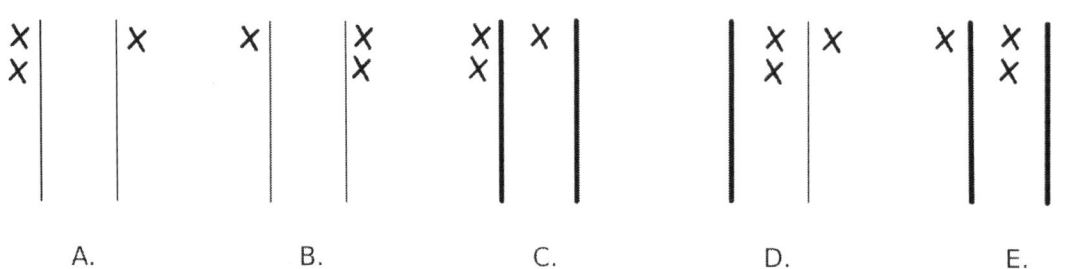

| A. | B. | C. | D. | E. |

3.

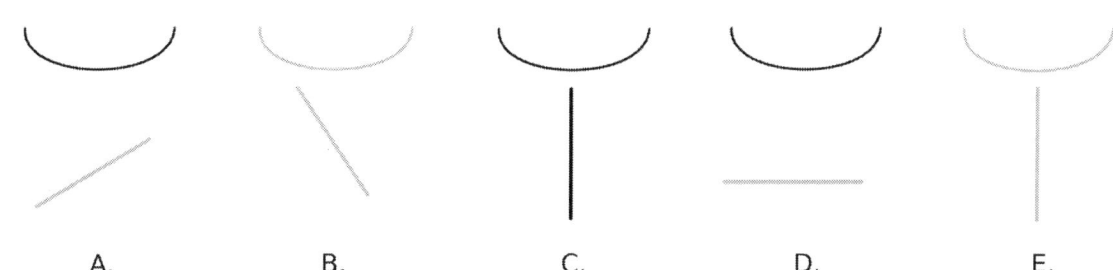

A.          B.          C.          D.          E.

4.

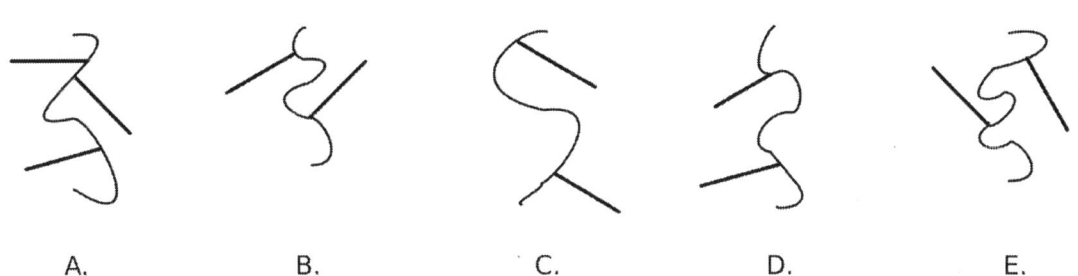

A.          B.          C.          D.          E.

5.

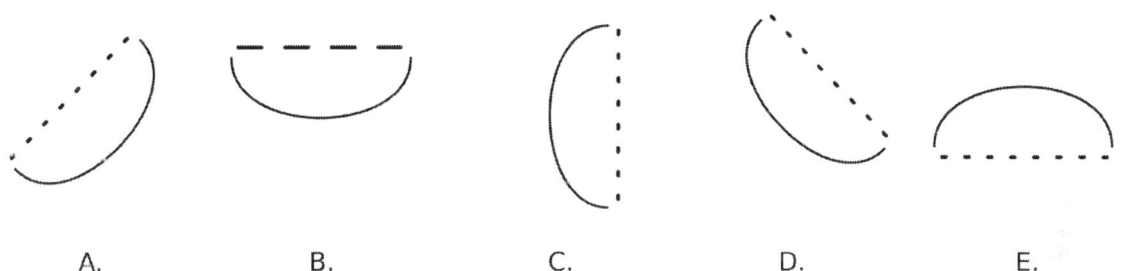

A.          B.          C.          D.          E.

Which shape is needed?

6.

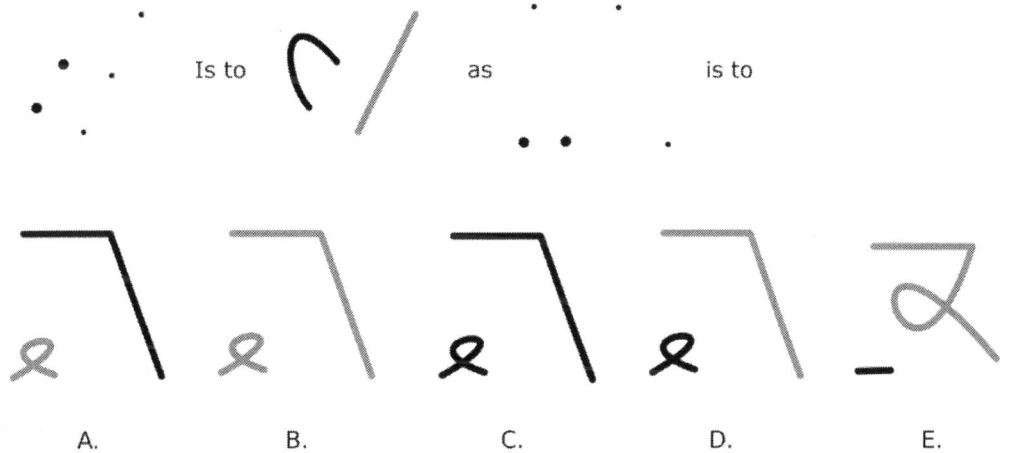

A.          B.          C.          D.          E.

11

7.

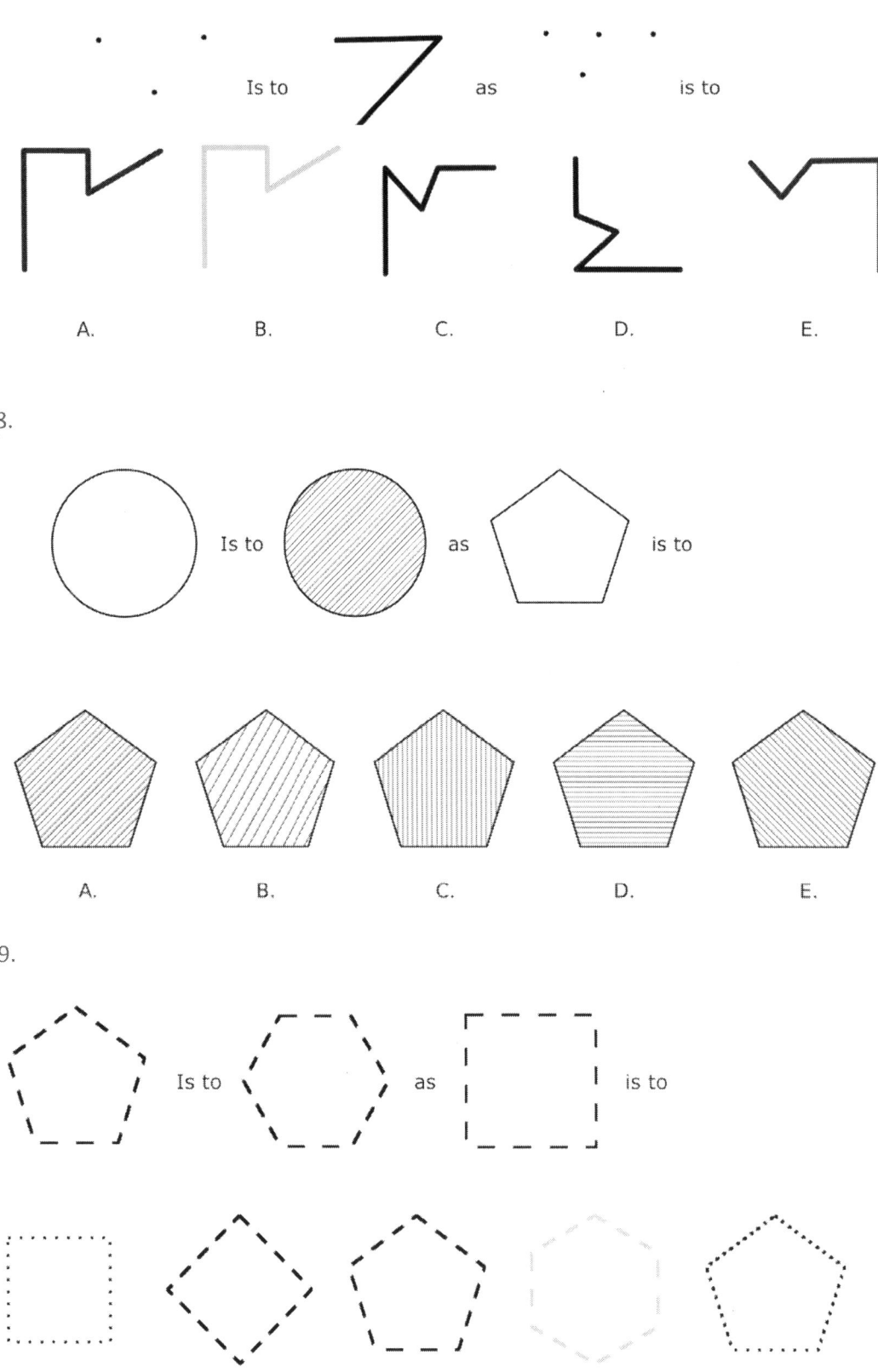

Is to · · · as · · · is to

A.    B.    C.    D.    E.

8.

Is to    as    is to

A.    B.    C.    D.    E.

9.

Is to    as    is to

A.    B.    C.    D.    E.

12

10.

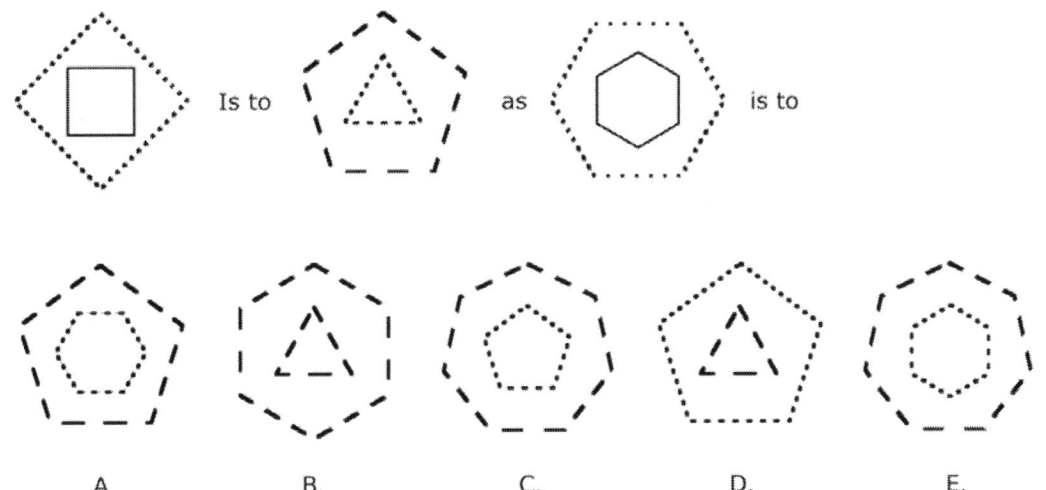

A.

B.

C.

D.

E.

# CHAPTER 3: ARROWS

A common shape occurring in NVR questions is the arrow:

Arrows can:

       Point to different shapes
       Point in different directions
       Point clockwise or anti clockwise
       Have different arrowheads
       Be curved or straight.

Besides arrows, other shapes such as triangles and chevrons ( &#8811; ) can point and are used in the same way.

Practice questions

    1.      Which arrow head is an equilateral triangle?

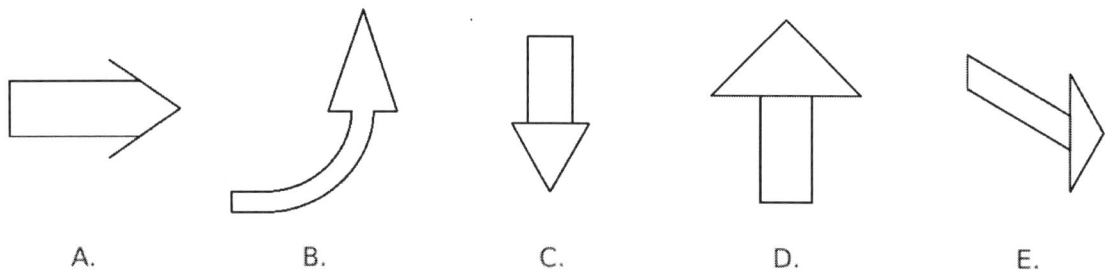

     A.            B.            C.            D.            E.

    2.      Which has three arrows pointing clockwise?

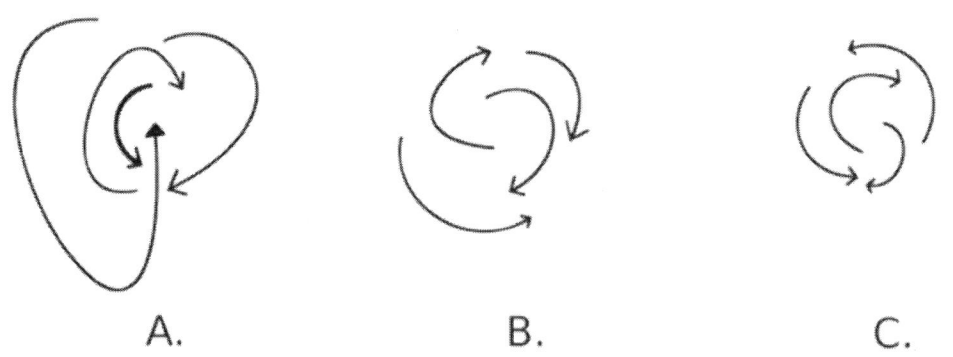

        A.                    B.                    C.

3. Which has the arrow pointing towards the circle?

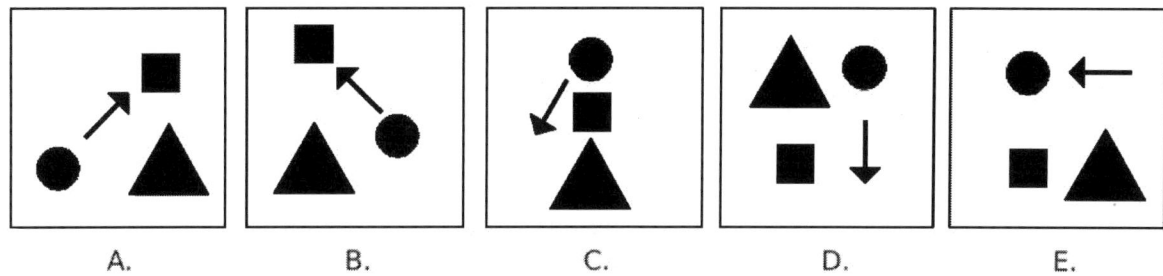

A.          B.          C.          D.          E.

4. In which of the following does the arrow point left?

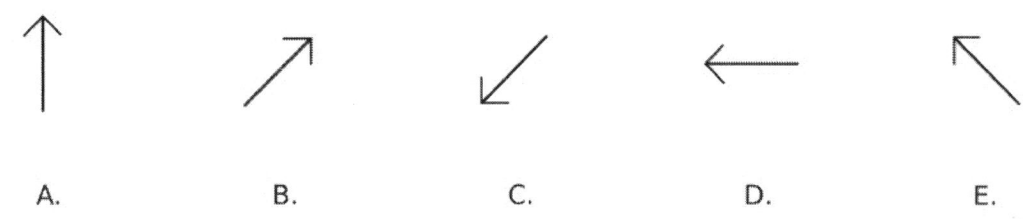

A.          B.          C.          D.          E.

# EXERCISE 3

Which of the figures on the right is most like the two example figures on the left:

1.

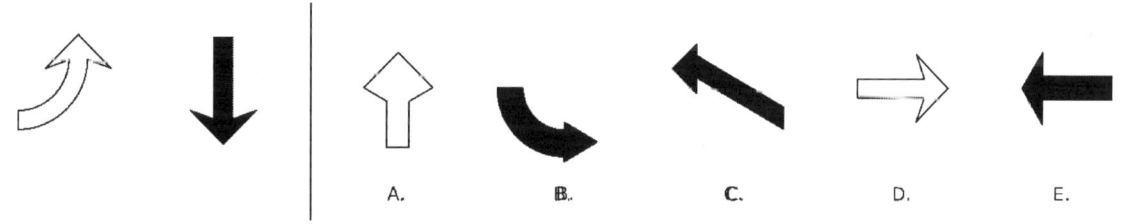

A.          B.          C.          D.          E.

2.

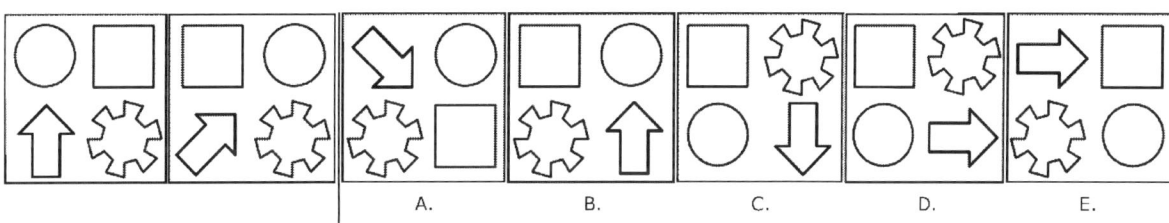

A.          B.          C.          D.          E.

15

3.

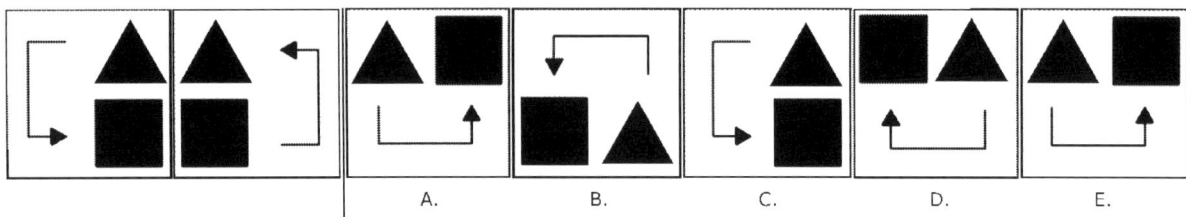

|  | A. | B. | C. | D. | E. |

4.

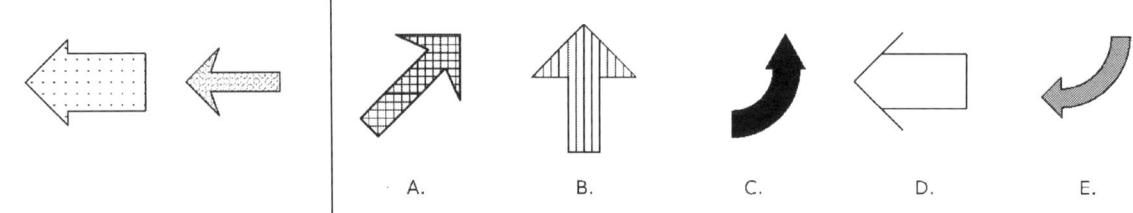

|  | A. | B. | C. | D. | E. |

5.

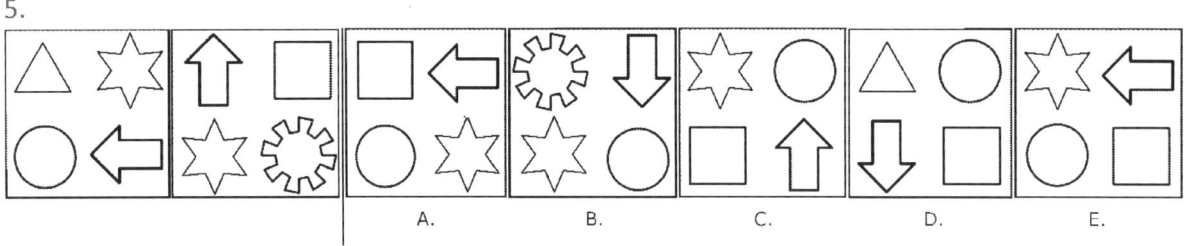

|  | A. | B. | C. | D. | E. |

There is one example that doesn't fit with the others below, find it:

6.

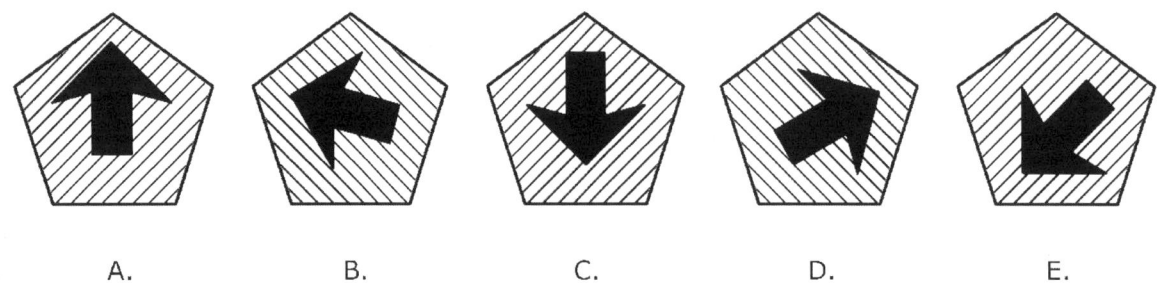

| A. | B. | C. | D. | E. |

7.

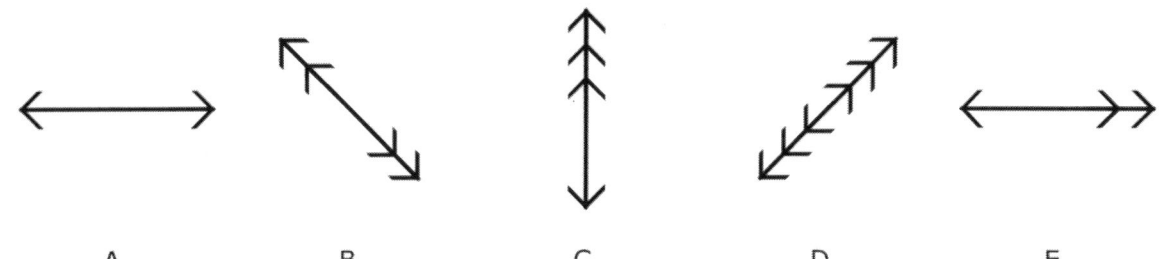

A.      B.      C.      D.      E.

8.

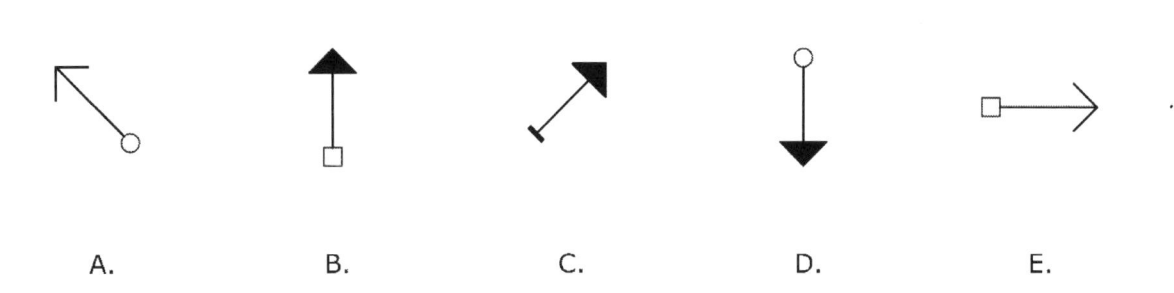

A.      B.      C.      D.      E.

9.

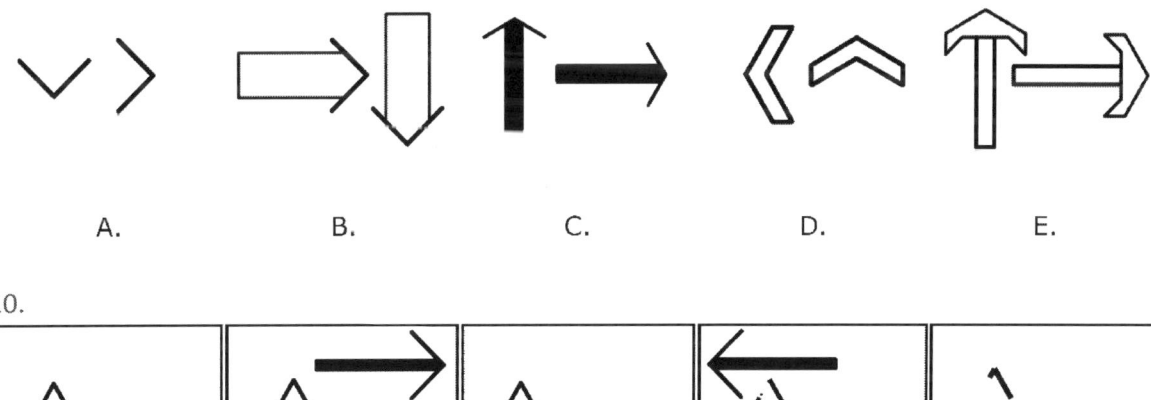

A.      B.      C.      D.      E.

10.

A.      B.      C.      D.      E.

# CHAPTER 4: ELIMINATION

The key to answering non-verbal reasoning questions is elimination.  Elimination should be used for all types of non-verbal reasoning questions except codes.


To answer a non-verbal reasoning question:

Look at one aspect of the question
Eliminate any answers that do not fit – crossing out the letter(s) underneath the figure (so you know that it is eliminated and don't waste time going back over it)
Look at another aspect of the question
Eliminate
Repeat until only one possible answer is left

Example:

Which figure (to the right) is most similar to the shapes on the left?

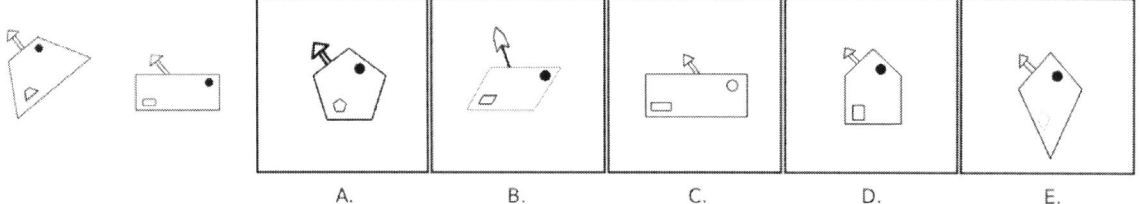

Looking at the two example shapes on the left: both large shapes have four sides; therefore, we can eliminate figures A and D.

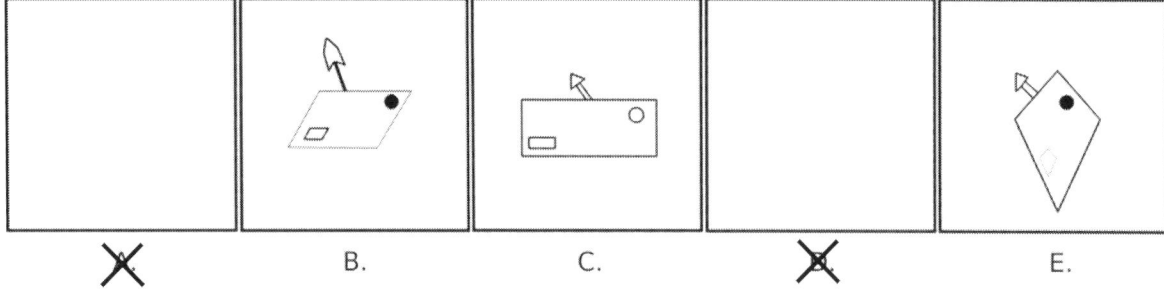

With the remaining shapes, only two of them have a solid black circle at the top, so we can eliminate C.

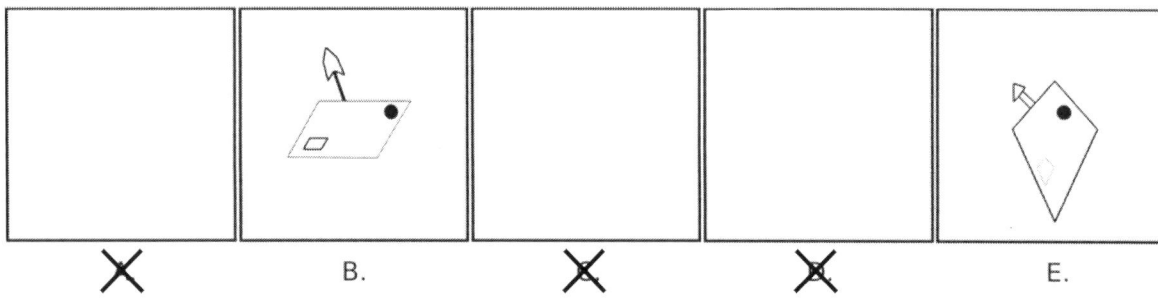

The bottom shape is the same as the outside shape, as all of the remaining possibilities have. The arrowheads are the same (a triangle) so we can eliminate B.

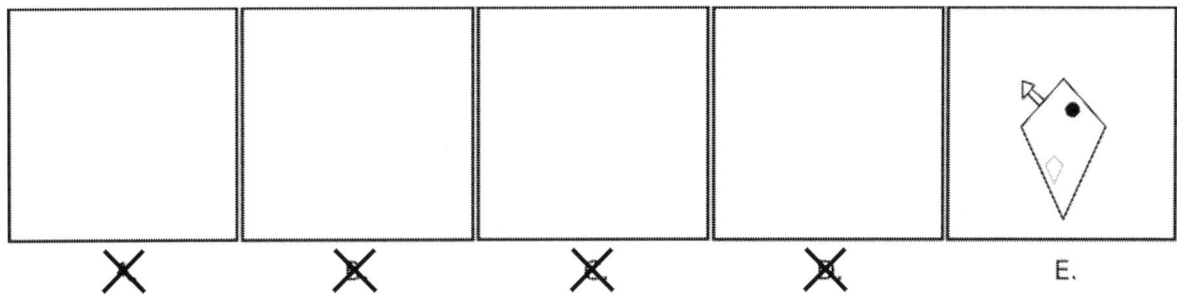

E.

Thus we have our answer, E. It helps to cross off each incorrect answer as you work the problem through, you will then know when you are left with only one (hopefully correct) alternative.

## EXERCISE 4
Which figure, on the right, is most similar to the two figures on the left?

1.

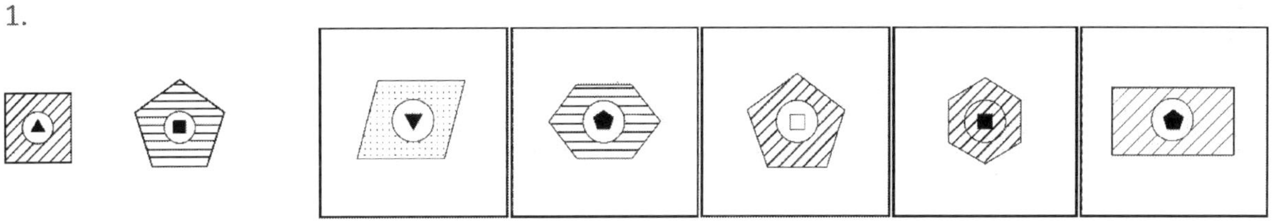

A.    B.    C.    D.    E.

2.

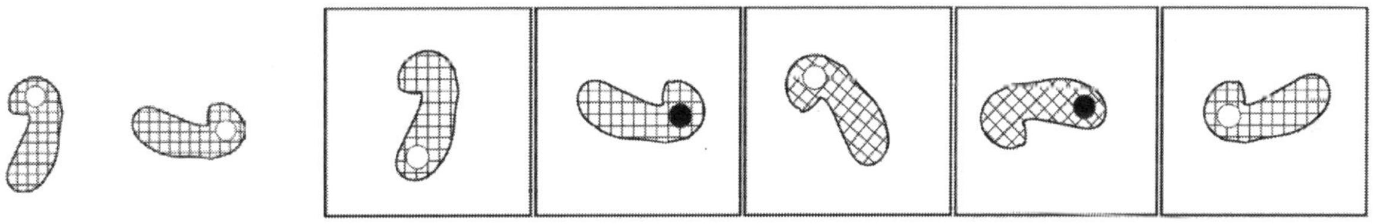

A.    B.    C.    D.    E.

3.

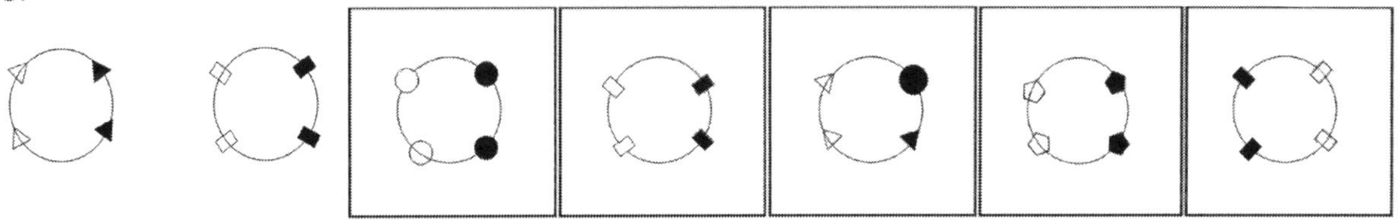

A.    B.    C.    D.    E.

4.

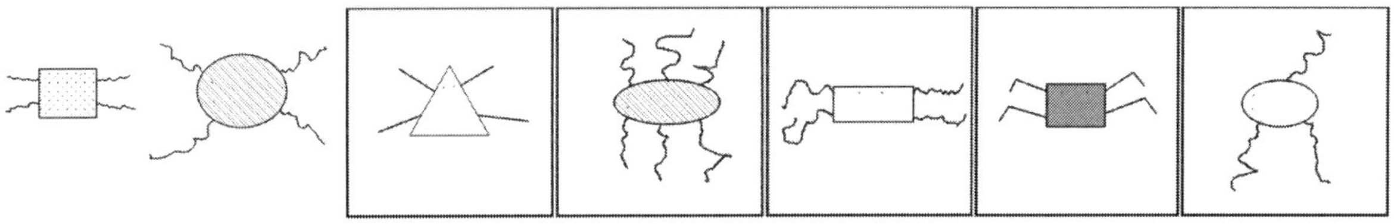

A.    B.    C.    D.    E.

5.

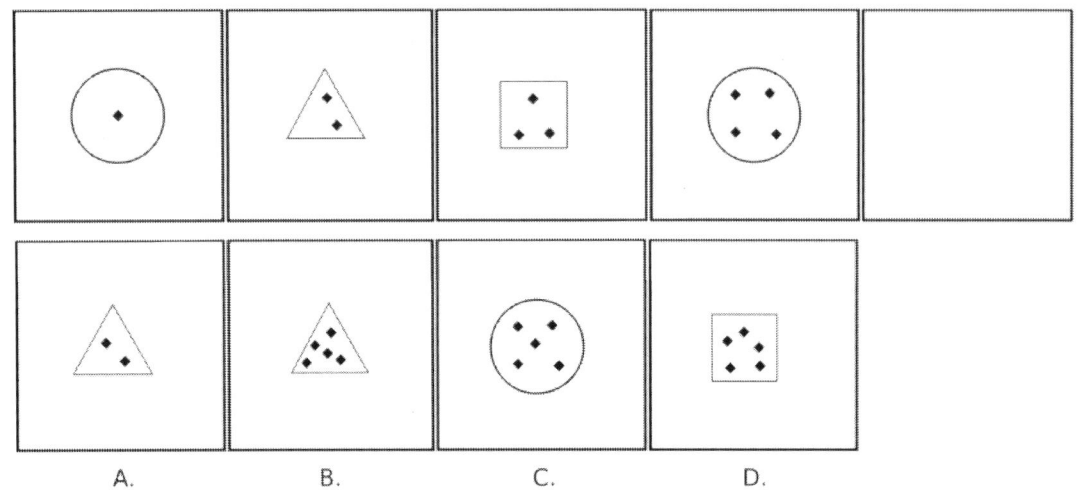

| | | | | |
|---|---|---|---|---|
| A. | B. | C. | D. | E. |

Which figure completes the series correctly?

6.

| | | | | |
|---|---|---|---|---|

| | | | |
|---|---|---|---|
| A. | B. | C. | D. |

7.

| | | | | |
|---|---|---|---|---|

| | | | |
|---|---|---|---|
| A. | B. | C. | D. |

8.

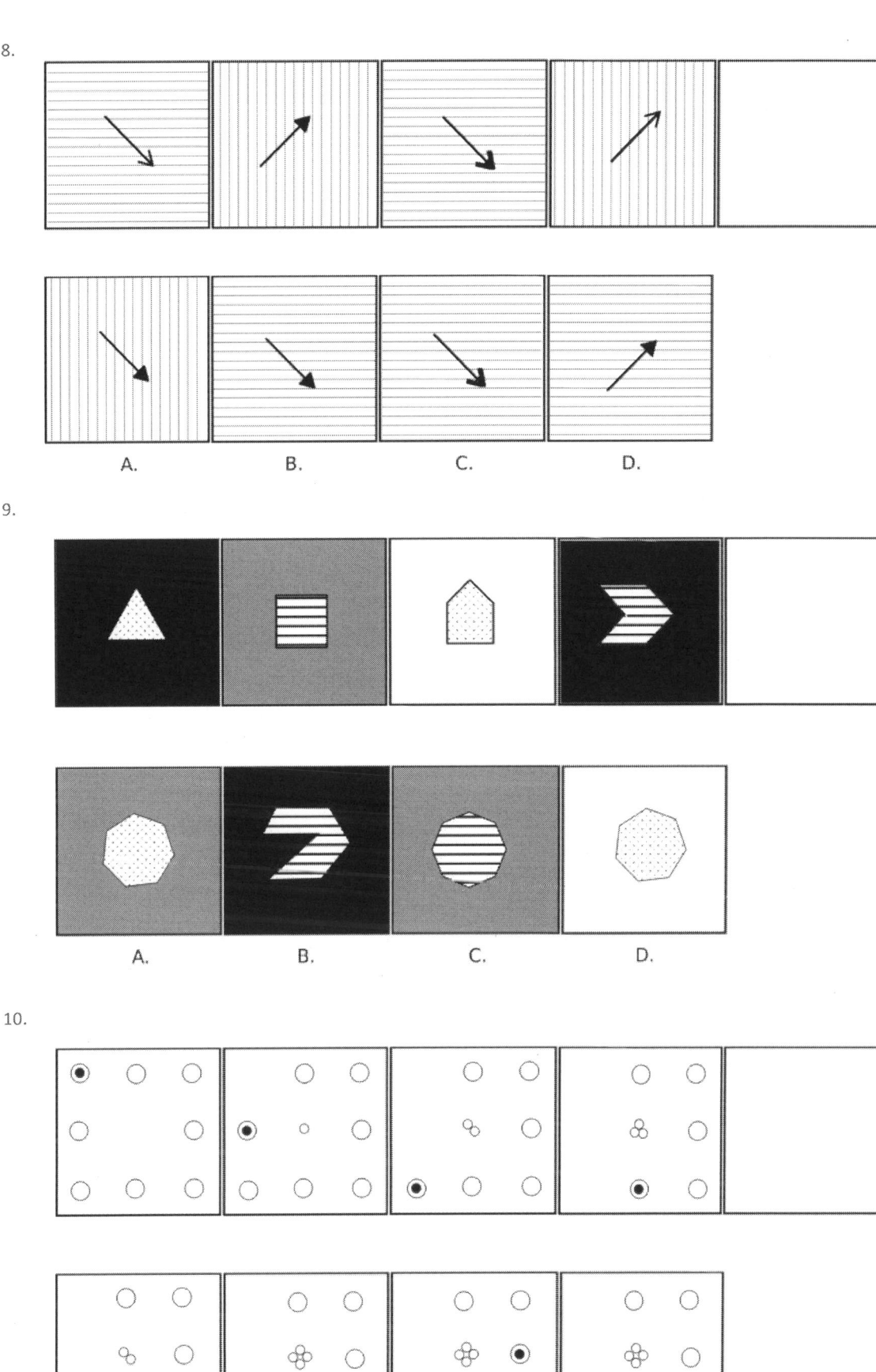

9.

10.

# CHAPTER 5: COUNTING

If you are unsure of where to start in solving a Non Verbal Reasoning question - start by counting.

This can include:

      Counting whole shapes.
      Counting parts of shapes (e.g. number of sides).
      Counting two things and finding the difference between them.
      Counting two or more things and seeing what happens when they are added together.

Example.

Which shape is the odd one out?

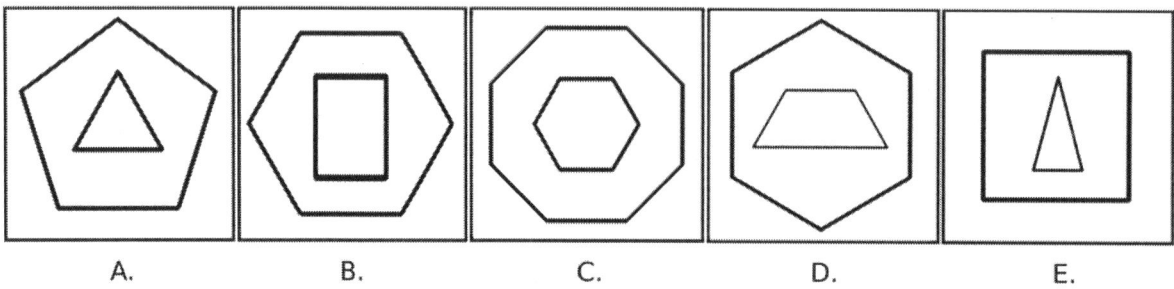

First we count the numbers of sides of the inside shapes.

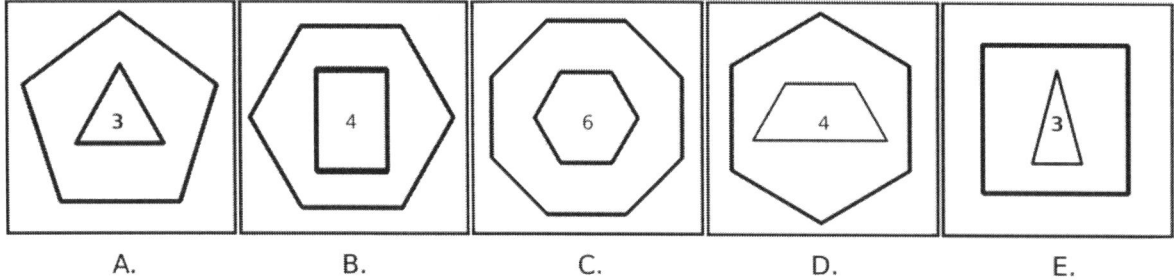

Next we count the number of sides of the outside shapes

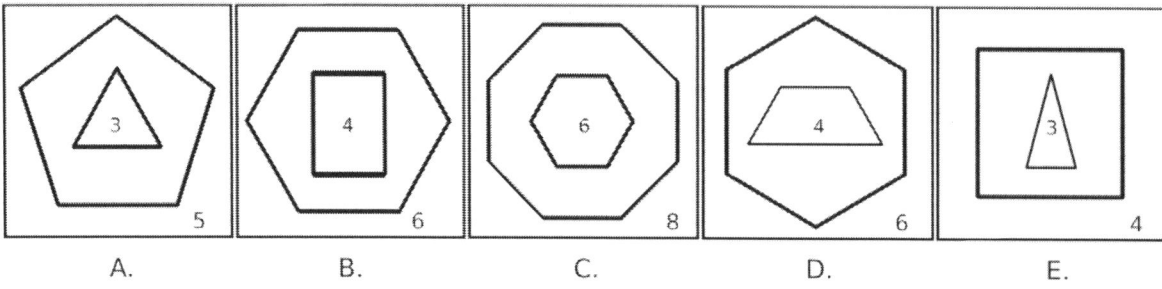

Now we observe that the all of the inside shapes (bar one) has two less sides than the outside shape. So we are left with the conclusion that E. is the odd one out.

# EXERCISE 5

Find the shape that completes the series.

1.

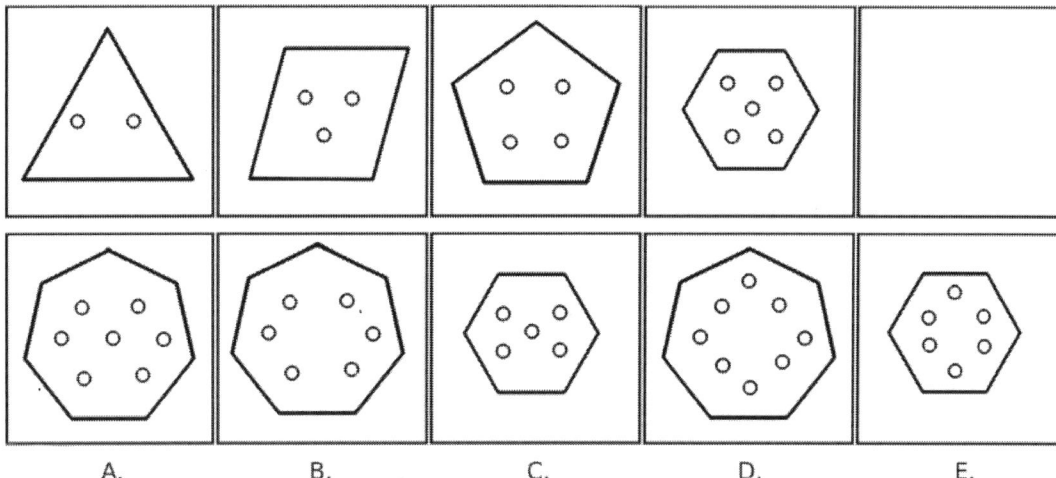

2.

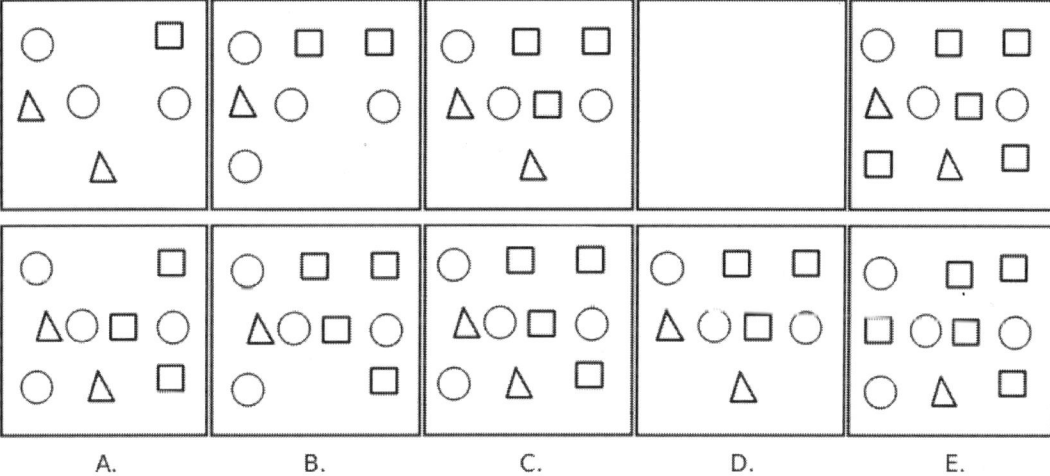

3.

4.

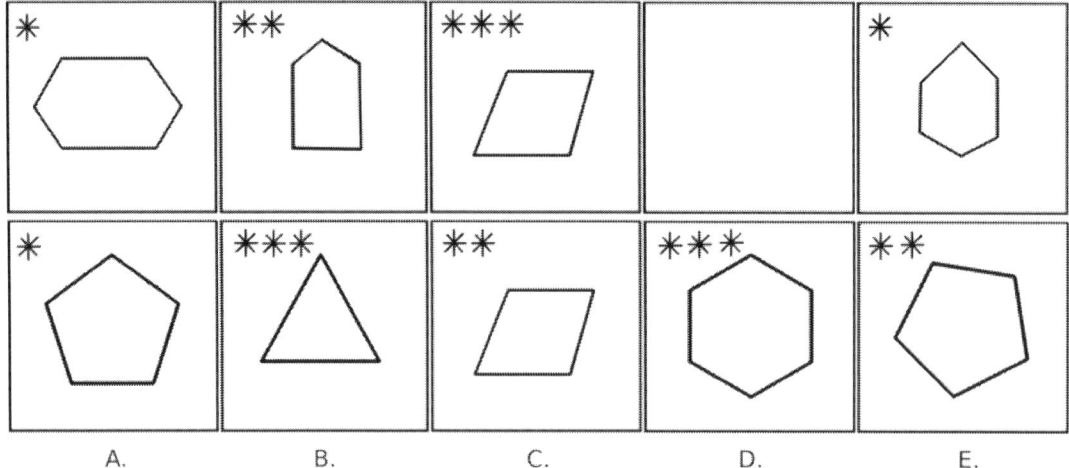

|   |   |   |   |   |
|---|---|---|---|---|
| A. | B. | C. | D. | E. |

5.

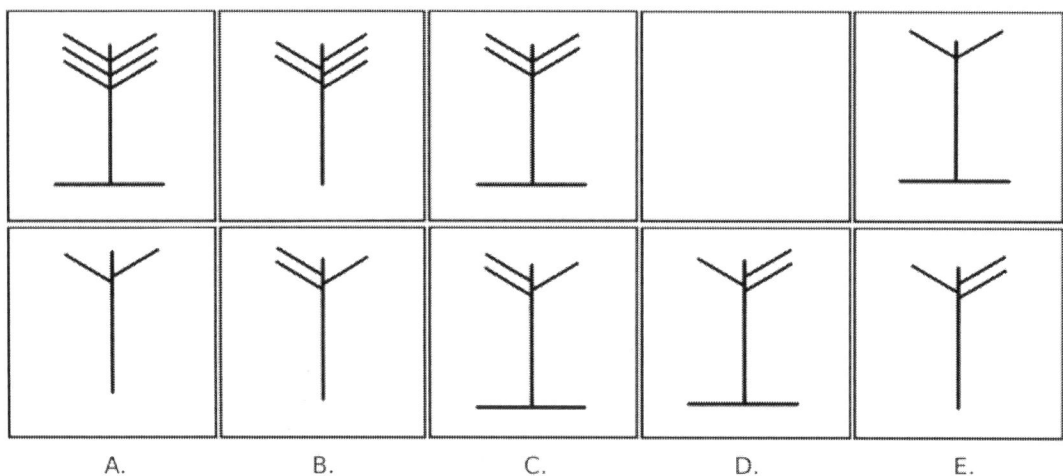

|   |   |   |   |   |
|---|---|---|---|---|
| A. | B. | C. | D. | E. |

Which shape is the odd one out?

6.

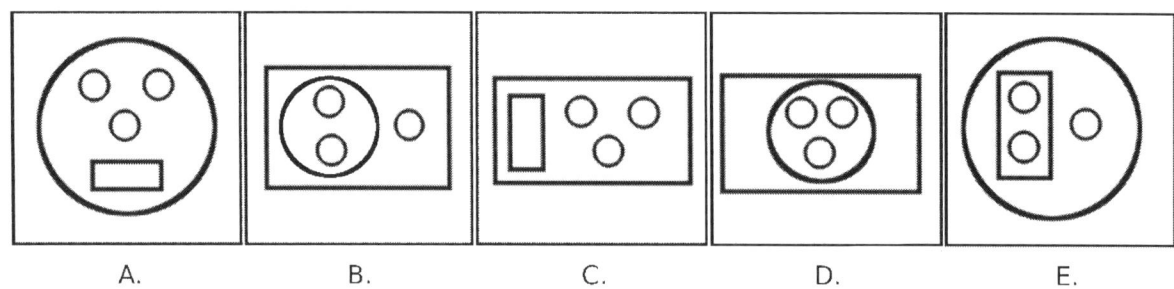

|   |   |   |   |   |
|---|---|---|---|---|
| A. | B. | C. | D. | E. |

7.

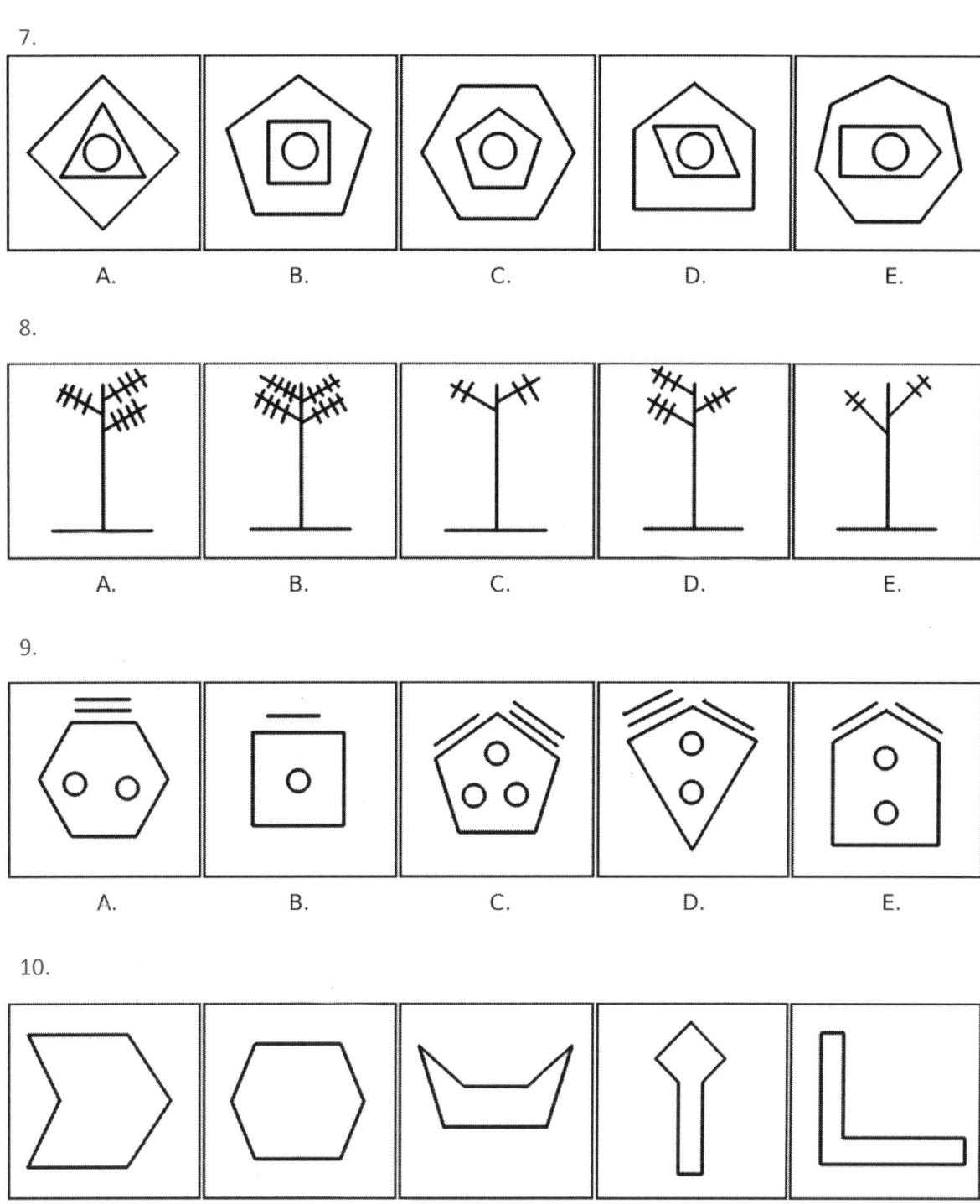

A.          B.          C.          D.          E.

8.

A.          B.          C.          D.          E.

9.

A.          B.          C.          D.          E.

10.

A.          B.          C.          D.          E.

25

# CHAPTER 6: REFLECTIONS

Reflections are very common in NVR, both as a question type and also incorporated into other question types.

A line of reflection can be thought of in three ways

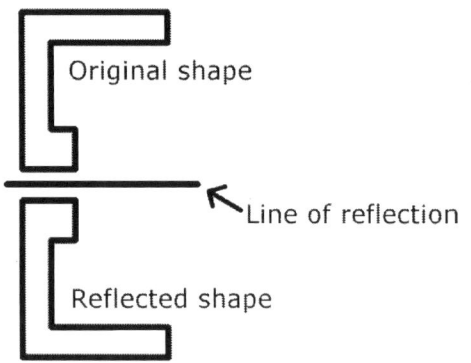

A mirror line.

A fold line - when folded along the line the two halves are on top of each other.

A line where every point one side of the line has a corresponding point the same distance from the line on the other side.

All of these points are the same distance from the line of reflection.

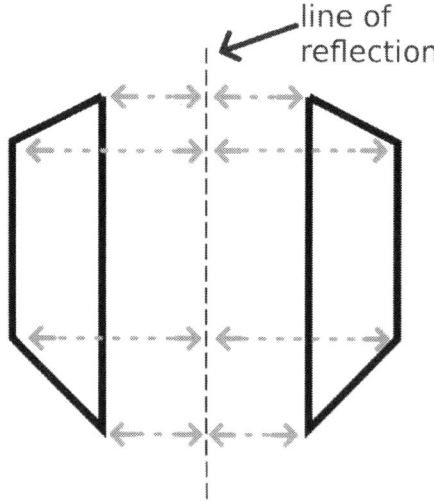

Remember that in shapes with shaded fills the fills can be reflected as well as the shape.

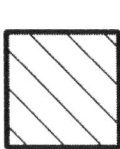 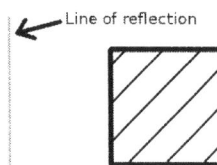

Sometimes in exams, reflections include inversions. An inversion is simply a reflection that is moved.

Note on the word flip. The word flip has been used to mean: a 180° rotation, a reflection and an inversion. For this reason, to avoid confusion, I would suggest avoiding the use of the word flip – but describe specifically what is happening.

If an exam paper uses the word flip treat it as an analogy.

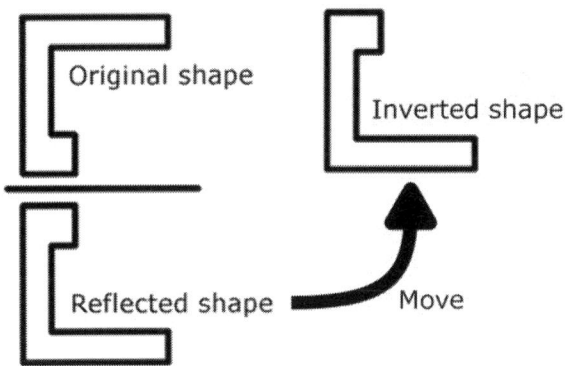

## EXERCISE 6

Choose the reflection of the shape on the left. In this exercise reflections include inversions.

1.

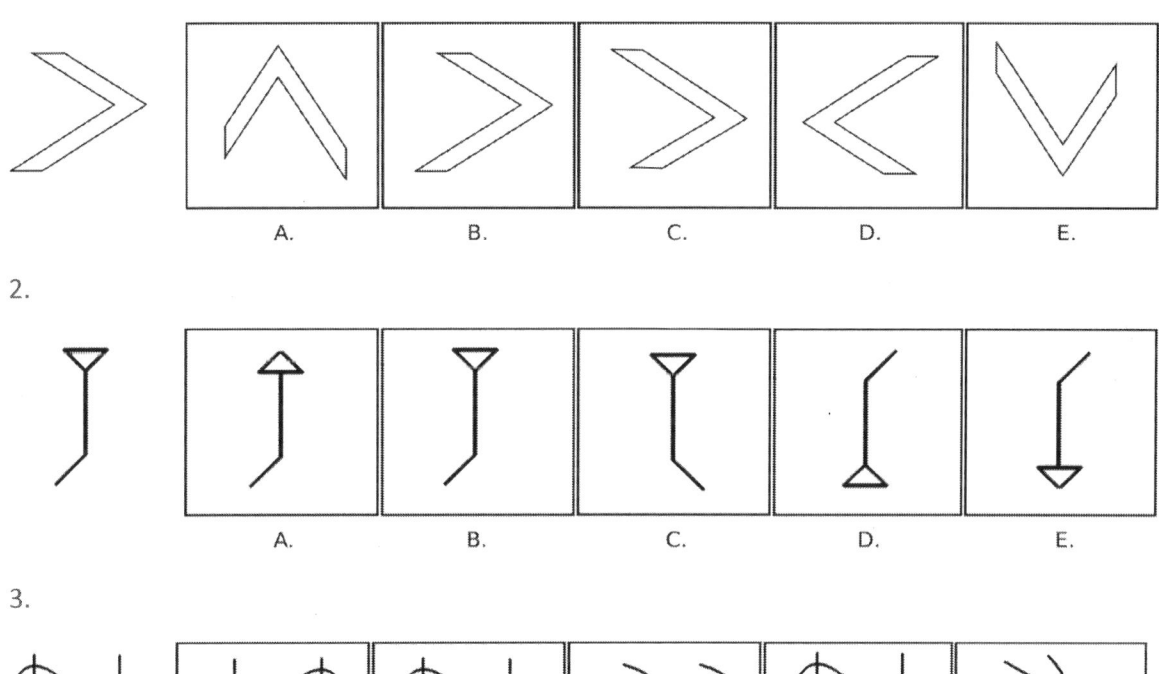

2.

3.

4.

A.  B.  C.  D.  E.

5.

A.  B.  C.  D.  E.

6.

A.  B.  C.  D.  E.

7.

A.  B.  C.  D.  E.

8.

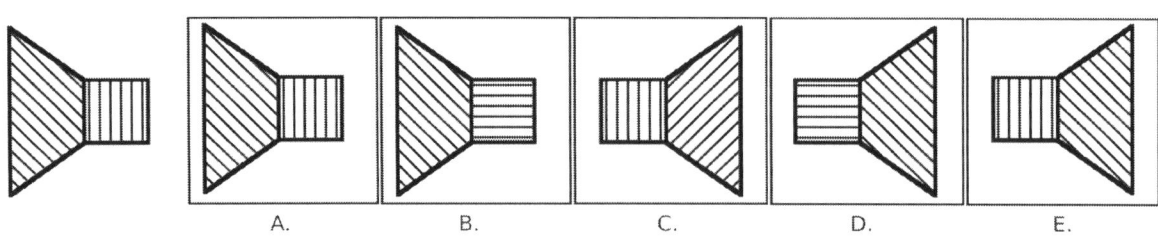

A.  B.  C.  D.  E.

9.

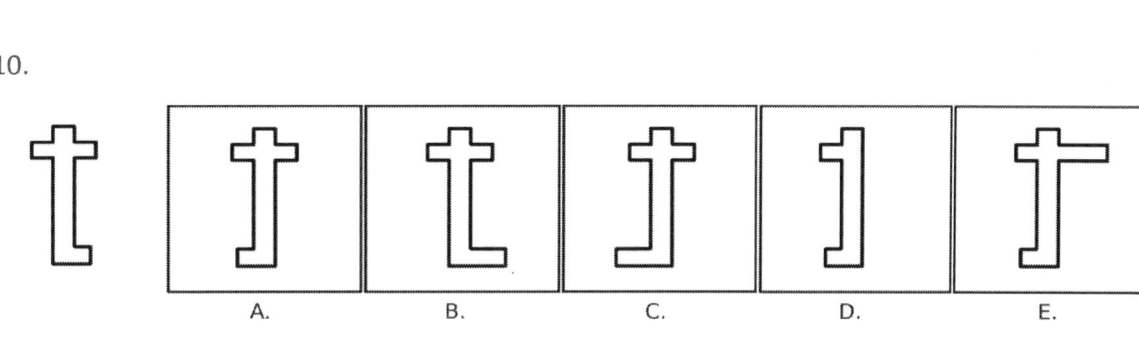

A.    B.    C.    D.    E.

10.

A.    B.    C.    D.    E.

# CHAPTER 7: 2D ROTATIONS

Rotations are also very common in NVR, both as a stand-alone question type and also incorporated into other questions.

Shapes can either be rotated:

Clockwise, in the same direction as a clock's hands turn,

or anticlockwise, (sometimes called counter clockwise), in the opposite direction.

or

Shapes and fills can also be rotated by different amounts, most commonly.

45°

90°

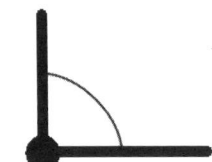

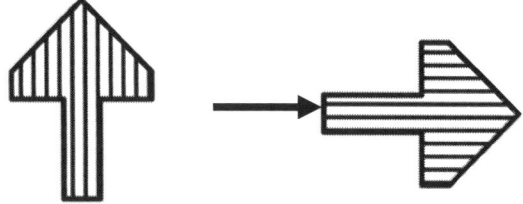

180°

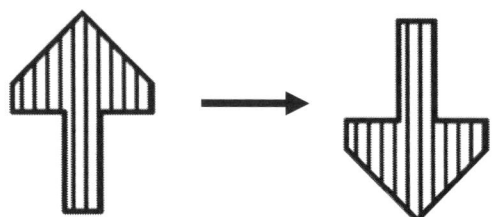

Practice questions

(Choose all that apply)

1. Which of these shapes are rotated by 90° clockwise?

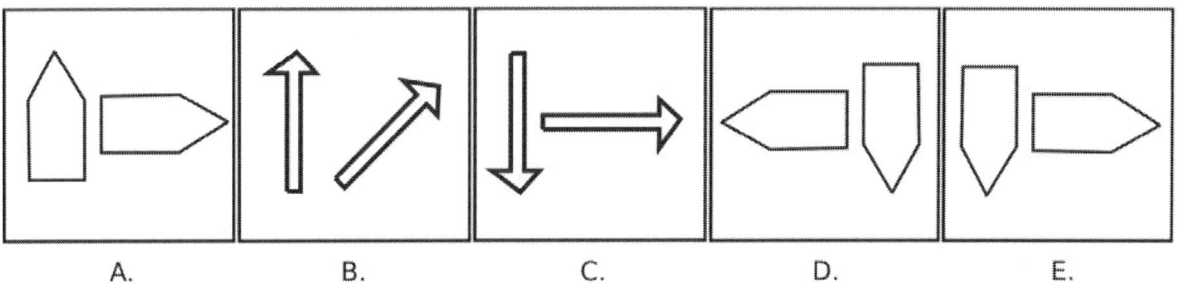

A.        B.        C.        D.        E.

2. Which of these shapes are rotated by 45° anticlockwise?

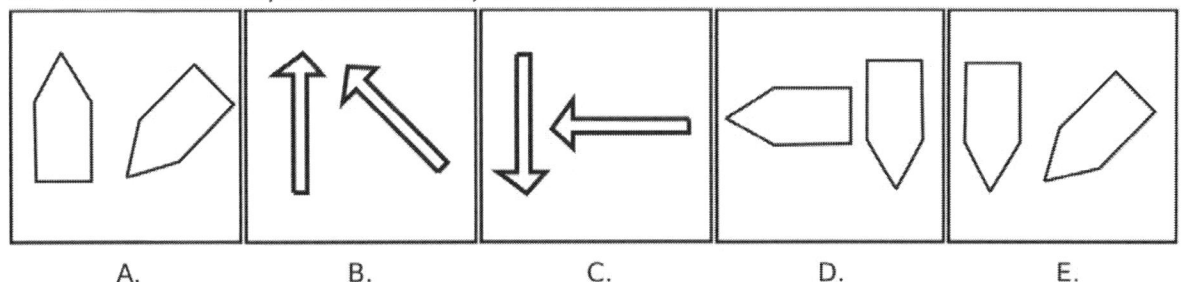

A.        B.        C.        D.        E.

3. Which of these shapes are rotated by 180° clockwise or anticlockwise (take your pick the answer will be the same)?

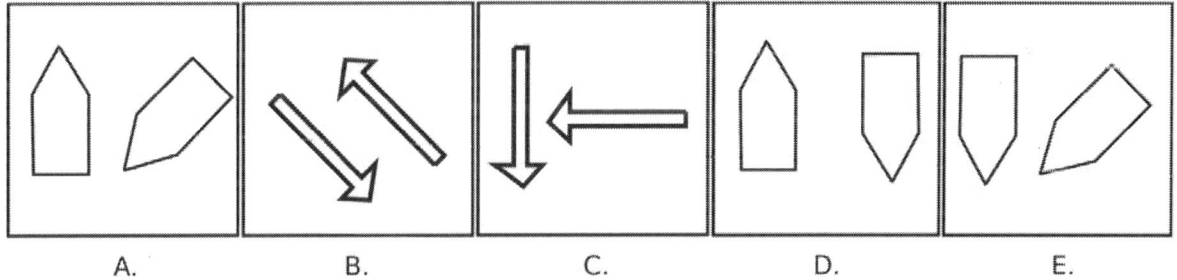

A.        B.        C.        D.        E.

4. In which of these shapes is the black arrow rotated 90° clockwise from the white?

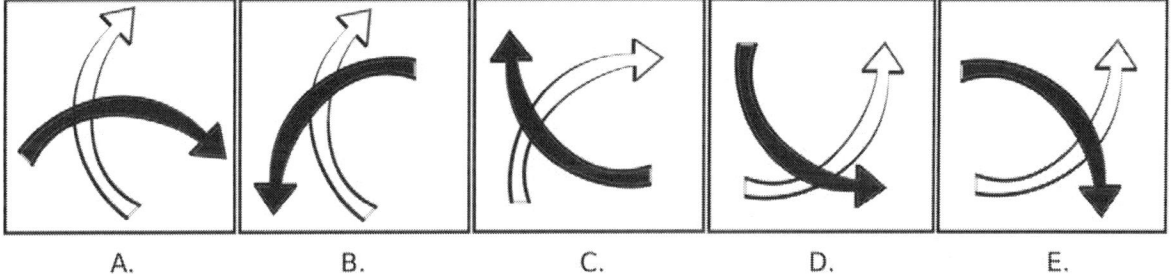

A.        B.        C.        D.        E.

## EXERCISE 7:
Which shape is a rotation of the shape on the left?

1.

2.

3.

4.

5.

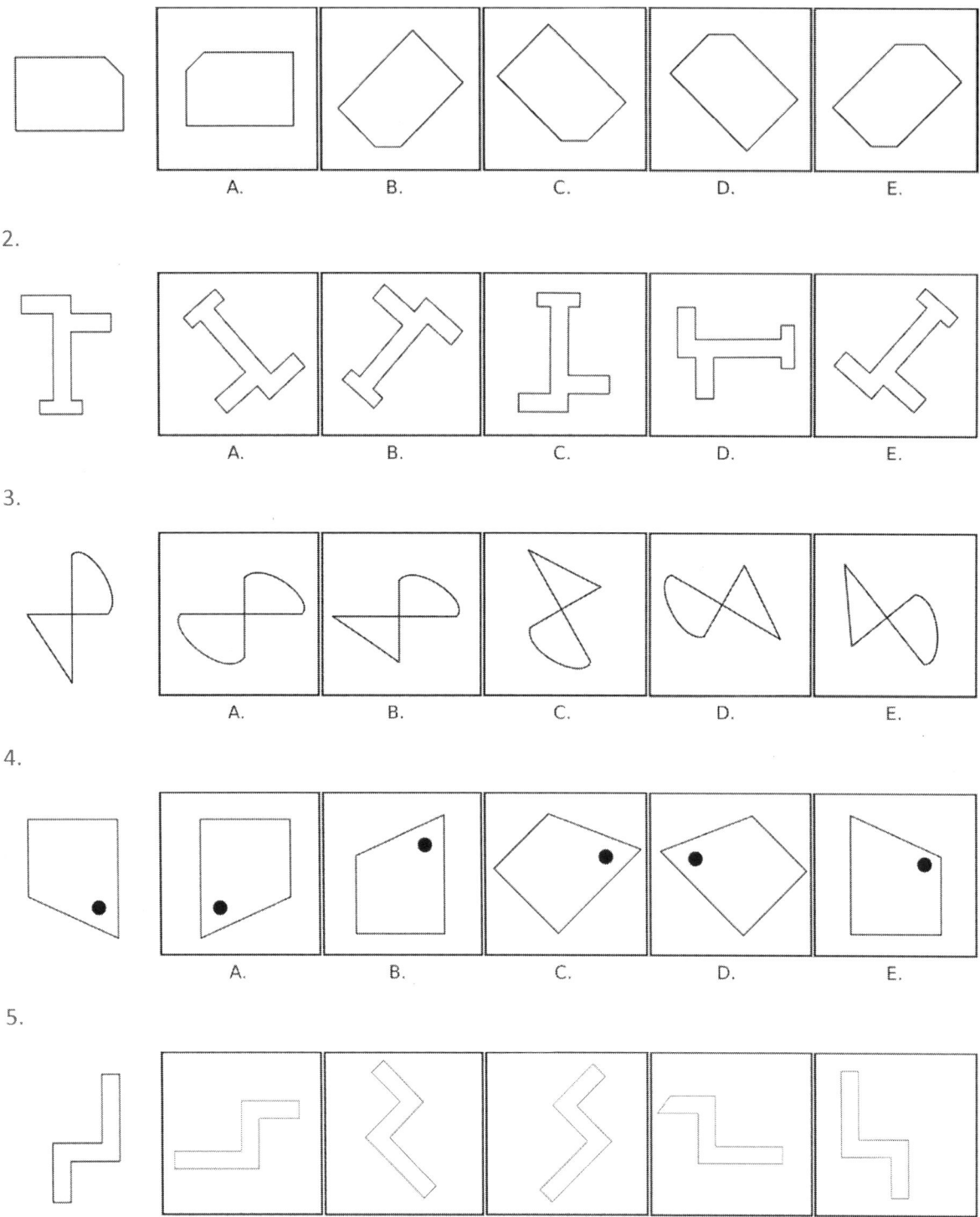

6.

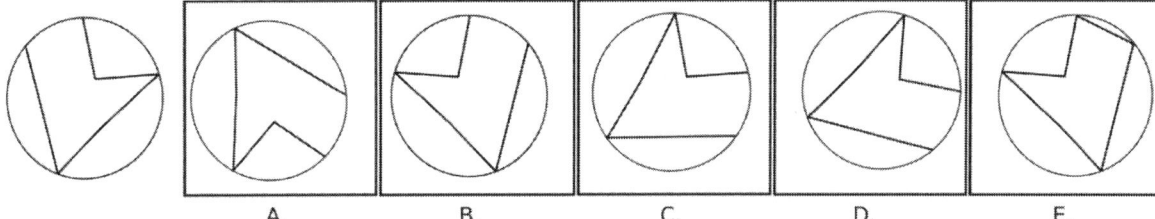

7.

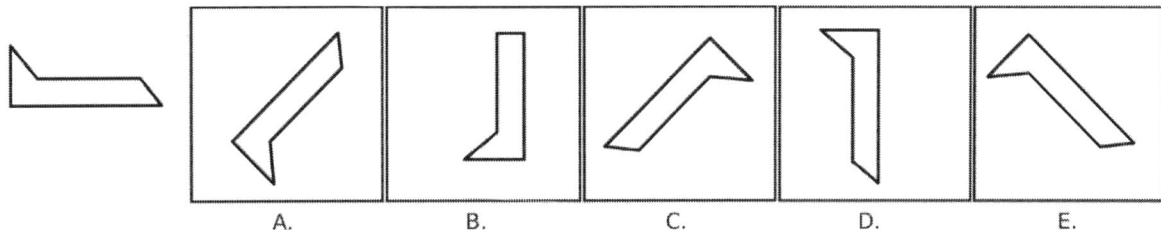

8.

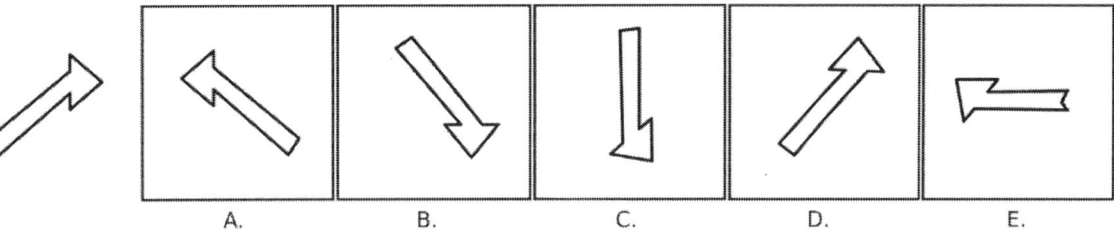

9.

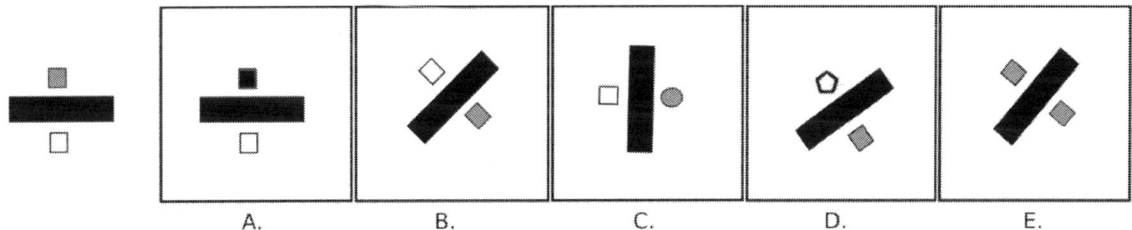

10.

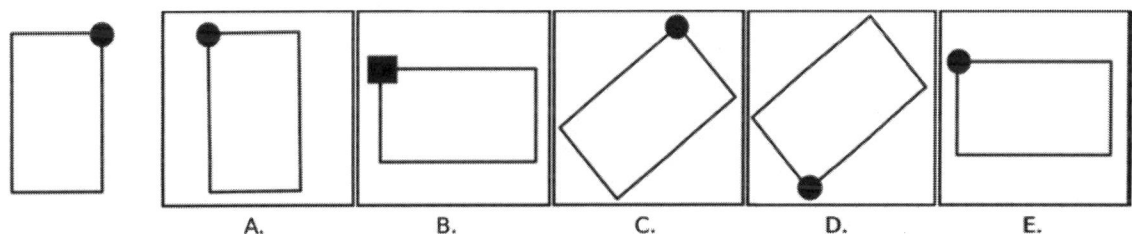

# CHAPTER 8: FURTHER ROTATIONS

Besides the rotation of a whole shape, other rotations that can occur include:

Rotation of the fill.
Rotation of smaller shapes inside or outside a larger shape.

For example.

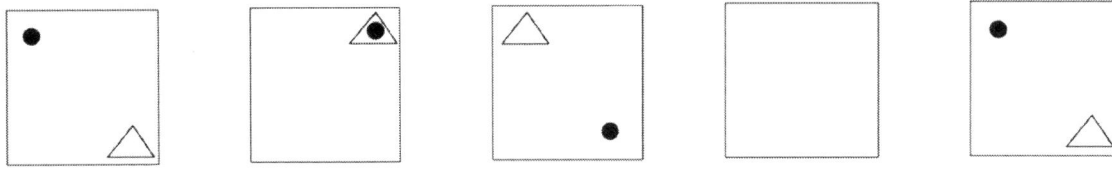

The circle is moving in a clockwise direction, so will next be in the bottom left corner.

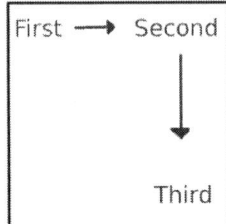

The triangle is moving in an anticlockwise direction – and will be next in the bottom left corner.

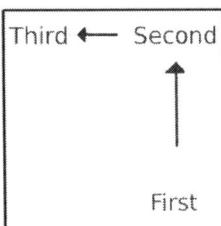

Sometimes, rotation is just one element of a question.

# EXERCISE 8:

Which shape is missing from the series below?

1.

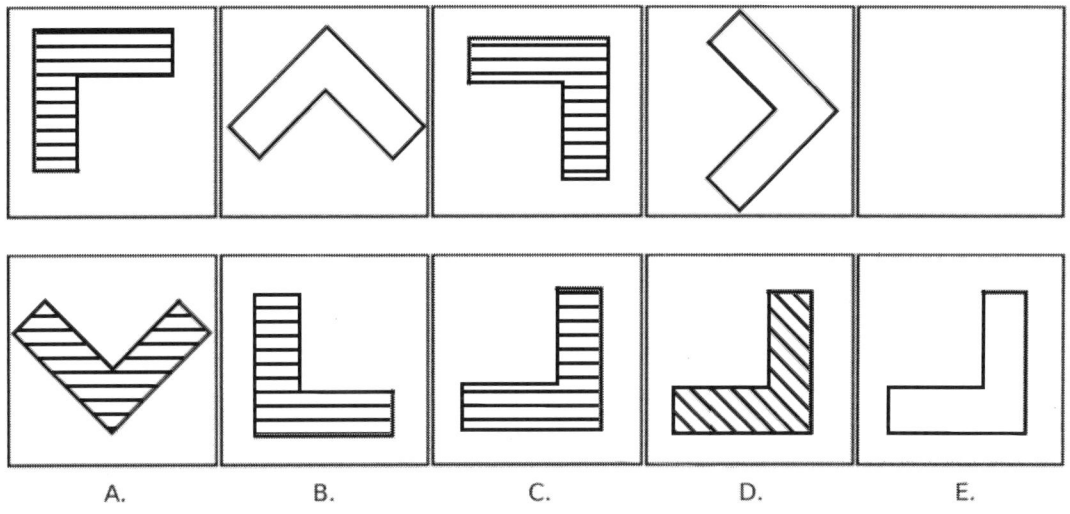

A.      B.      C.      D.      E.

2.

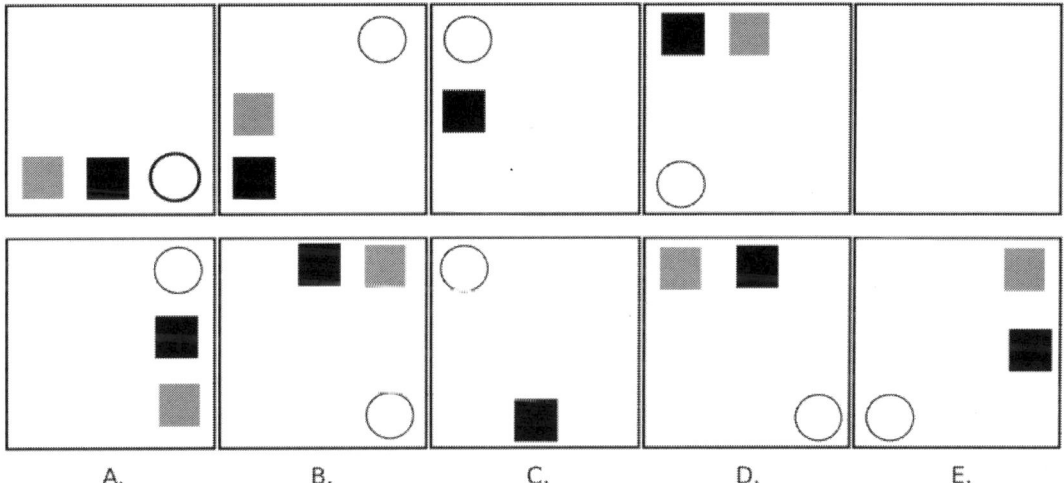

A.      B.      C.      D.      E.

3.

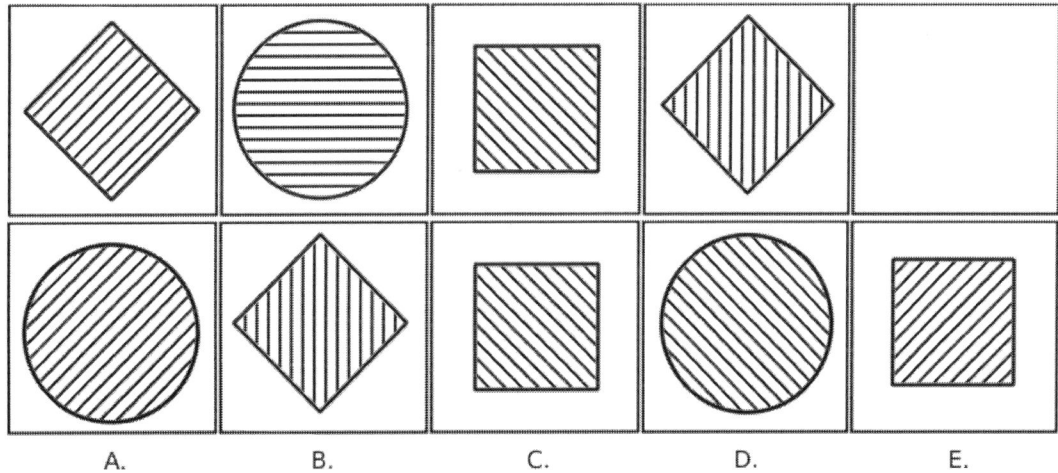

A.      B.      C.      D.      E.

4.

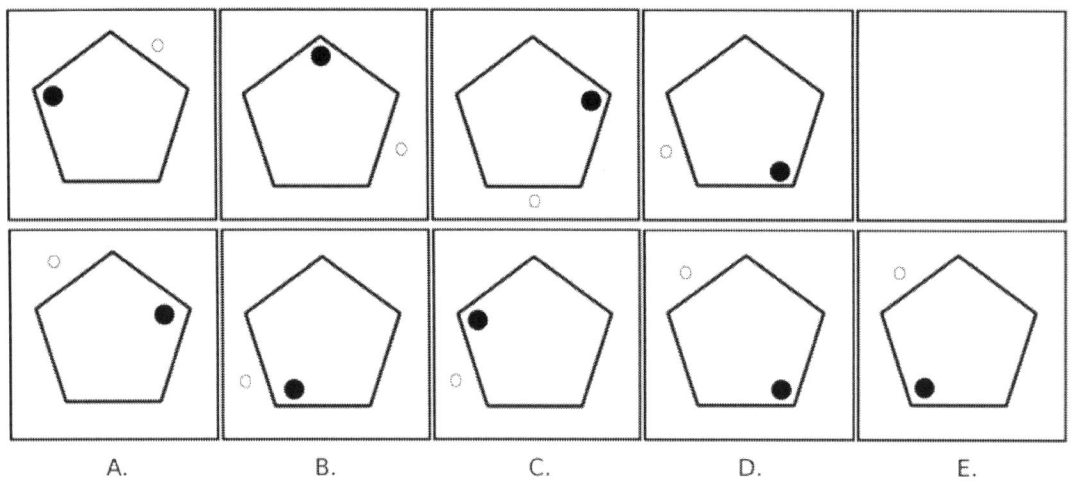

A.     B.     C.     D.     E.

5.

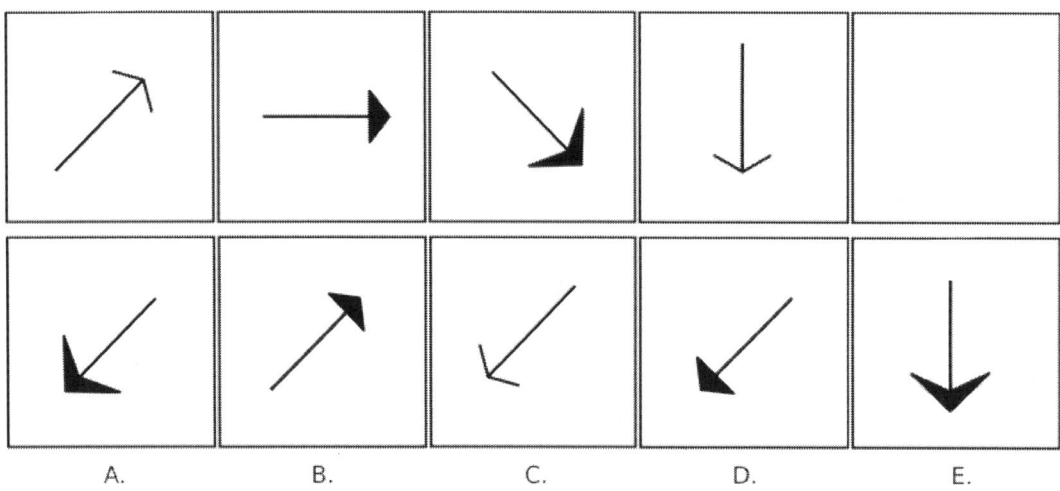

A.     B.     C.     D.     E.

6.

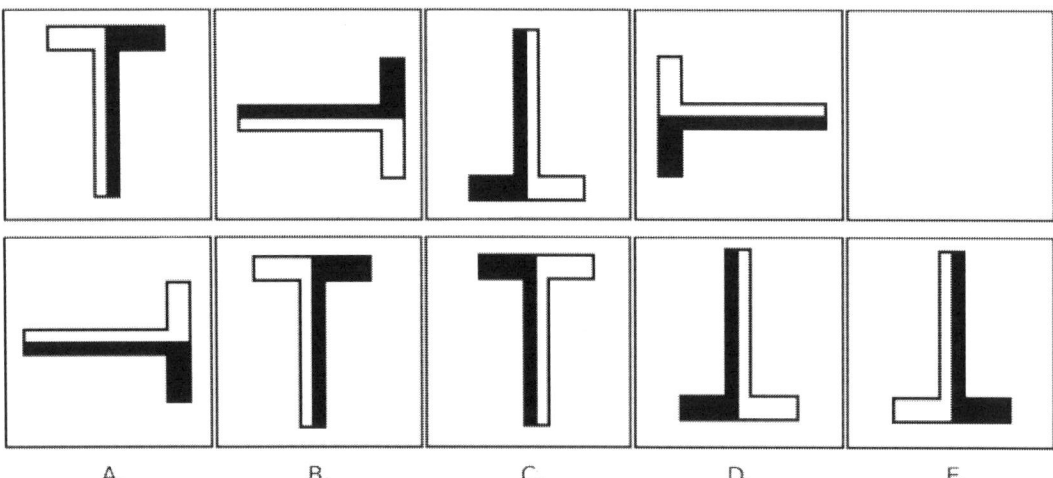

A.     B.     C.     D.     E.

Which is the odd one out?

7.

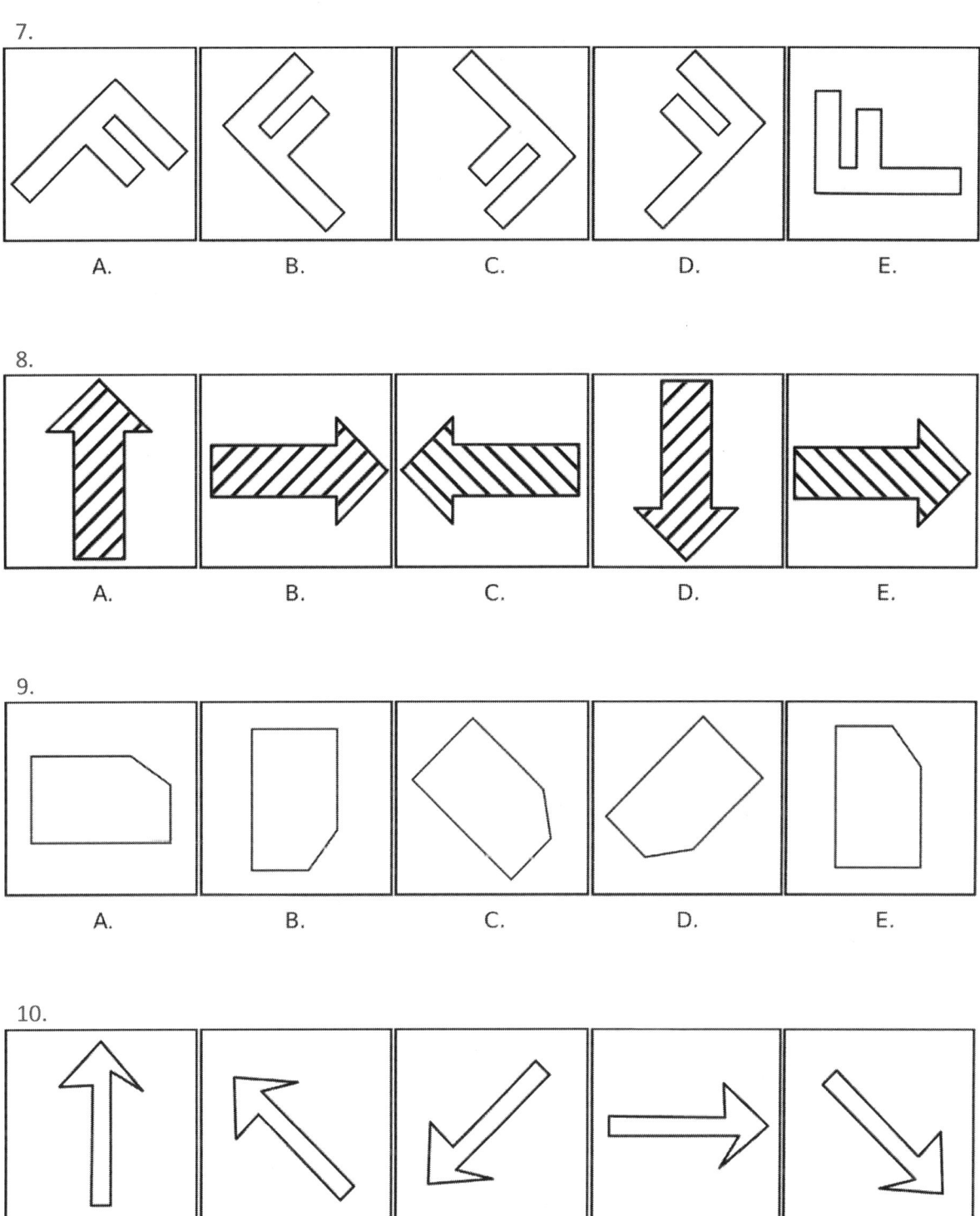

|  A. | B. | C. | D. | E. |

8.

|  A. | B. | C. | D. | E. |

9.

|  A. | B. | C. | D. | E. |

10.

|  A. | B. | C. | D. | E. |

# CHAPTER 9: SIZE

The size of a shape can change in four ways:

The shapes can become bigger or smaller.

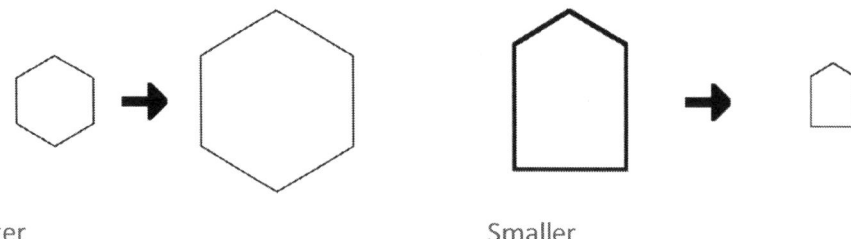

Bigger                                      Smaller

Sometimes shapes stay the same size in one direction but the other direction can get bigger (stretched) or smaller (squashed).

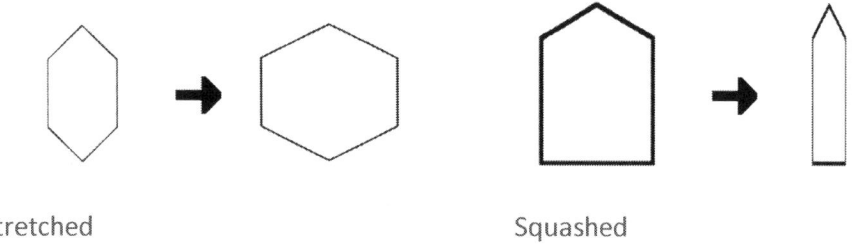

Stretched                                   Squashed

EXERCISE 9

1.

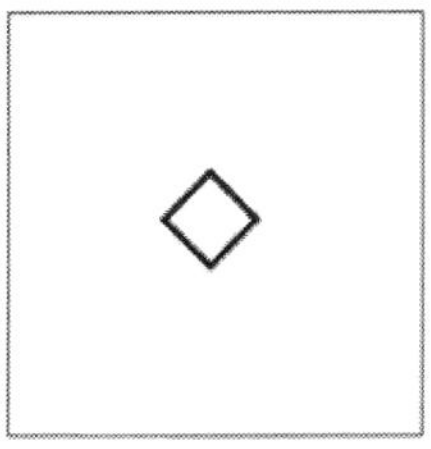

is to

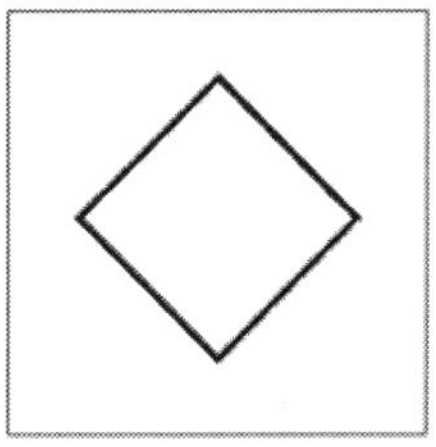

as

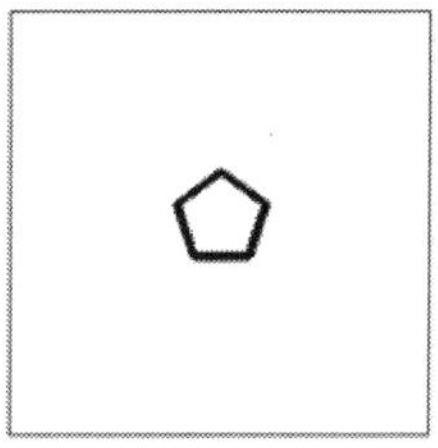

is to

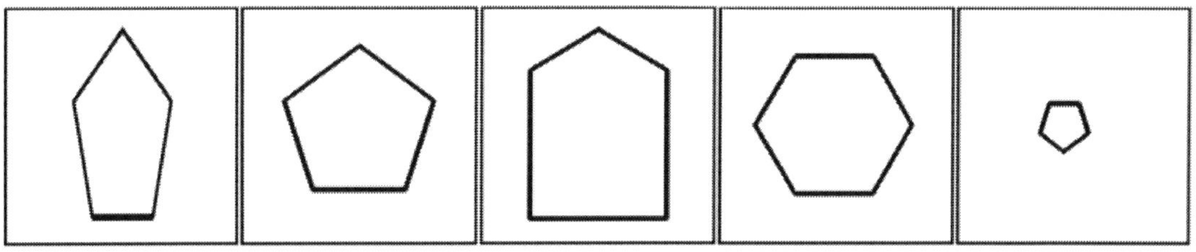

A.  B.  C.  D.  E.

2.

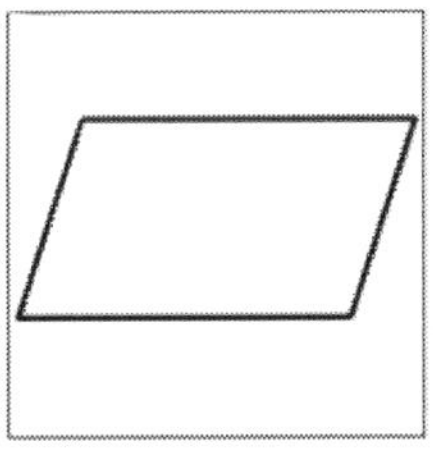

is to

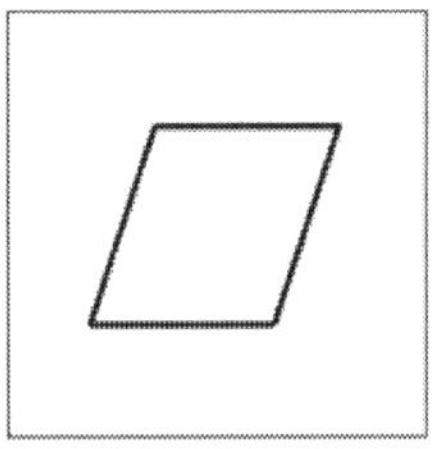

as

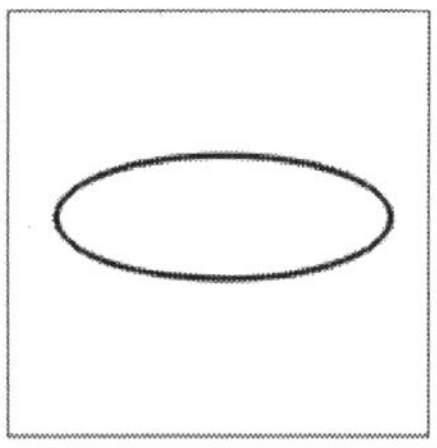

is to

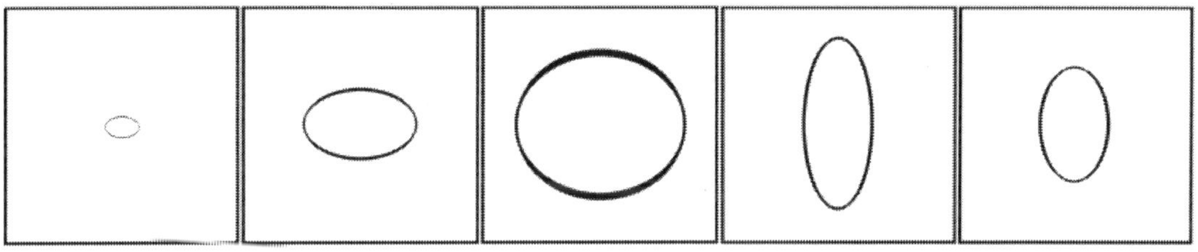

A.  B.  C.  D.  E.

3.

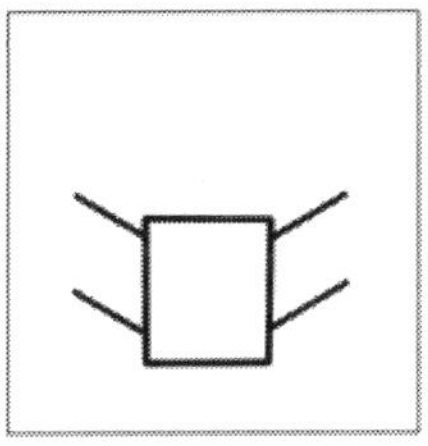

is to

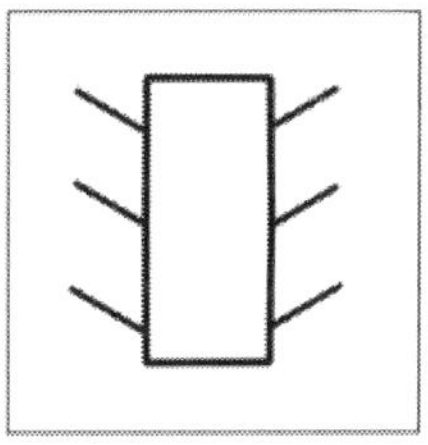

as

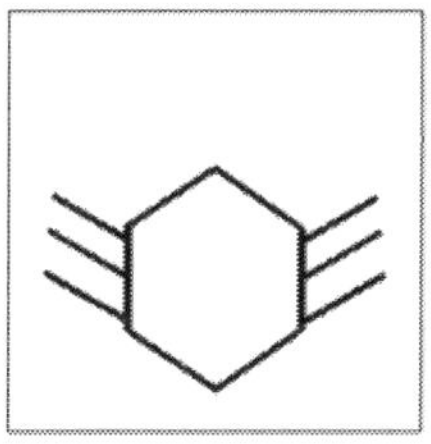

is to

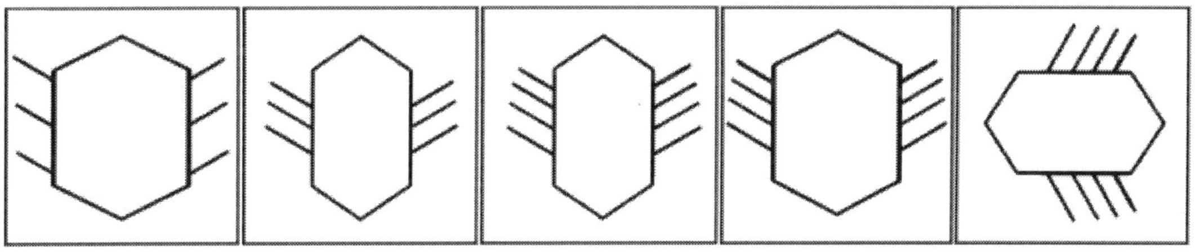

A.  B.  C.  D.  E.

4.

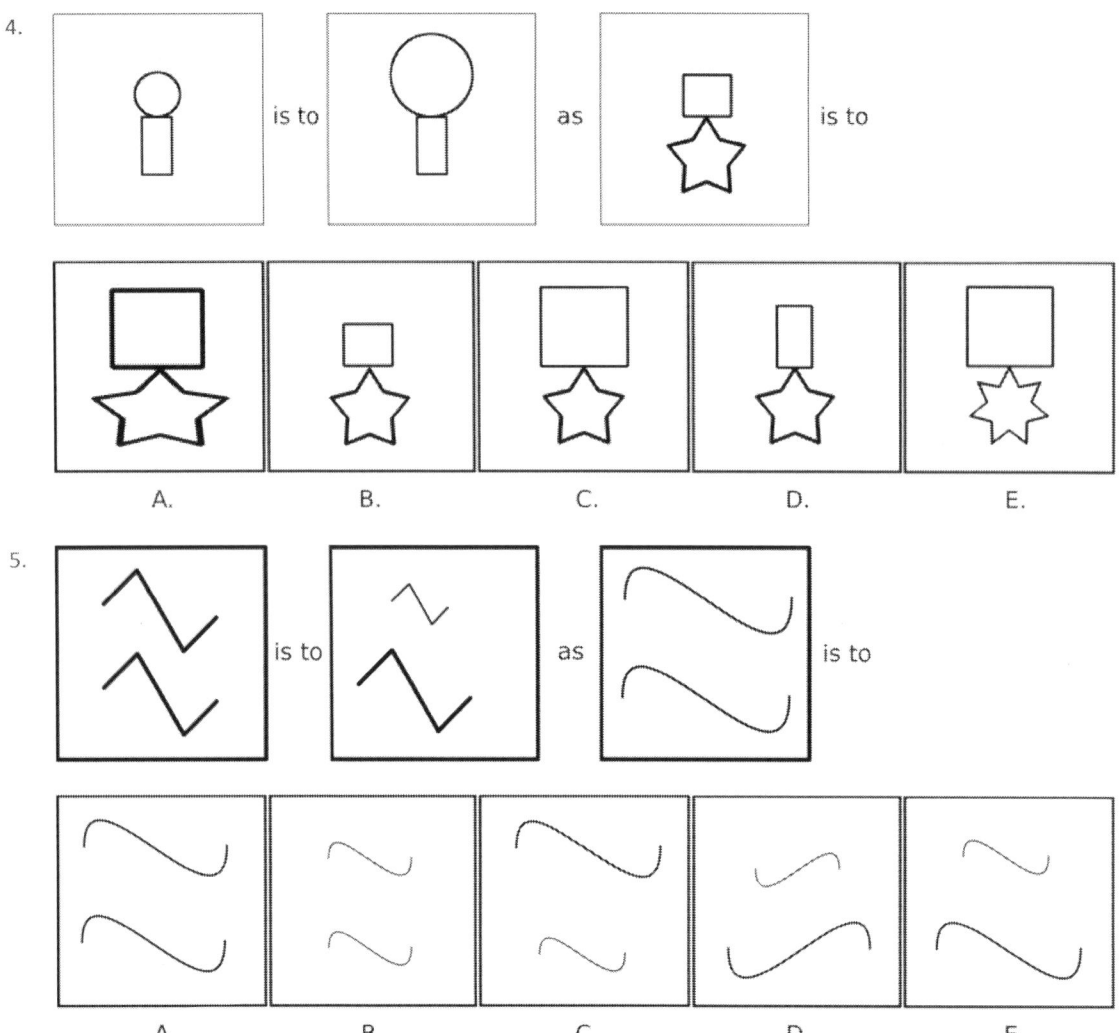

5.

Which shape is the odd one out?

6.

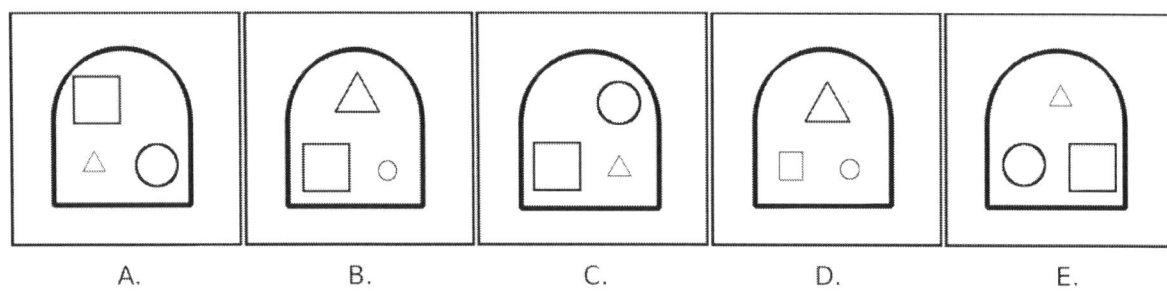

7.

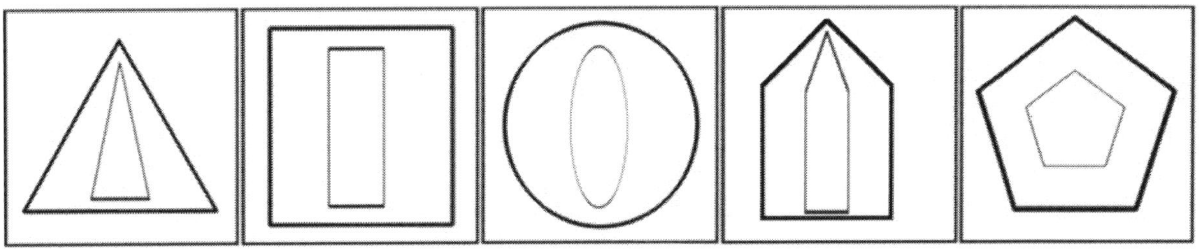

A.　　　　B.　　　　C.　　　　D.　　　　E.

8.

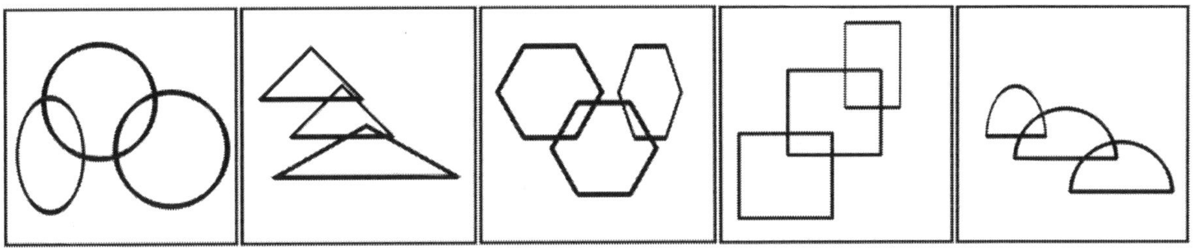

A.　　　　B.　　　　C.　　　　D.　　　　E.

9.

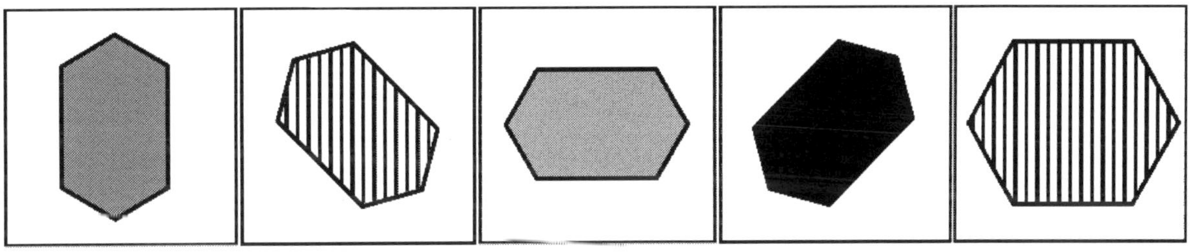

A.　　　　B.　　　　C.　　　　D.　　　　E.

10.

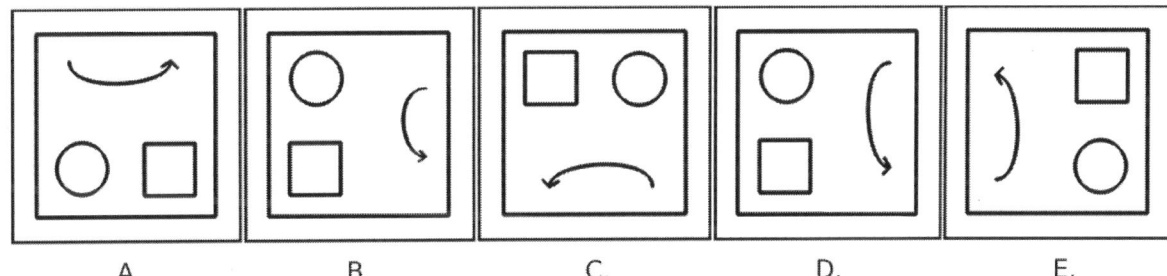

A.　　　　B.　　　　C.　　　　D.　　　　E.

# CHAPTER 10: OVERLAPPING SHAPES

There are two ways that shapes can overlap:

1. **Links**: all lines of both linked shapes can be seen.

2. **Overlays**: one shape 'hides' part of the other shape.

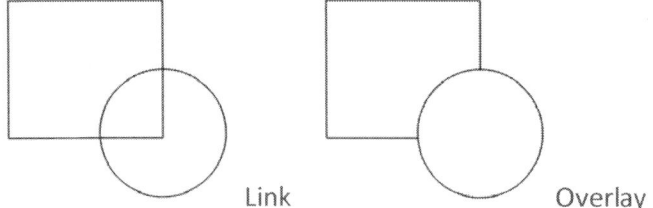

Link          Overlay

Besides noticing if two shapes are connected with a link or an overlay, it is important to also note.

Does the second shape go all the way across, or part of the way across the first shape?

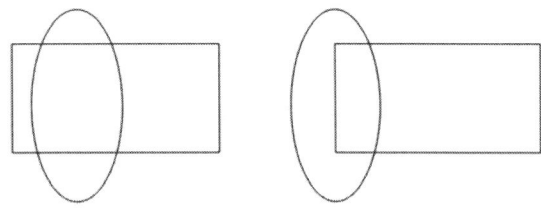

In an overlay which shape can you see all of, and which shape can you only see part of?

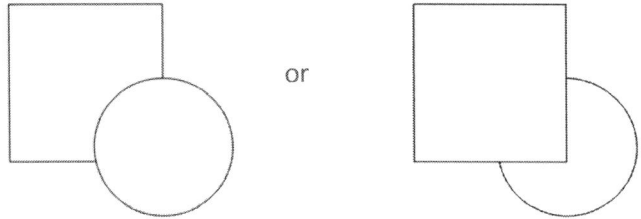

or

Sometimes, the shape made by the link, may be the same or different:

Both of these overlaps make a shape with four sides.

# EXERCISE 10:
Which shape is the odd one out?

1:

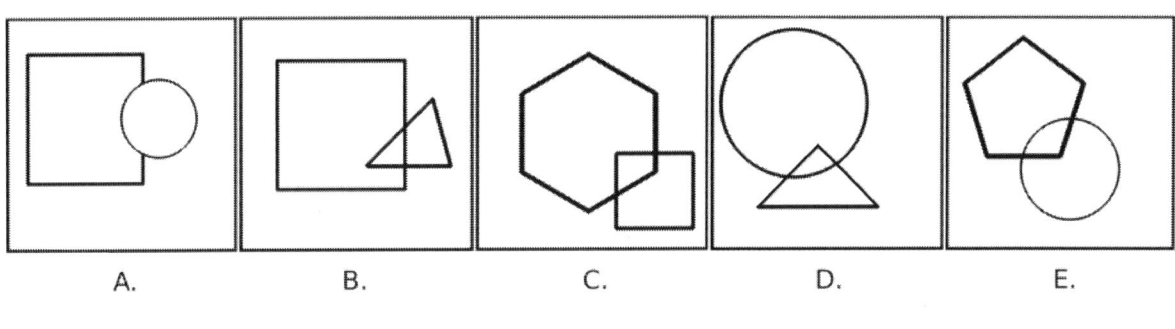

A.  B.  C.  D.  E.

2:

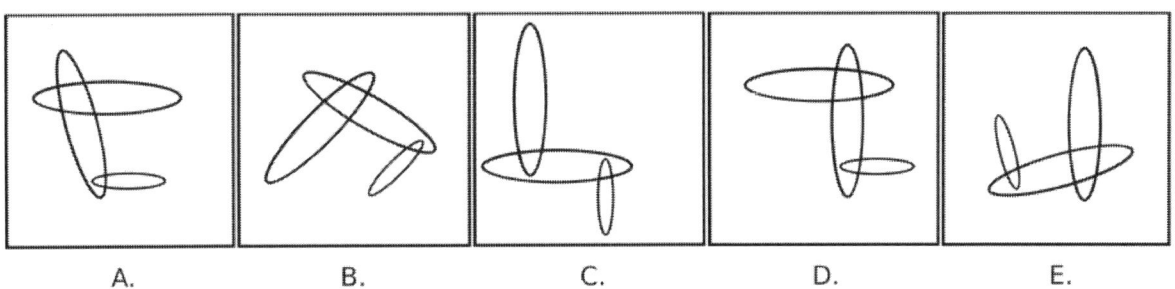

A.  B.  C.  D.  E.

3.

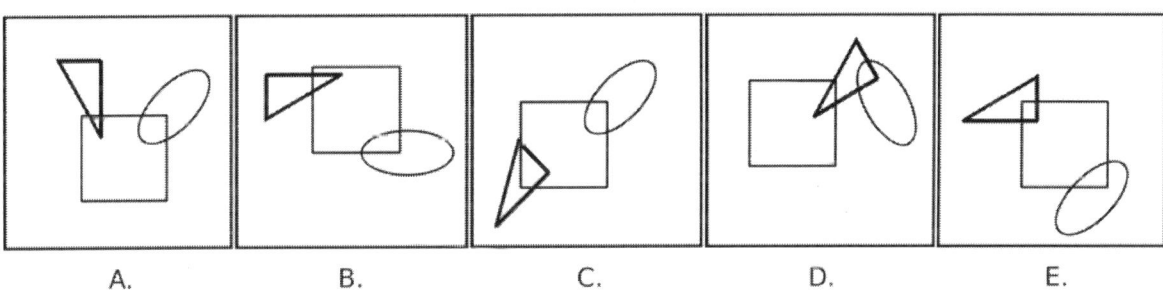

A.  B.  C.  D.  E.

4.

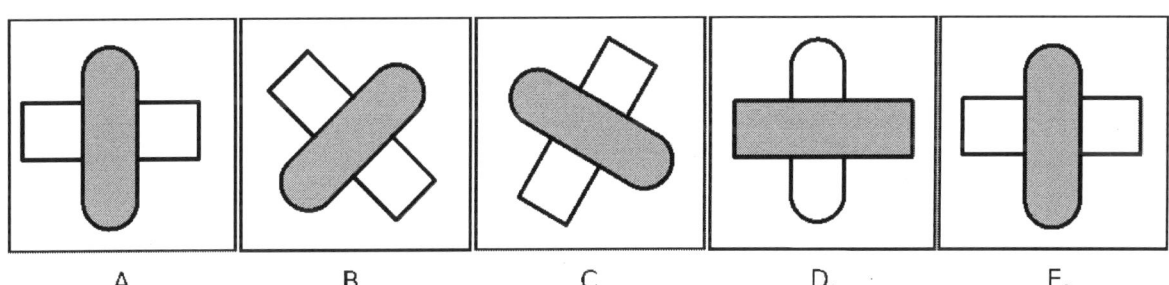

A.  B.  C.  D.  E.

5.

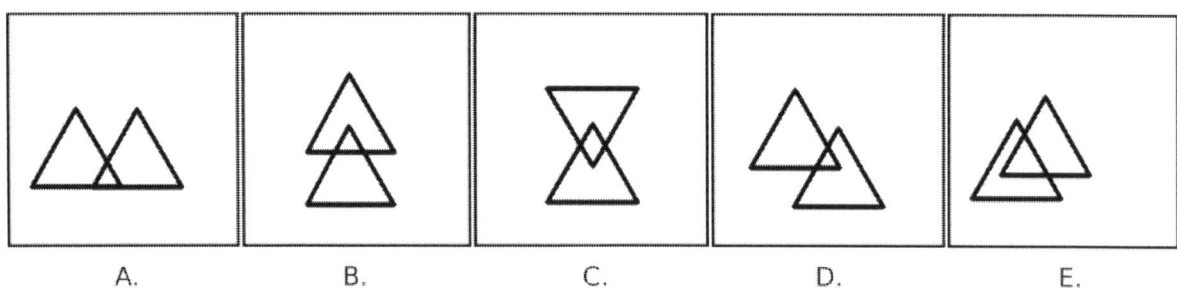

A.  B.  C.  D.  E.

6.

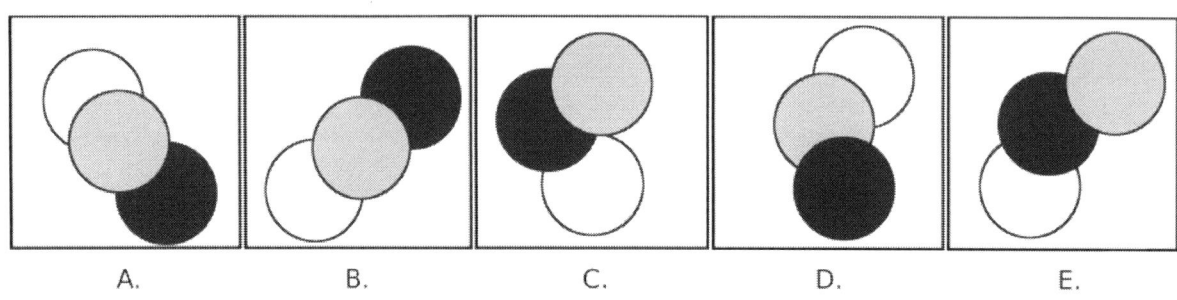

A.  B.  C.  D.  E.

Which shape fits best with the family of shapes shown?

7.

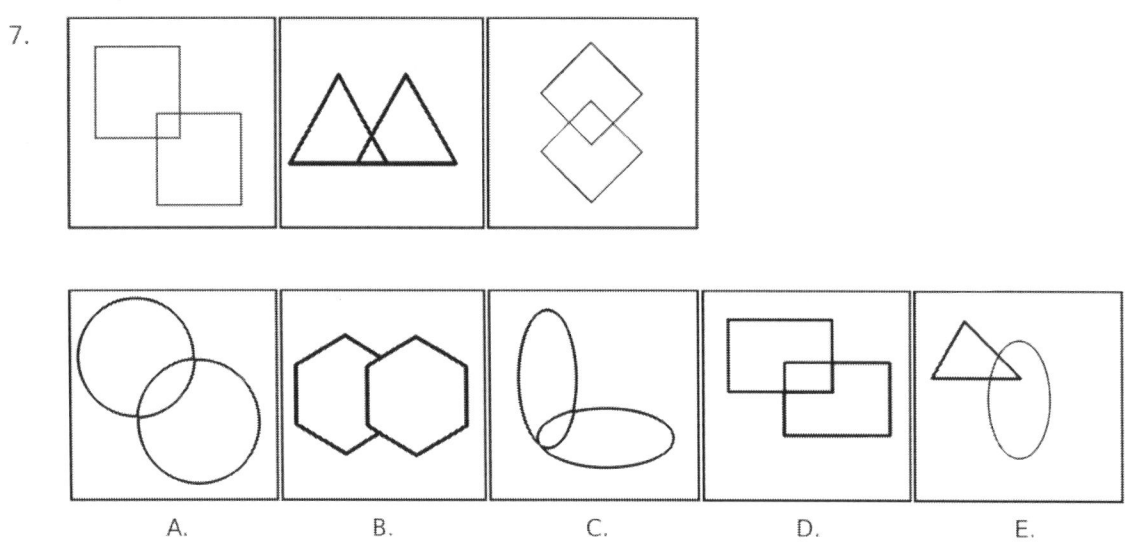

A.  B.  C.  D.  E.

8.

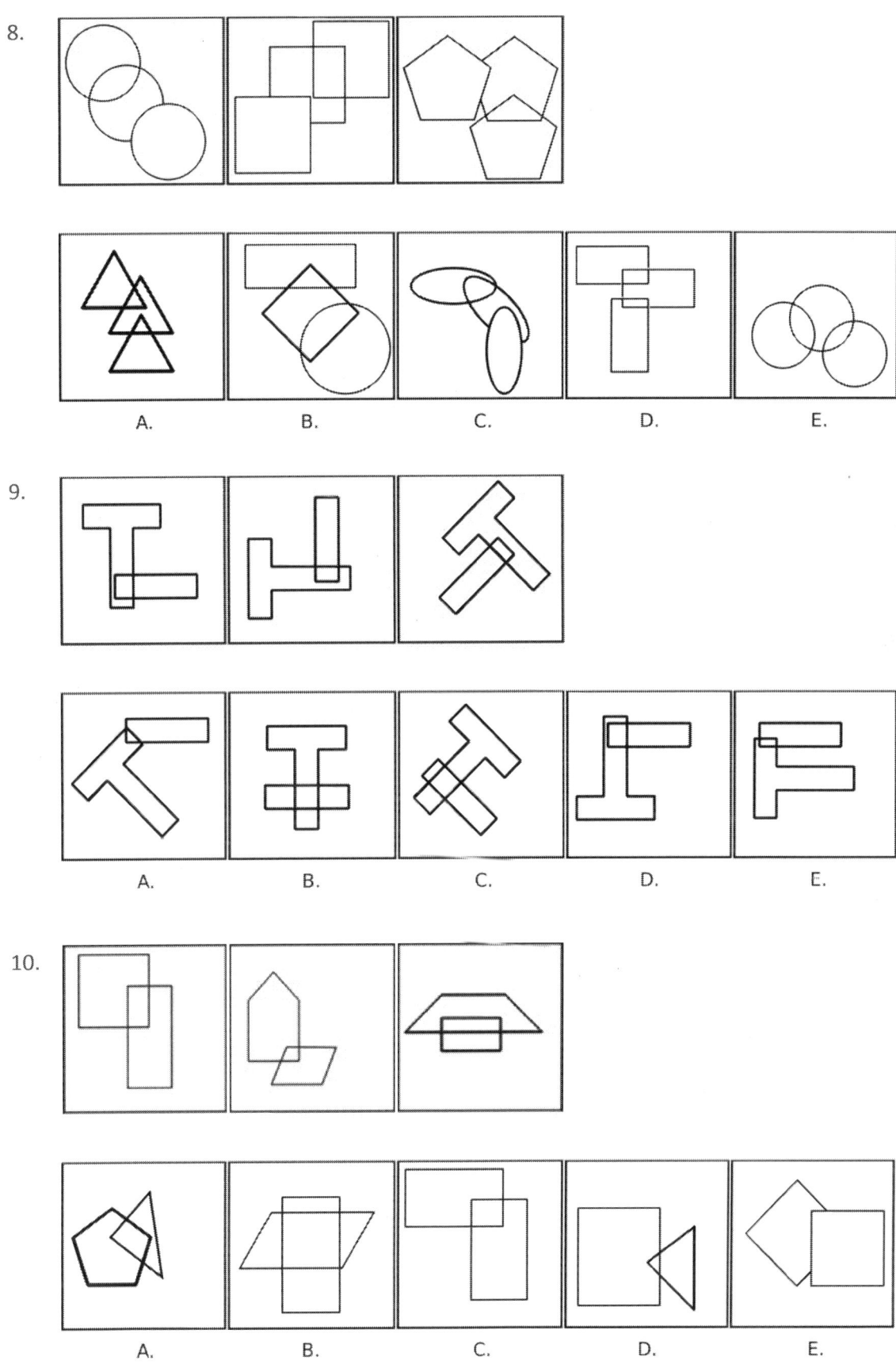

A.     B.     C.     D.     E.

9.

A.     B.     C.     D.     E.

10.

A.     B.     C.     D.     E.

45

# CHAPTER 11: MOVE

In Non-Verbal Reasoning, shapes can move in the following ways:

Horizontally (side to side)
Vertically (up and down)
Diagonally
Clockwise
Anticlockwise

In series questions, it can be helpful to write in the first box where a shape moves.

Example which shape is the next in the series?

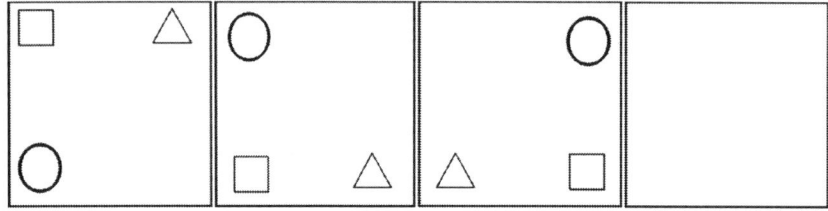

If I follow the square, it is top left corner of in the first box, then bottom left, and then bottom right. So, I would write the numbers like this.

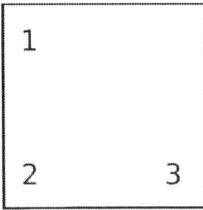

It is now clear that the square is moving around in an anticlockwise manner.

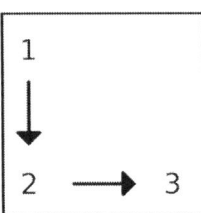

The next square will be in the top right.

If necessary, I can do the same thing with a second shape.

# EXERCISE 11:

Which shape completes the series below?

1.

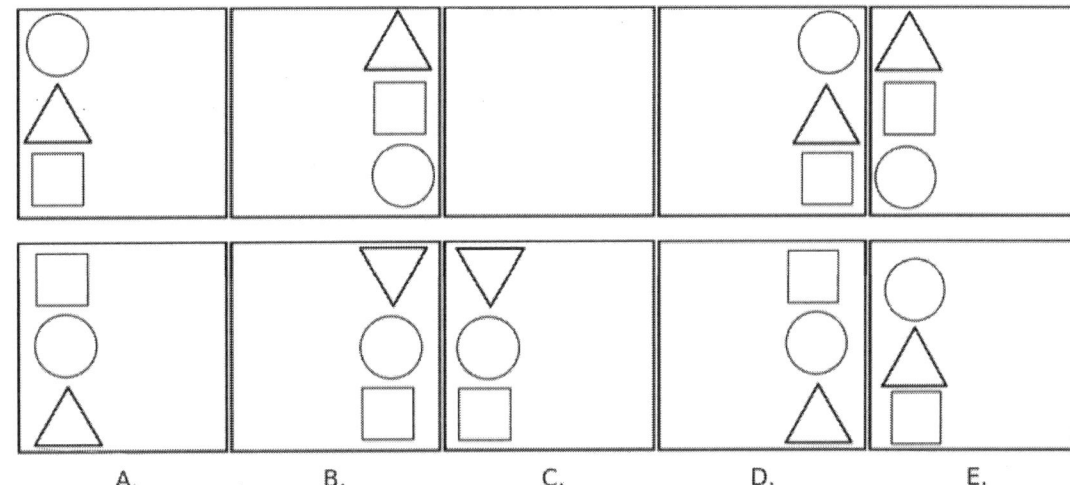

A.          B.          C.          D.          E.

2.

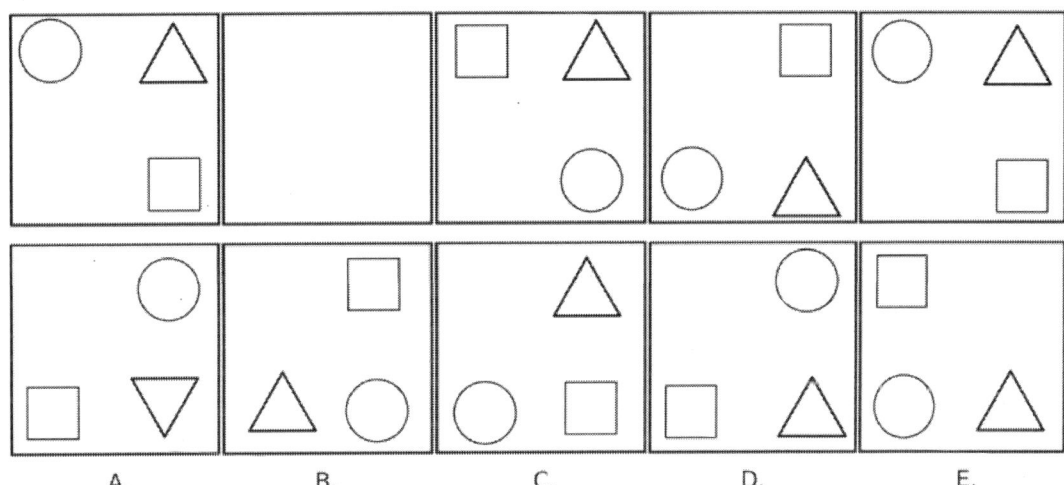

A.          B.          C.          D.          E.

3.

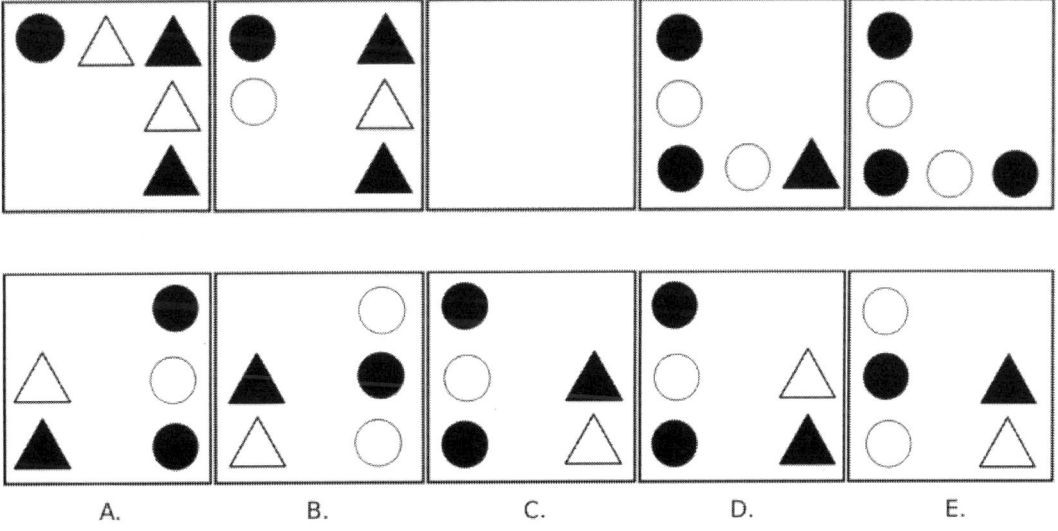

A.          B.          C.          D.          E.

4.

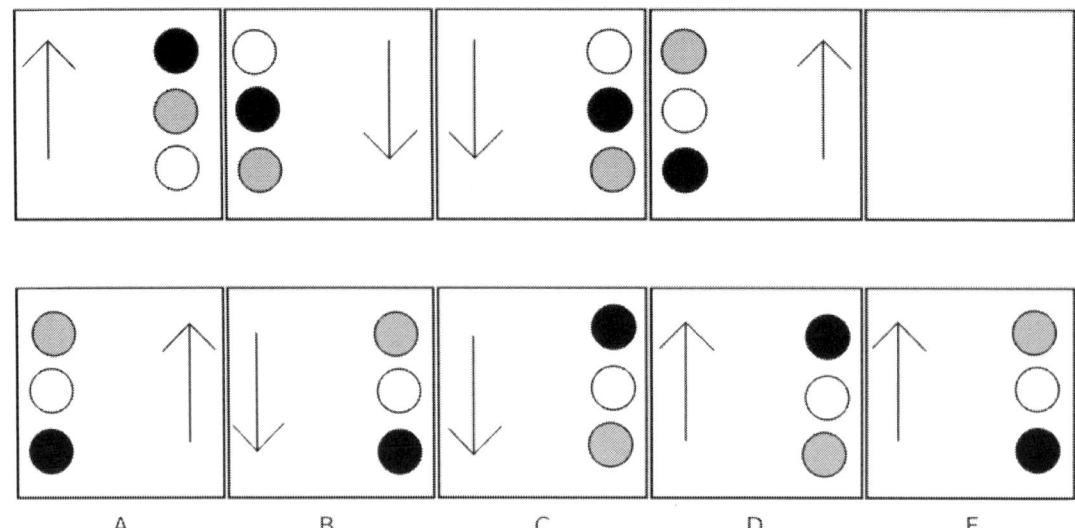

A.      B.      C.      D.      E.

5.

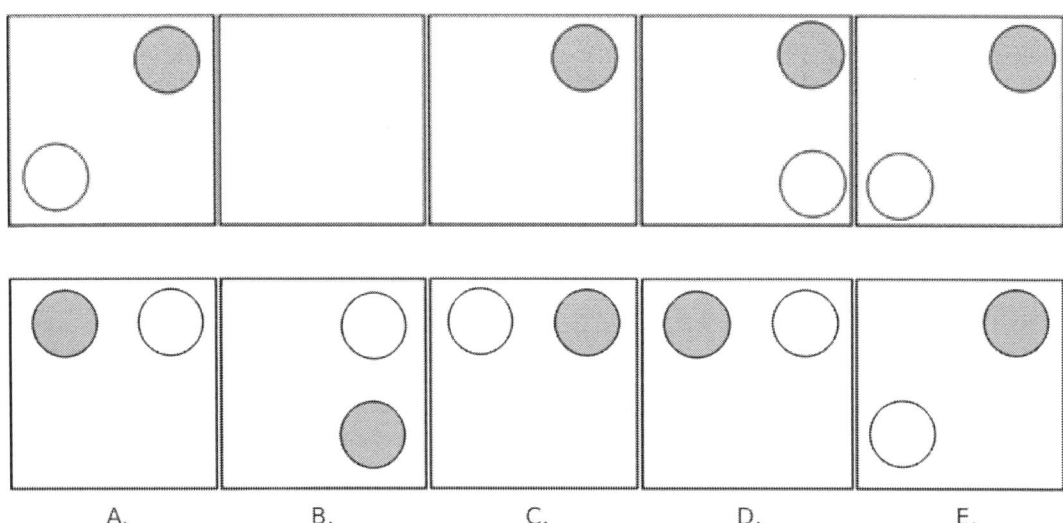

A.      B.      C.      D.      E.

Determine the codes for the following (if you have trouble with the codes, please return to this section after completing chapter 14):

6.

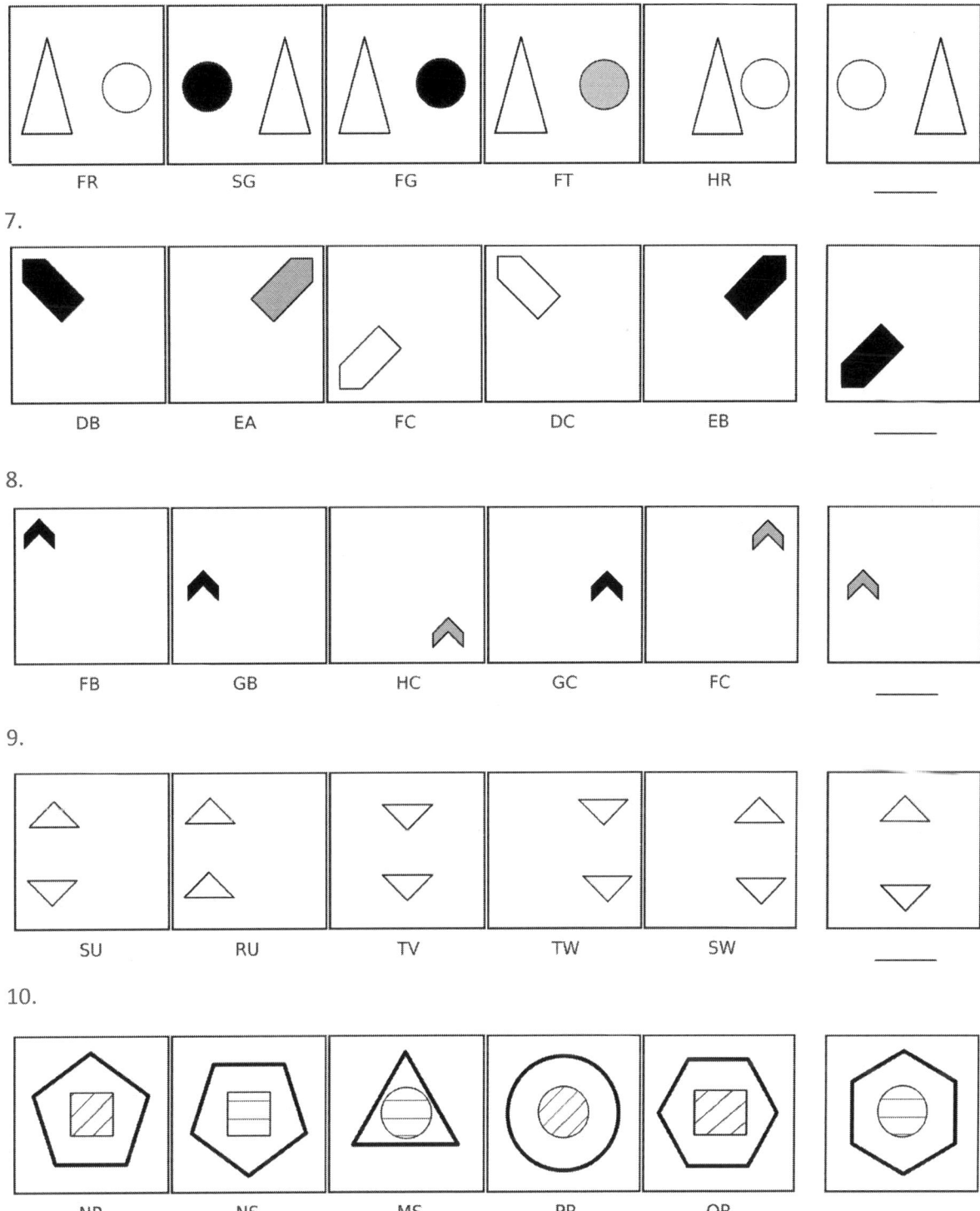

| FR | SG | FG | FT | HR | _____ |

7.

| DB | EA | FC | DC | EB | _____ |

8.

| FB | GB | HC | GC | FC | _____ |

9.

| SU | RU | TV | TW | SW | _____ |

10.

| NR | NS | MS | PR | QR | _____ |

49

# CHAPTER 12: ODD ONE OUT

In this type of NVR problem you must find something that is the same in all of the options, except one. Odd one out is one of the most difficult problem types because there are many different things to consider.

Some of the things that can change include:

> Type of lines
> Symmetry
> Shading
> Size
> Overlaps
> Number of lines or shapes
> Directions
> Reflections vs rotations

## EXERCISE 12: WHICH IS THE ODD ONE OUT?

1.

4.

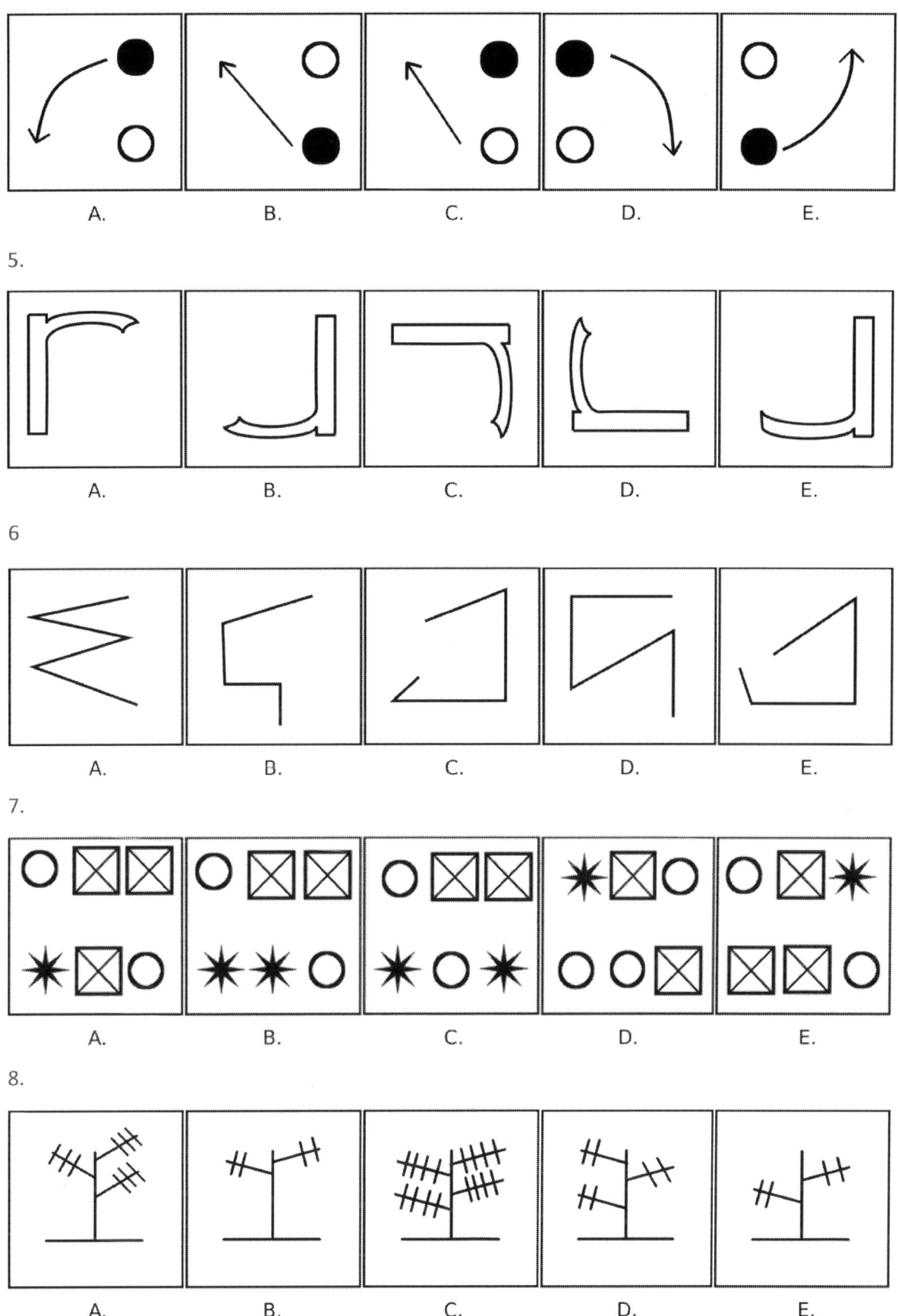

A.  B.  C.  D.  E.

5.

A.  B.  C.  D.  E.

6

A.  B.  C.  D.  E.

7.

A.  B.  C.  D.  E.

8.

A.  B.  C.  D.  E.

9.

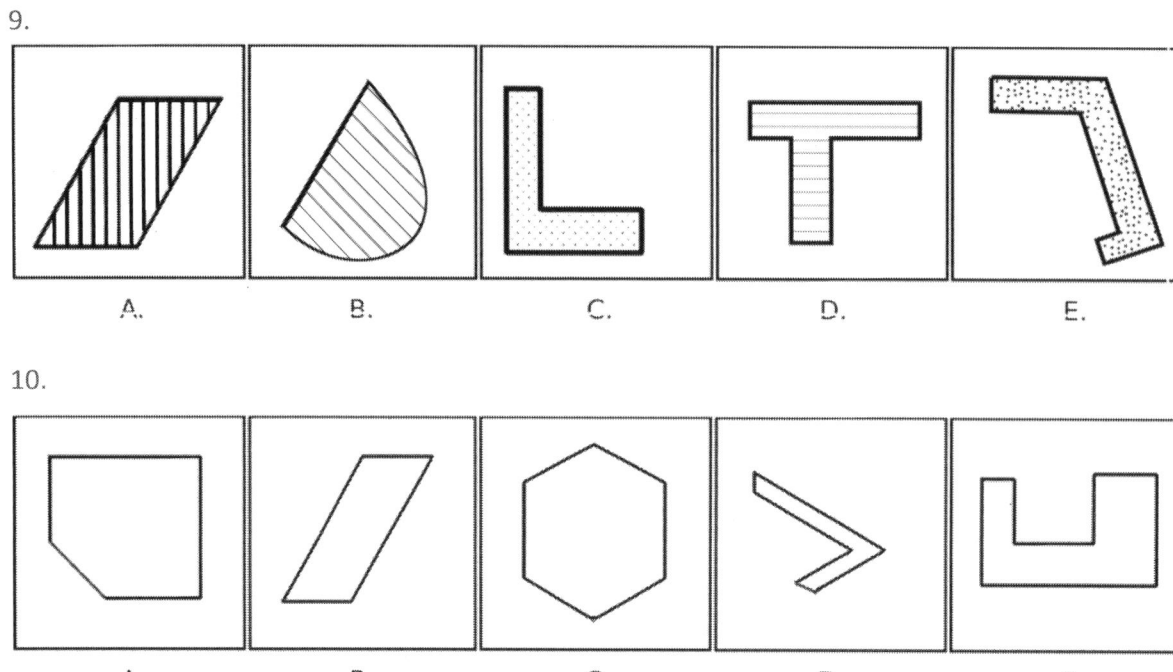

| A. | B. | C. | D. | E. |

10.

| A. | B. | C. | D. | E. |

# CHAPTER 13: SIMILARITIES

In this type of NVR problem, you need to find which option fits in with the two or three examples (normally on the left)

To work out similarity type questions, find one thing that is the same in the examples; then eliminate any shapes that do not share that one characteristic. Then find something else that's the same. Keep repeating this process until there is only one possibility left. Characteristics that can be the same include type of lines, shading, number of sides (total or difference between two shapes), number of shapes, position of shapes and symmetry.

Example:

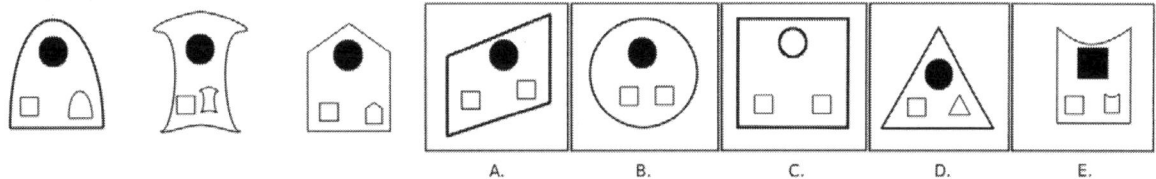

All of the example shapes have a black circle at the top, therefore it can't be C or E.

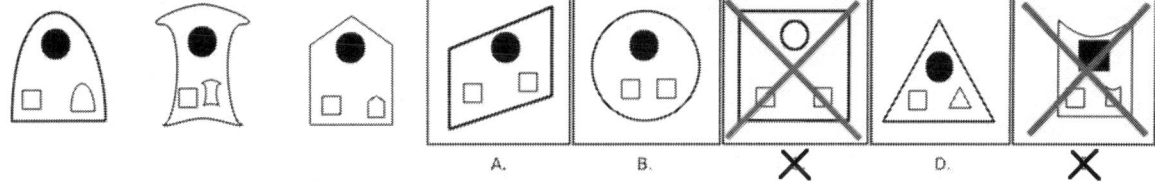

Next, all three of the outer shapes have a vertical line of symmetry, so it cannot be A.

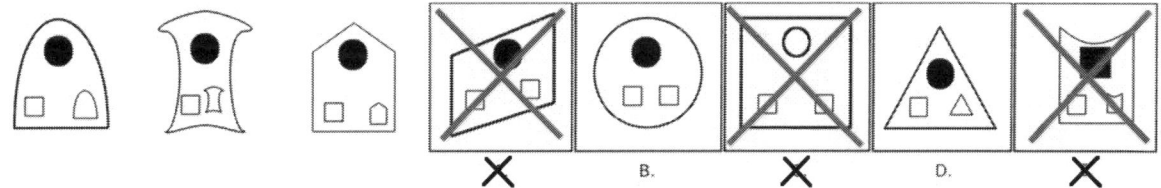

The shape at the bottom right is the same as the large outer shape, so it cannot be B. Therefore the only answer that is left is D. D is therefore the answer.

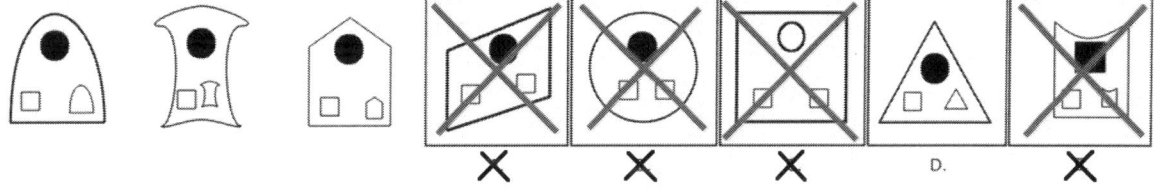

EXERCISE 13: SIMILARITIES.

1.

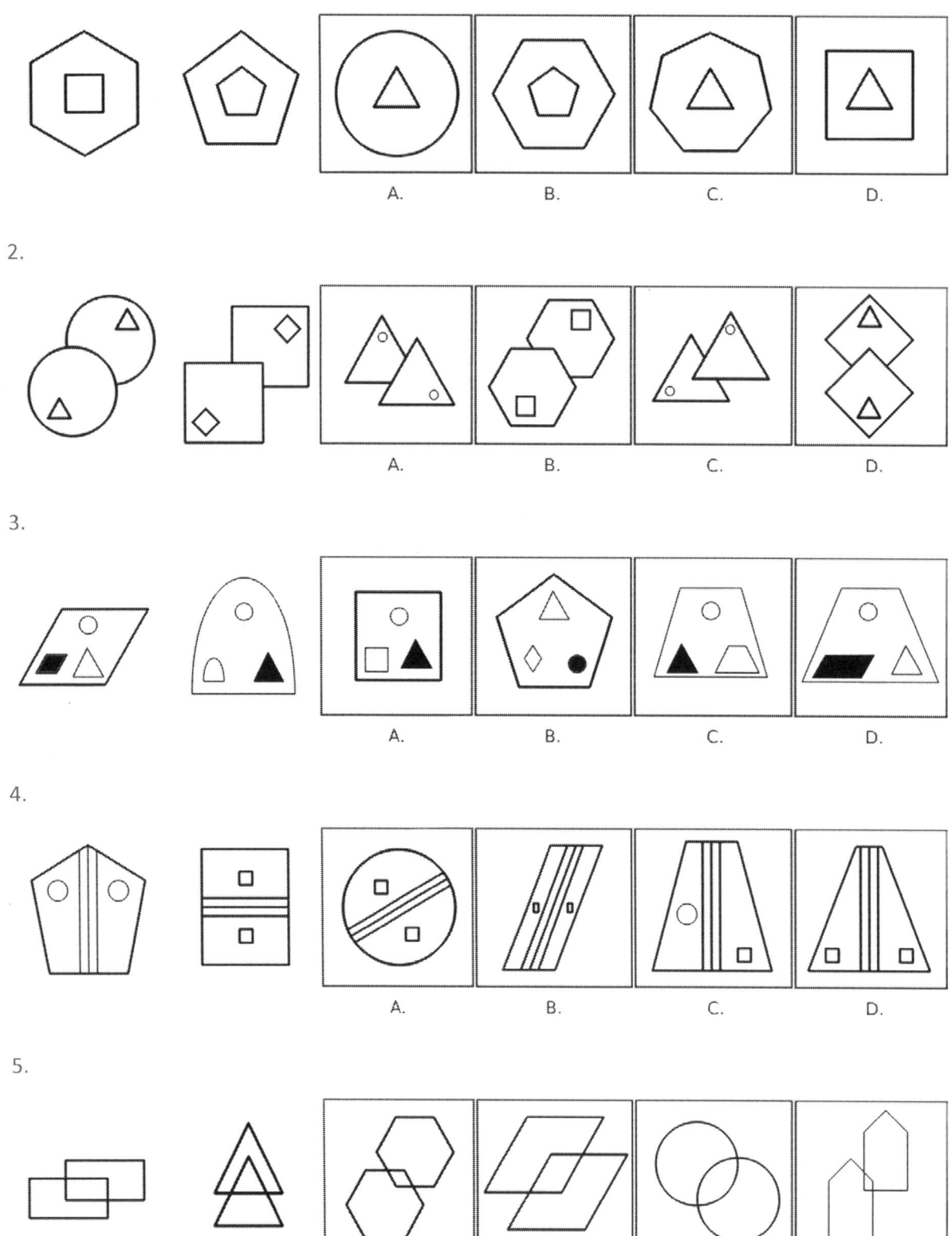

2.

3.

4.

5.

6.

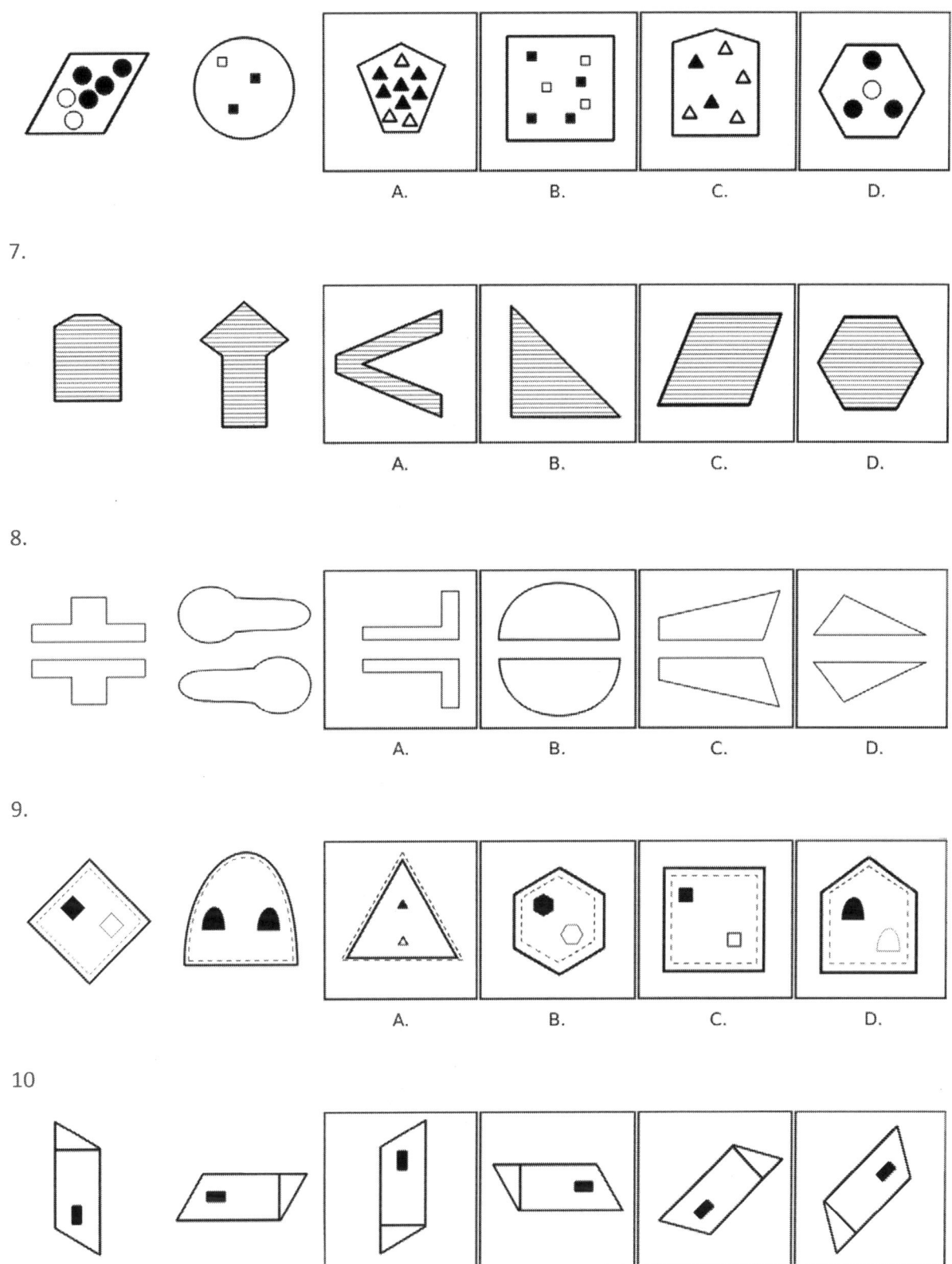

A.　　　B.　　　C.　　　D.

7.

A.　　　B.　　　C.　　　D.

8.

A.　　　B.　　　C.　　　D.

9.

A.　　　B.　　　C.　　　D.

10

A.　　　B.　　　C.　　　D.

# CHAPTER 14: CODES

In codes, the code of the test shape is determined from the codes of the other shapes.

The procedure for working out codes is always the same.

Look at the first letter first:

1. Look for two or more shapes that are the same.

2. Work out what is the same about them.

3. Work out what the first letter is.

4. Write the letter below the test shape.

Look at the second shape and repeat the steps above. Repeat for any remaining letters.

If, for one letter they are all different, then we need to ask what is different about them all.

Example:

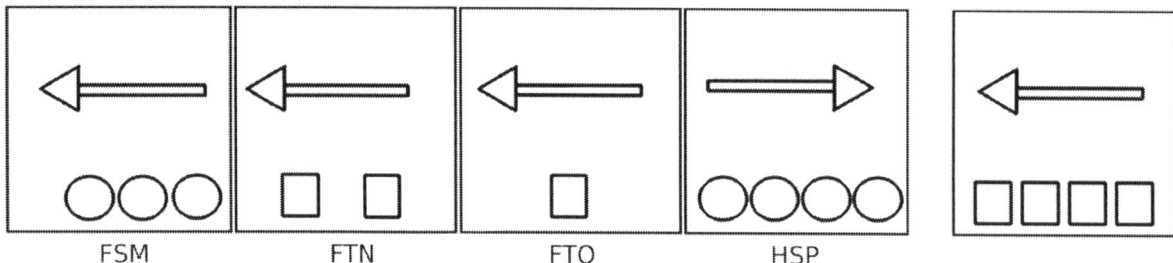

| FSM | FTN | FTO | HSP | |

Look at the first letter first. There are three 'F's.

In all of the 'F's the arrow points to the left. So the first letter stands for the direction. So the first letter is 'F' and I can write 'F' below the test shape.

Now we move on to the second letter; there are two 'S's. Both of the 'S's have circles below the arrows. So the second letter is the shape below the arrows. So the second letter is 'T' and I write 'T' after the 'F' below the test shape.

Finally, I come to the third letter. All of the letters are different; so I ask what is different about them all. They all have a different number of shapes below the arrow. There are four shapes under the arrow in my test shape – so the third letter is 'P', and I write 'P' under the test shape. The answer is 'FTP'.

EXERCISE 14:

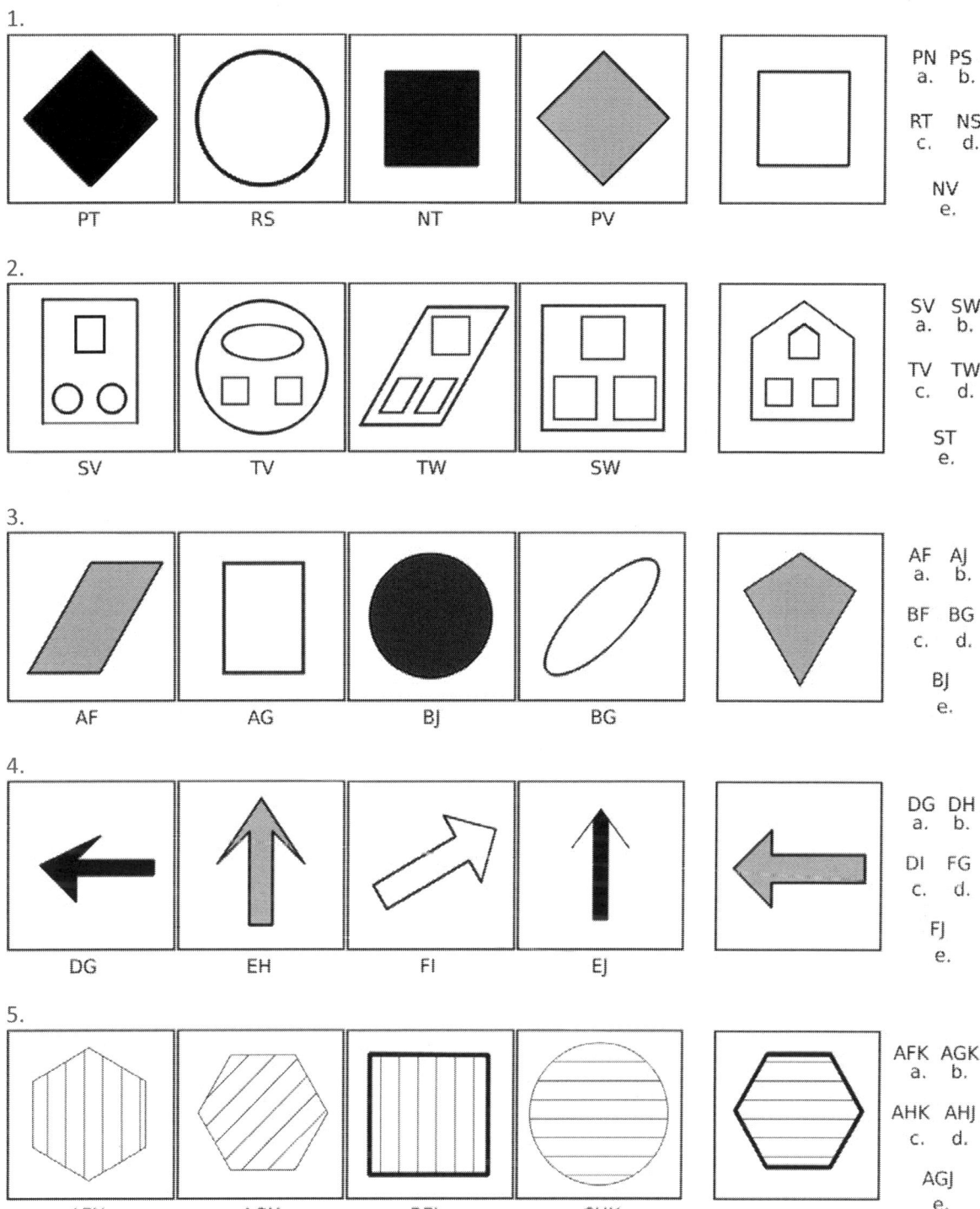

1.

| PT | RS | NT | PV | |
|----|----|----|----|---|

PN PS
a.   b.

RT  NS
c.   d.

NV
e.

2.

| SV | TV | TW | SW | |
|----|----|----|----|---|

SV SW
a.   b.

TV  TW
c.   d.

ST
e.

3.

| AF | AG | BJ | BG | |
|----|----|----|----|---|

AF  AJ
a.   b.

BF  BG
c.   d.

BJ
e.

4.

| DG | EH | FI | EJ | |
|----|----|----|----|---|

DG DH
a.   b.

DI  FG
c.   d.

FJ
e.

5.

| AFK | AGK | BFJ | CHK | |
|-----|-----|-----|-----|---|

AFK AGK
a.    b.

AHK AHJ
c.    d.

AGJ
e.

57

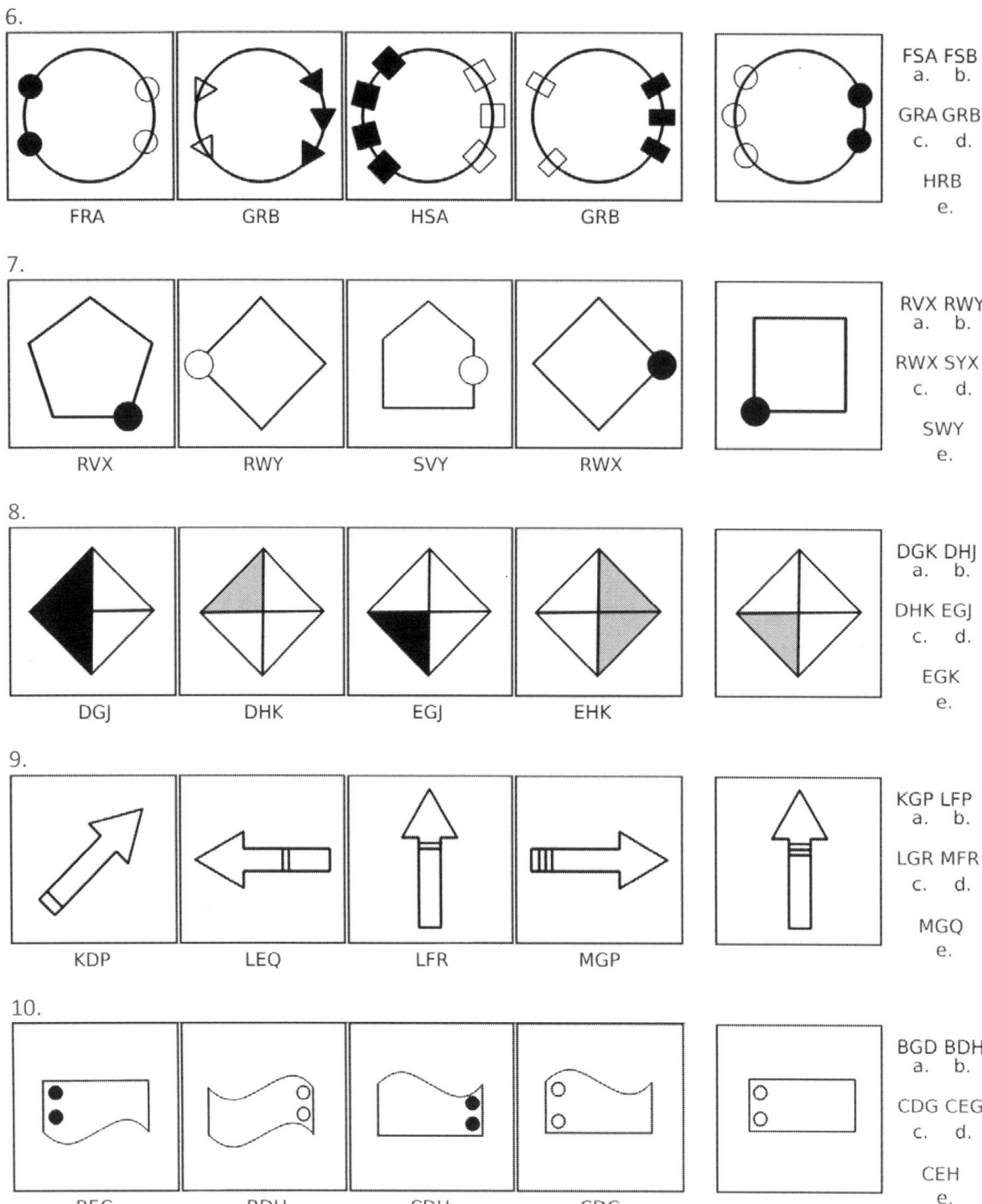

6.

FRA GRB HSA GRB

FSA FSB
a. b.

GRA GRB
c. d.

HRB
e.

7.

RVX RWY SVY RWX

RVX RWY
a. b.

RWX SYX
c. d.

SWY
e.

8.

DGJ DHK EGJ EHK

DGK DHJ
a. b.

DHK EGJ
c. d.

EGK
e.

9.

KDP LEQ LFR MGP

KGP LFP
a. b.

LGR MFR
c. d.

MGQ
e.

10.

BEG BDH CDH CDG

BGD BDH
a. b.

CDG CEG
c. d.

CEH
e.

# CHAPTER 15: MATRICES

There are a number of different types of matrices or grid questions.

The main types being:

    4 Square matrix
    9 Square matrix
    Segments
    Hexagon grid

We will deal with Segments and Hexagon grids in the next chapter. As with all NVR type questions, matrices involve finding a pattern and eliminating the wrong options.

However, the different types of matrices work differently.

## Four Square Matrix

Four square matrices can be done either horizontally or vertically. Four square matrices work in the same way as analogies: whatever happens in one row/column, you must do exactly the same in the other row/column.

Example

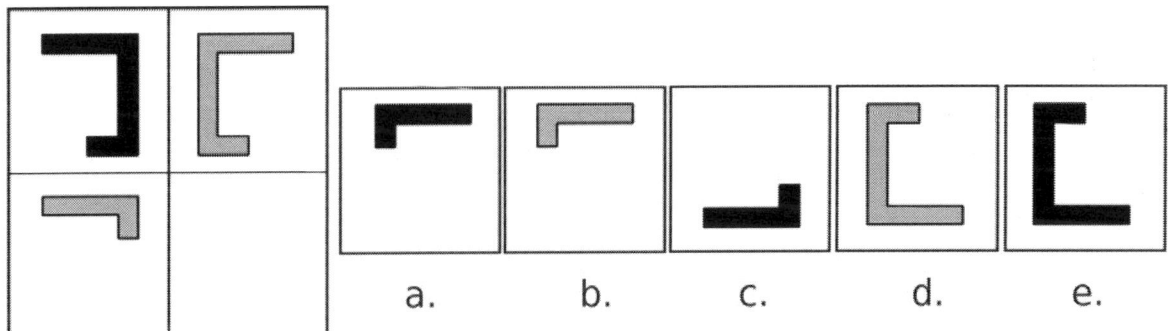

a.     b.     c.     d.     e.

This can be completed either horizontally or vertically.

## Horizontally

Going left to right:

    1, Top row – shapes reflected.

    So: the bottom row is also reflected. Therefore we eliminate c, d and e.

59

2, Top row coloured fill goes from black to grey.

The bottom row colour goes from grey to black. Therefore eliminate b (grey and black swap).

Therefore the answer is a.


Vertically

Going down:

1, in the first column, the bottom shape is the top half of the shape in the top square.

So: in the second column. The shape in the bottom square must be the top half of the shape in the top square. Therefore we can eliminate c, d and e.

2. In the first column, the coloured fill goes from black to grey.

So: in the second column, the colours will swap from grey to black. Therefore eliminate b.

Therefore the answer is a.


Nine Square Matrix

Nine square matrices work in three ways. A single question may involve, one, two or all three methods:

1. Each row and column contains one of each shape or shading.

2. Each row has a particular characteristic.

3. Each column has a particular characteristic.

Example

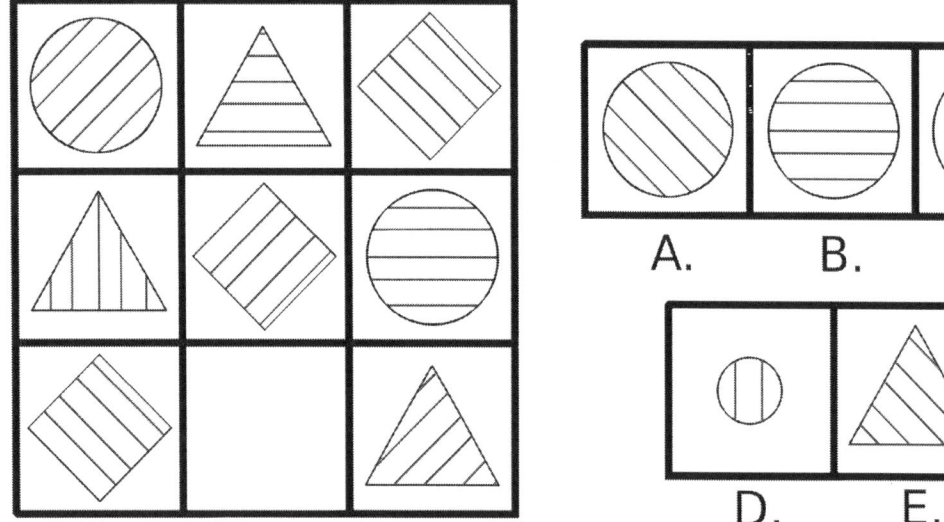

1. Each row and column has a circle, triangle and diamond: What is missing is a circle, so we can eliminate, E.

2. All of the triangles are the same size, as are all of the diamonds, so all of the circles will be the same size, so we can eliminate D.

3. Looking across each row, the shading rotates 45° clockwise each time. So the shading of the diamond in the third row needs to be rotated 45° clockwise, so we can eliminate A and B.

Therefore the answer is C

## EXERCISE 15

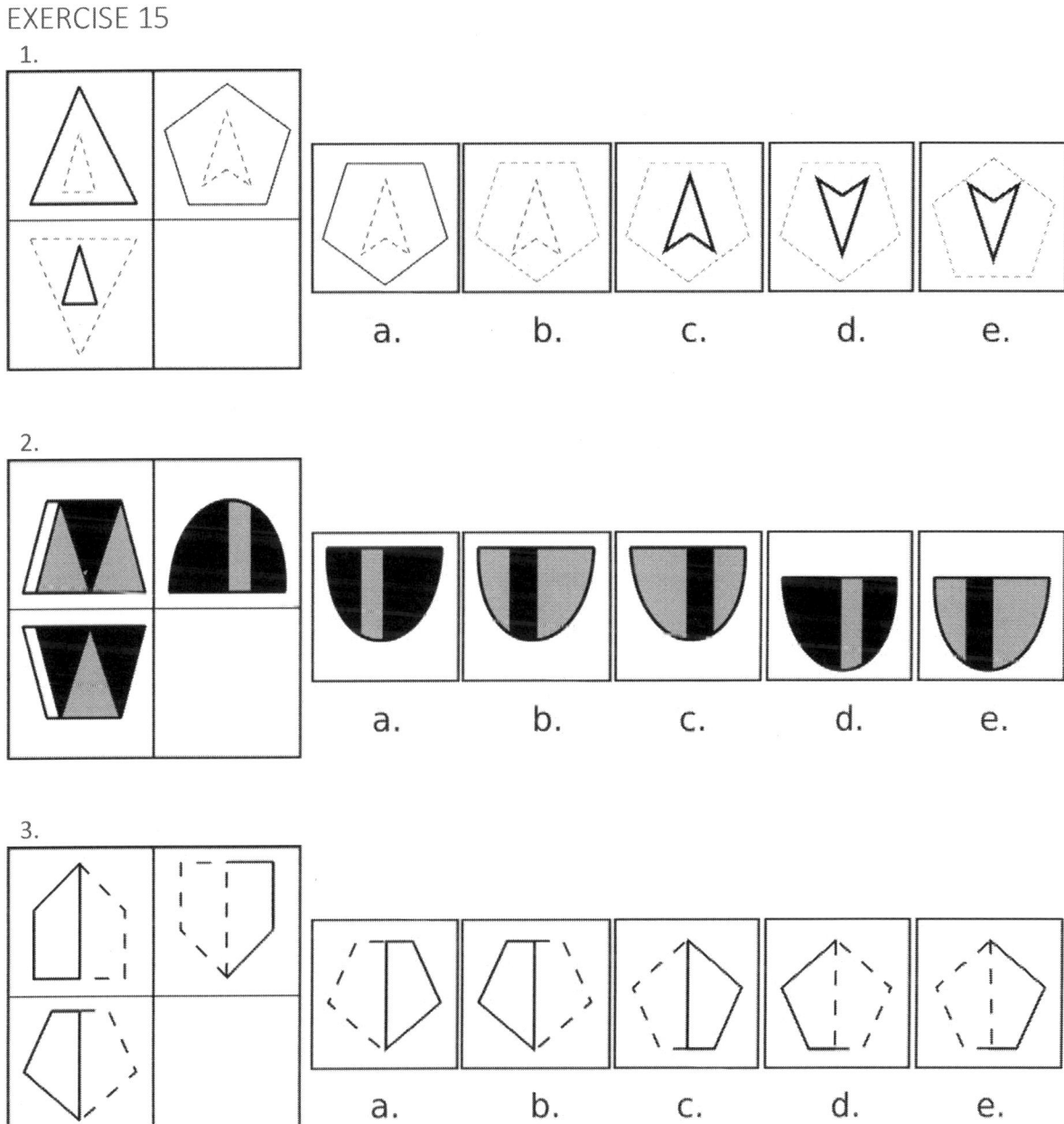

4.

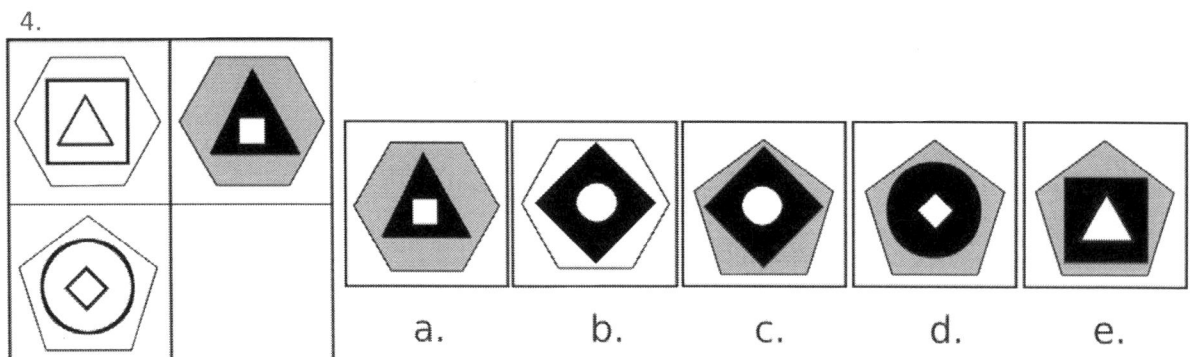

a.    b.    c.    d.    e.

5.

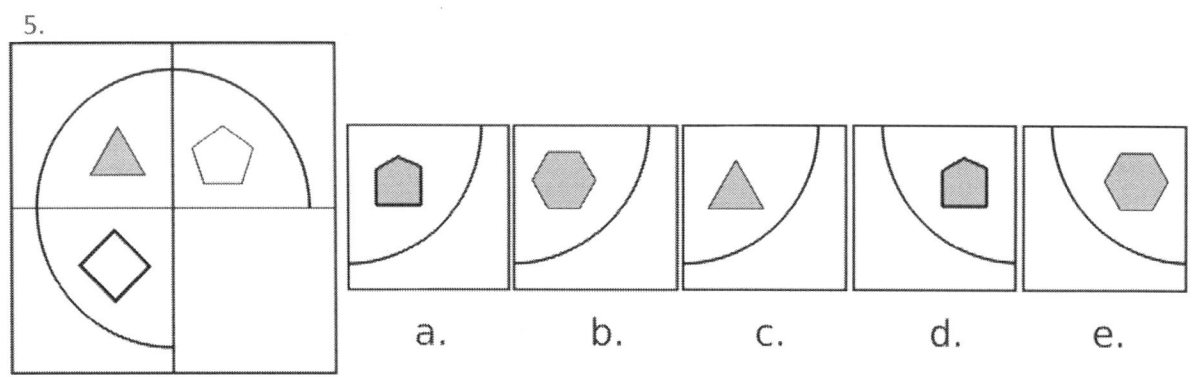

a.    b.    c.    d.    e.

6.

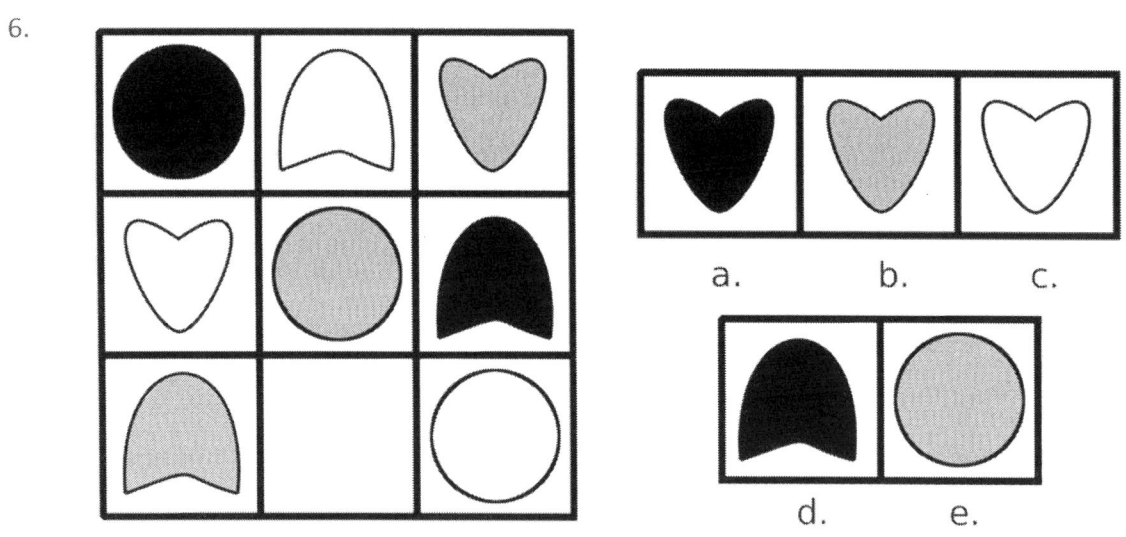

a.    b.    c.

d.    e.

7.

a.      b.      c.

d.      e.

8.

a.      b.      c.

d.      e.

9.

a.      b.      c.

d.      e.

10.

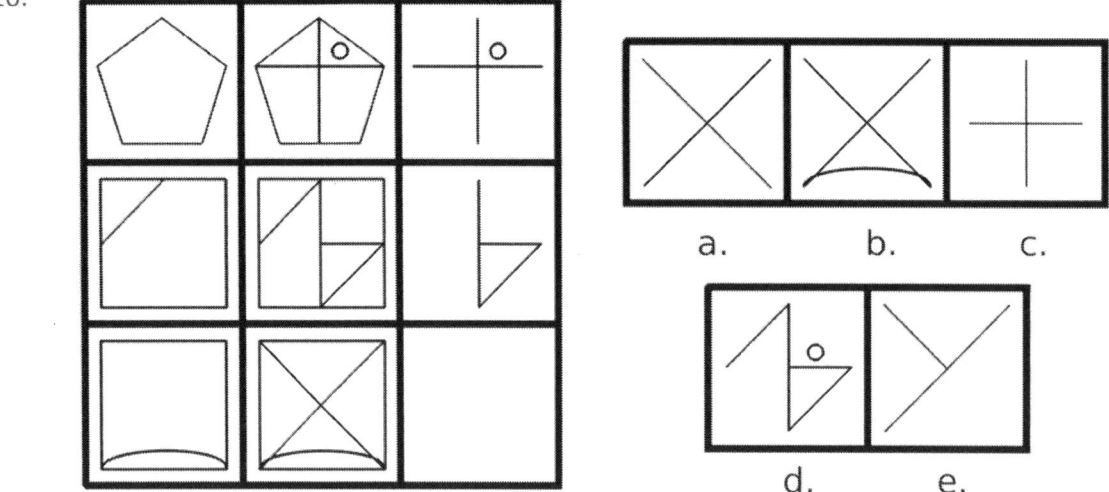

a.          b.          c.

d.          e.

# CHAPTER 16: SEGMENT AND HEXAGONS

Segments and hexagonal grids work in two ways:

A series that forms a loop.

Connections between opposite shapes.

Example

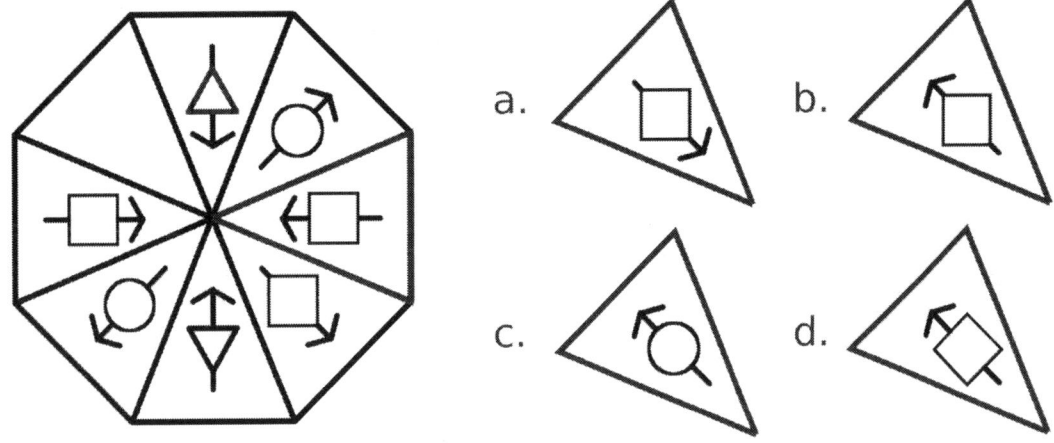

Answer:

Going around the octagon the arrows alternately point towards the centre and

then outwards.

Shapes on each of the arrows, are reflections of the shapes of their opposite segments.

Therefore the answer is B.

EXERCISE 16.

1.

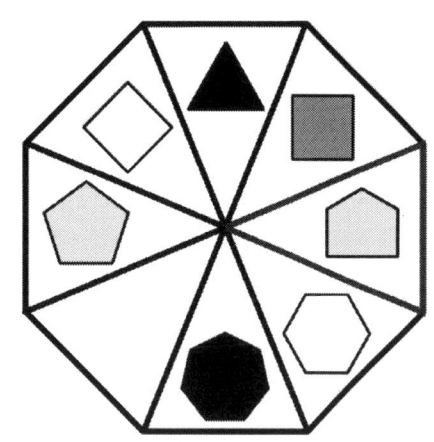     a. 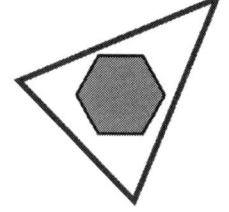     b.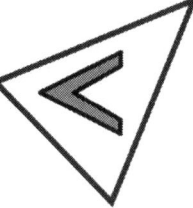

c. 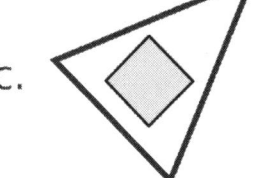     d.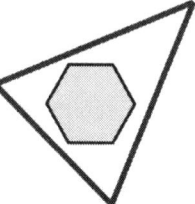

2.

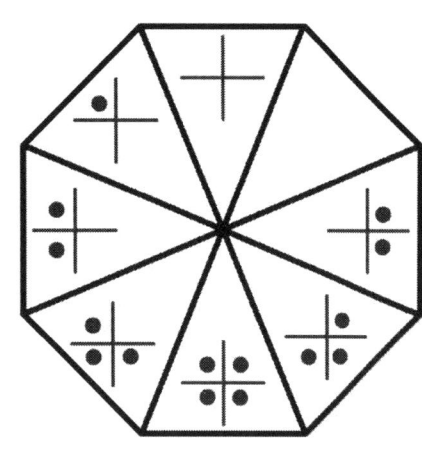     a. 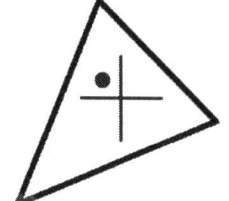     b.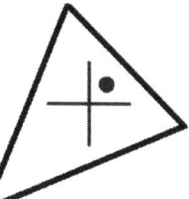

c. 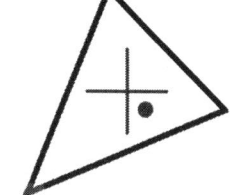     d.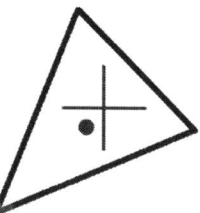

3.

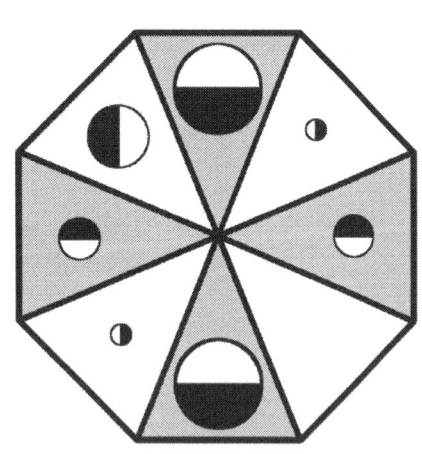     a. 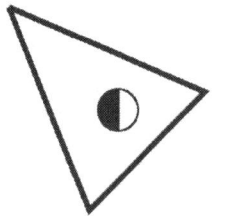     b.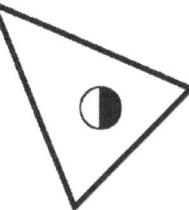

c. 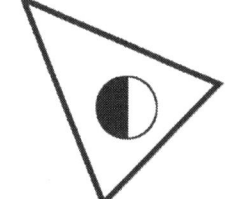     d.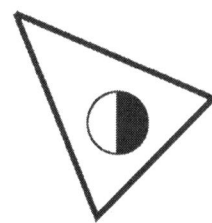

4.

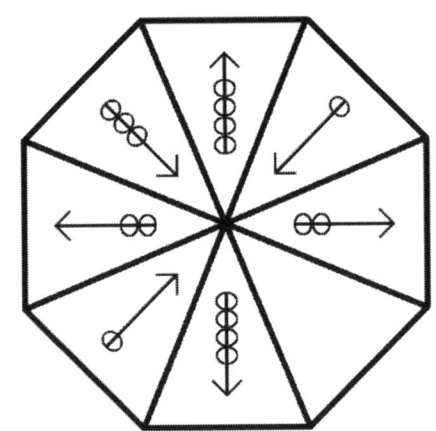

a.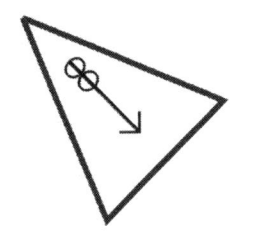

b.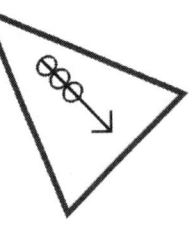

c.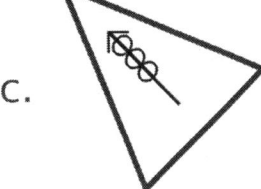

d.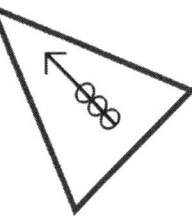

5.

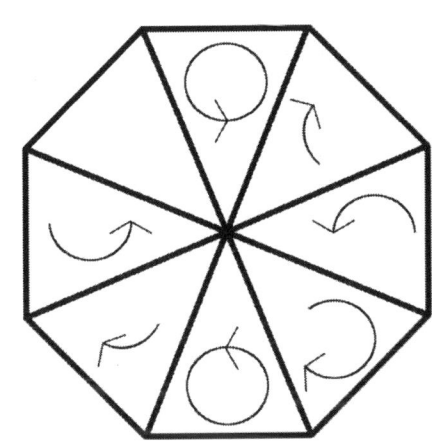

a.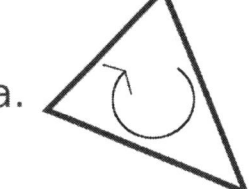

b.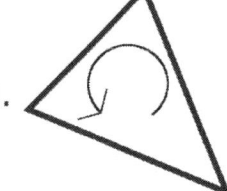

c.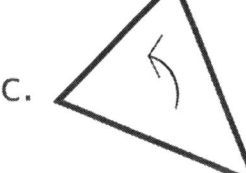

d.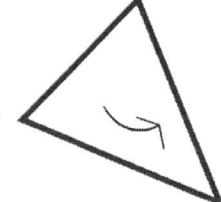

6.

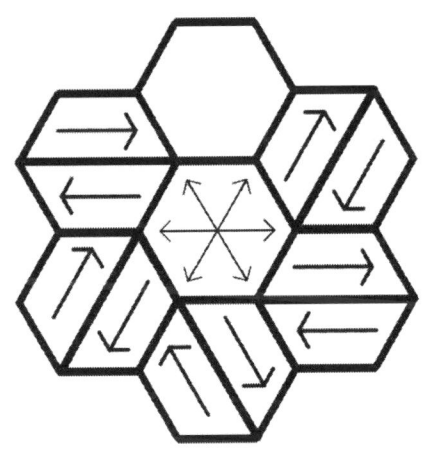

a.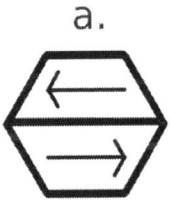

b.

c.

d.

e.

7.

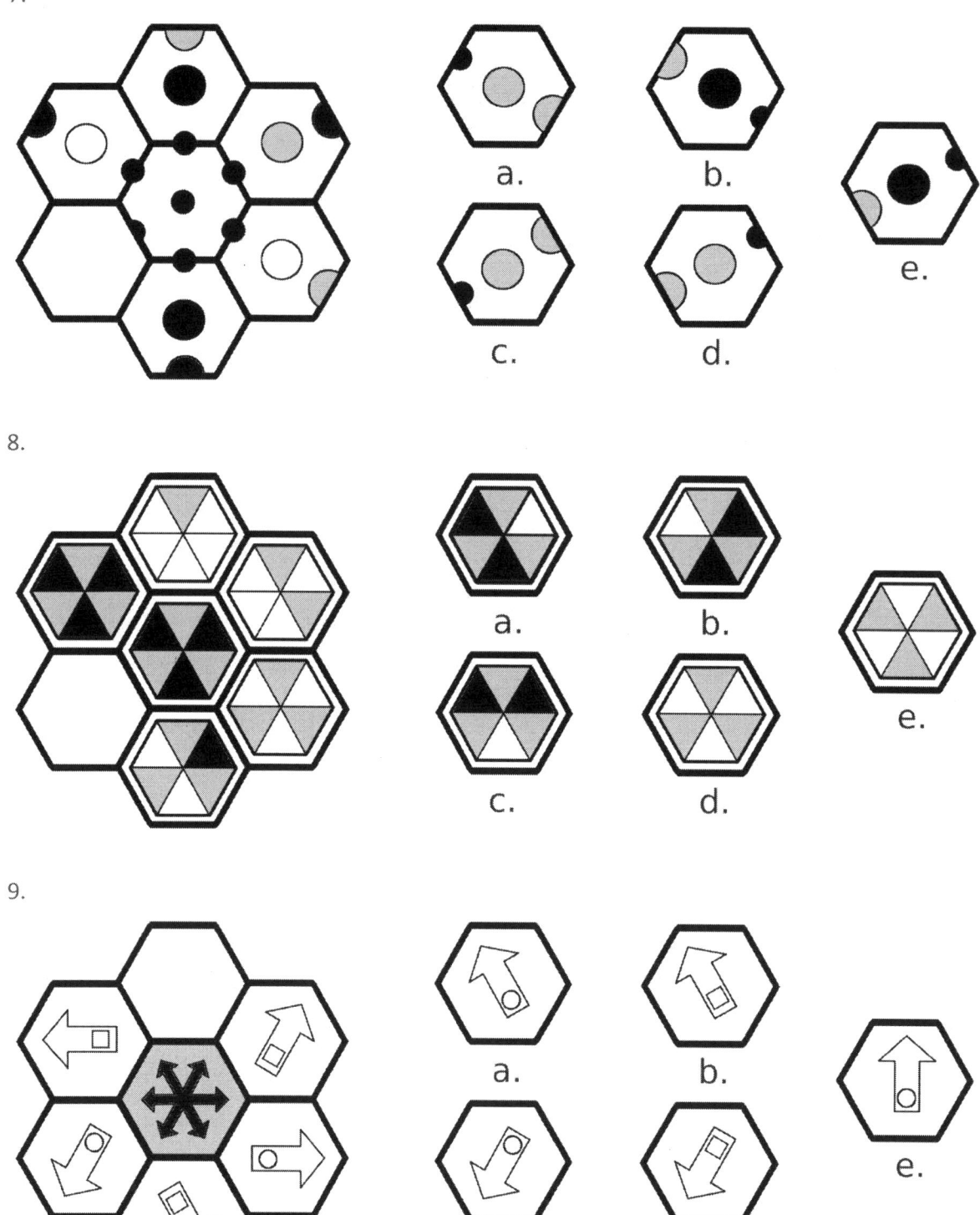

8.

9.

10.

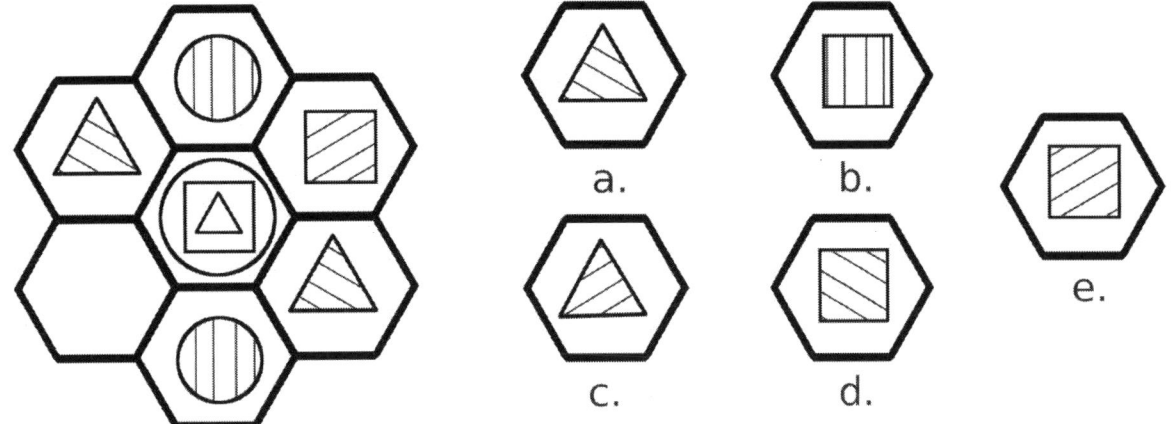

# CHAPTER 17: SERIES

In a series question, work out what the pattern is and then find the shape that is missing.

There are two types of series:

        Repetitive – a, b, c, a, b, c, a, b, c.
        Cumulative – keeps going up, or going down.

If there is a repetitive pattern of only two items, we can say that they alternate.

Example

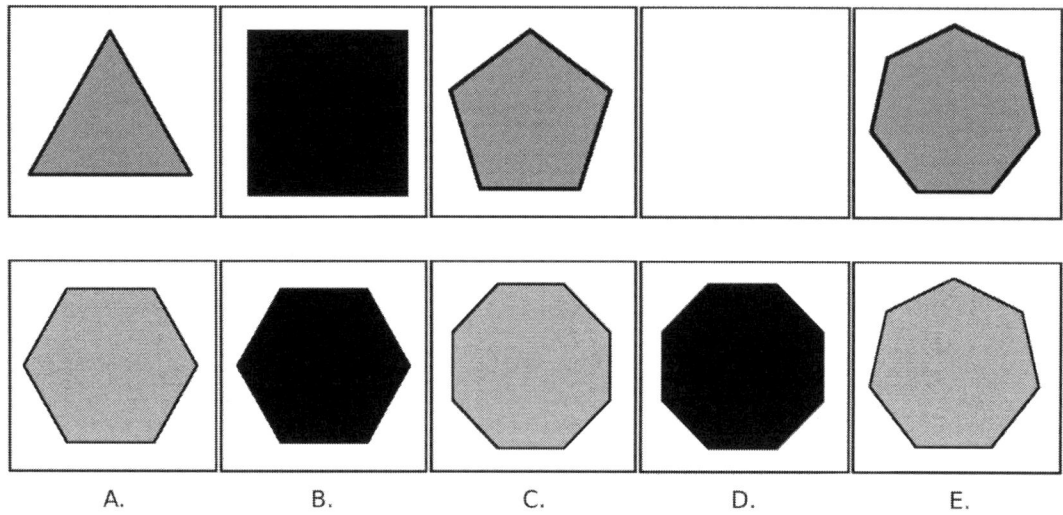

A.        B.        C.        D.        E.

        The shading is a repetitive pattern; grey/ black/ grey/ black
        So the missing colour is black.
        Therefore we eliminate: A, C, E.
        The number of sides is a cumulative pattern: 3, 4, 5, 6, and 7.
        So the missing shape will have six sides.
        Therefore: eliminate D.

        The answer is B.

1.

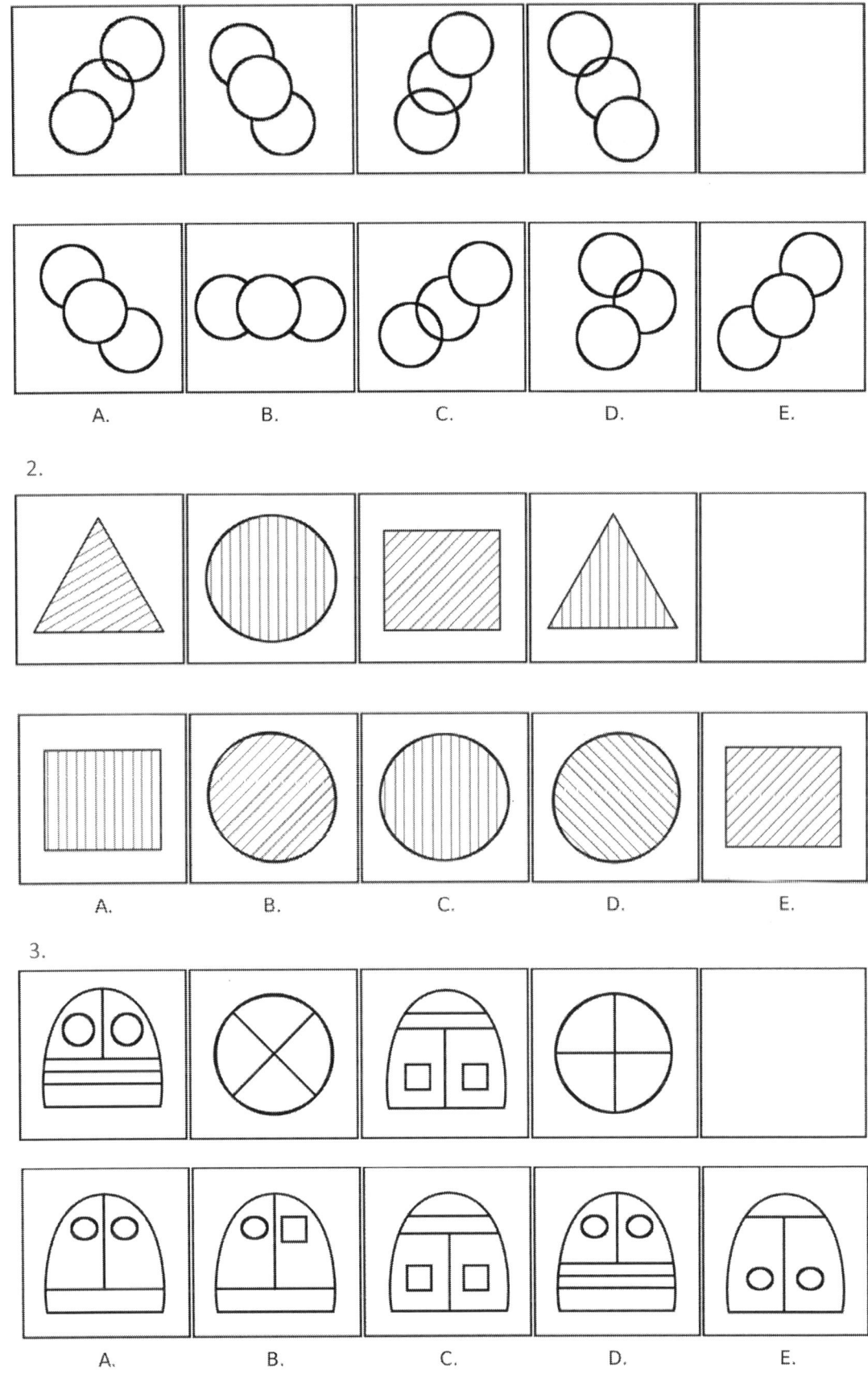

2.

3.

4.

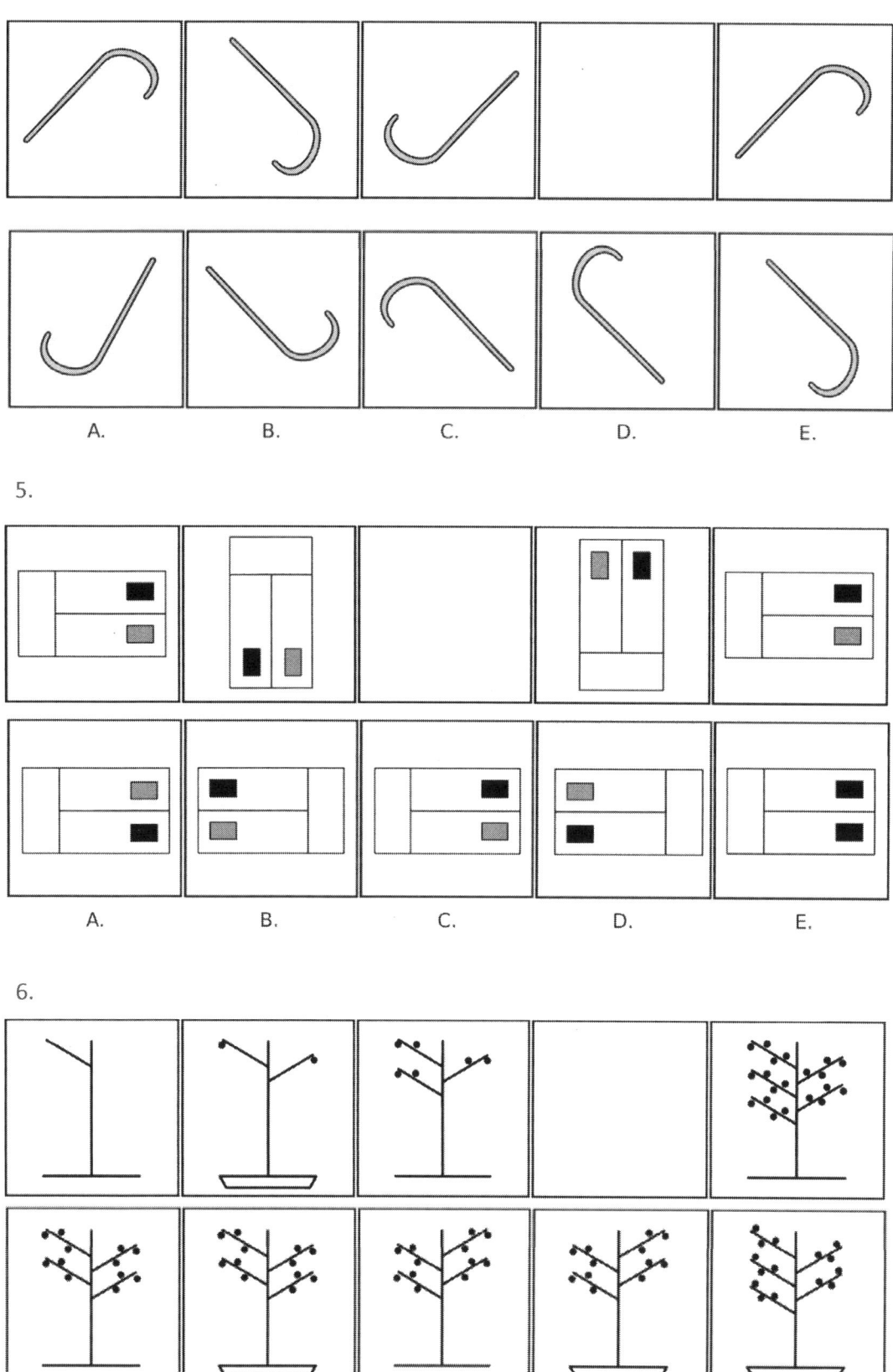

5.

6.

7.

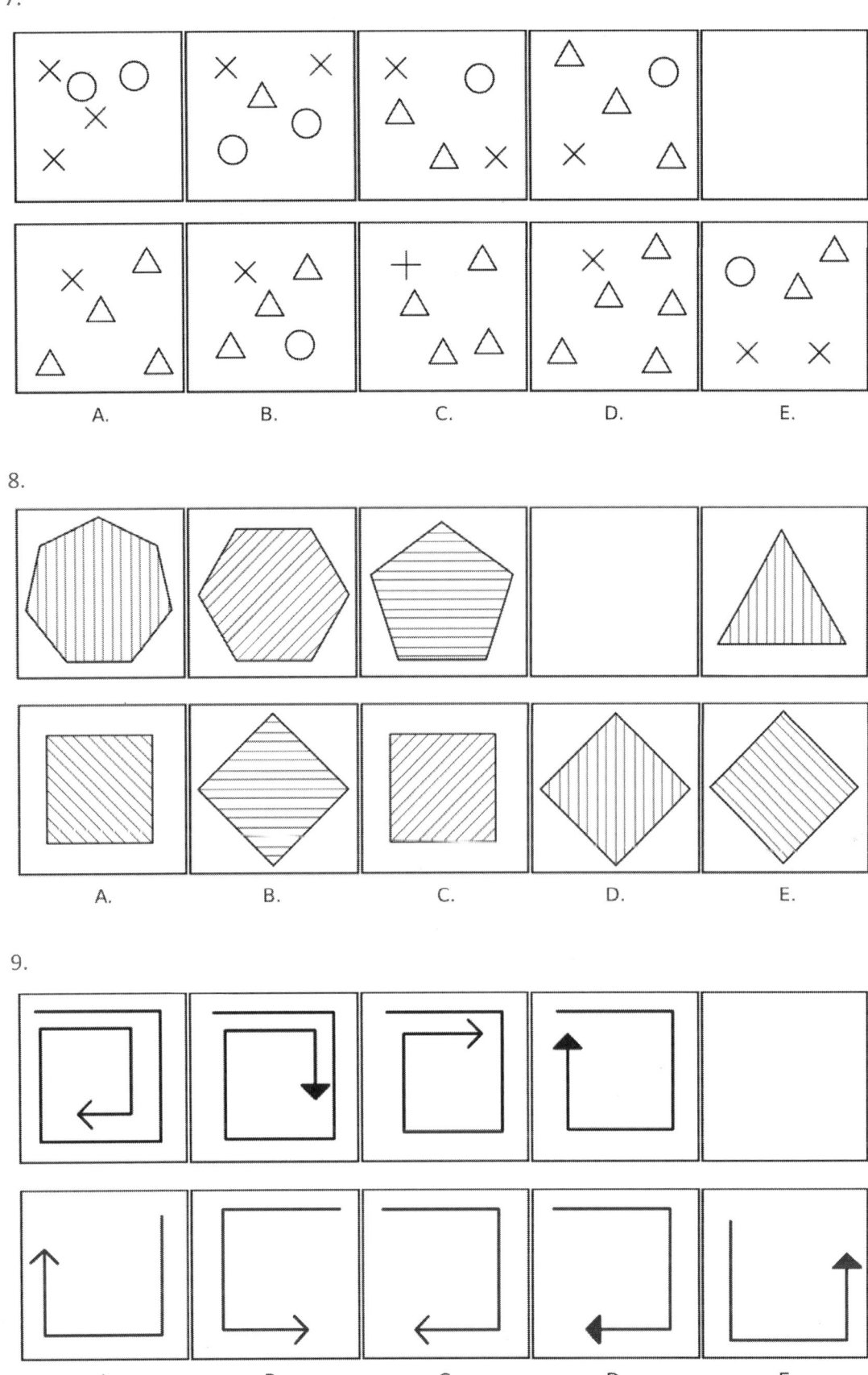

A.   B.   C.   D.   E.

8.

A.   B.   C.   D.   E.

9.

A.   B.   C.   D.   E.

10.

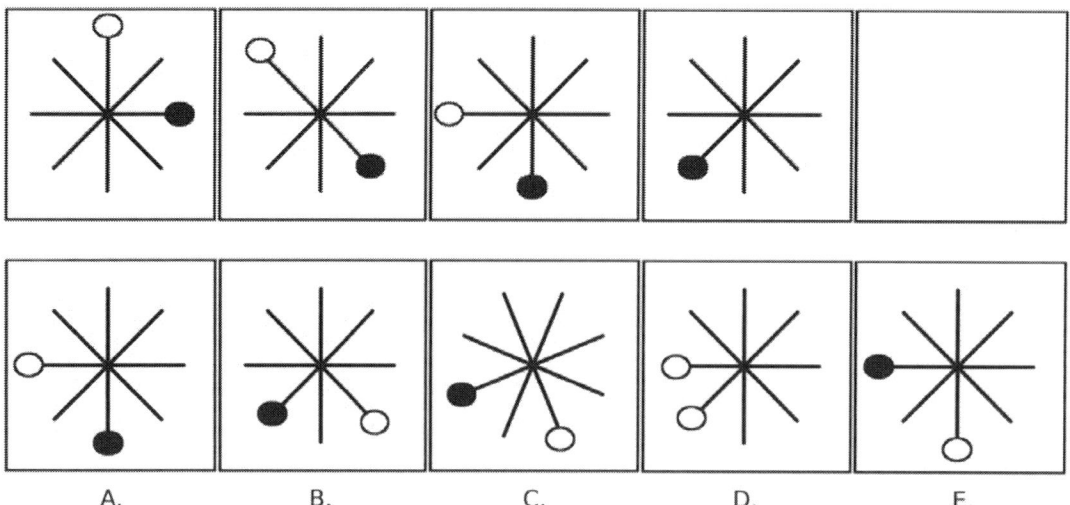

A.         B.         C.         D.         E.

# CHAPTER 18: SEQUENCES

In these questions, there are two squares left blank. However, together they make the one series. You need to decide which of the answers should replace each of the black squares, in turn. Each of the black squares will have a different question number. Generally, each black square will be a different answer.

The same possible answers apply to both questions. This means you need to be careful when eliminating, as you will need to reconsider the same options for the next black square in the series.

Make sure when you answer the questions you make it clear, which answer relates to which question number.

## EXERCISE 18
What images best complete the series below?

1 and 2

A.    B.    C.    D.    E.    F.

3 and 4

A.    B.    C.    D.    E.    F.

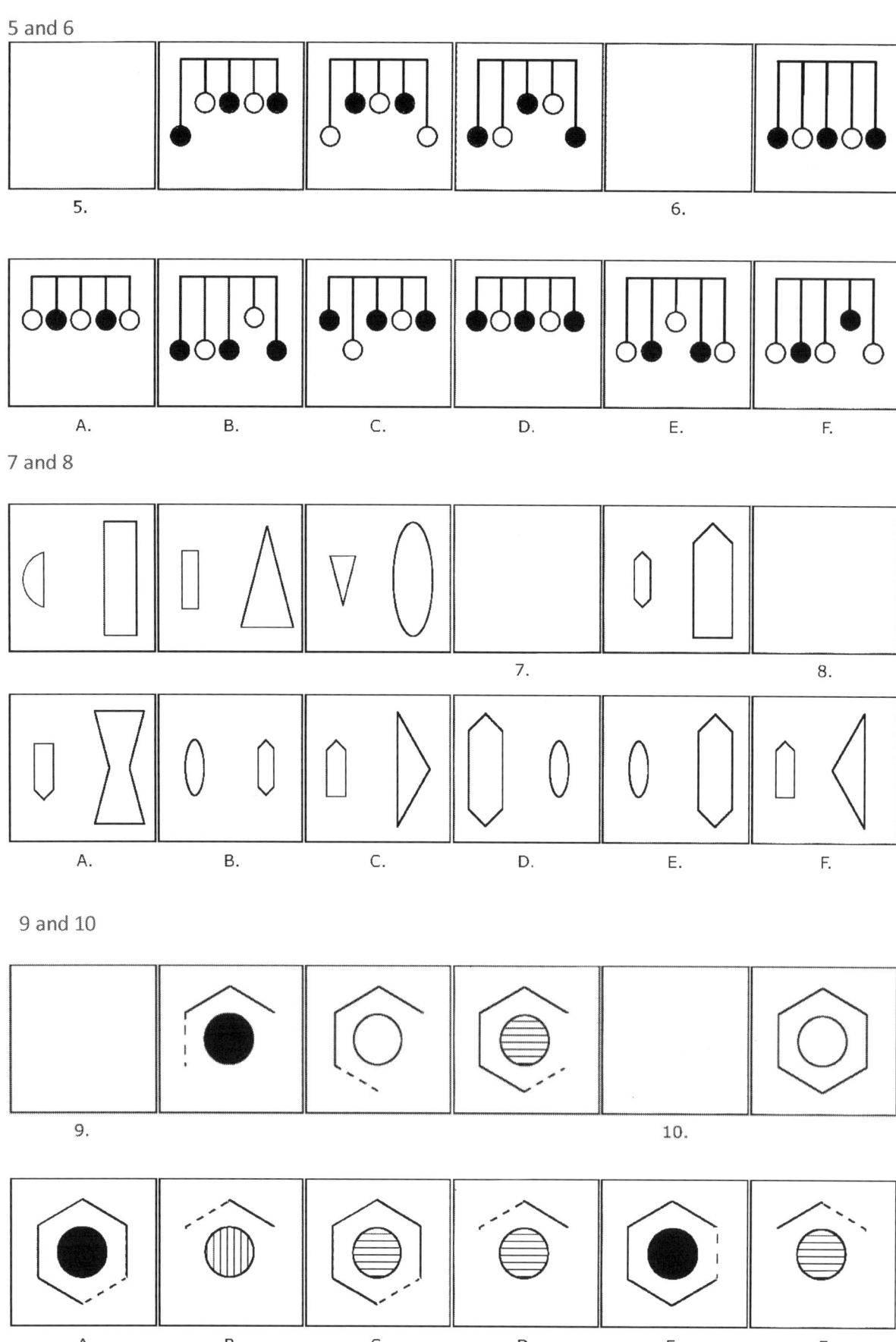

# CHAPTER 19: ANALOGIES

Analogies can be thought of as "this is to that, as this is to that."  In these questions whatever happens to the first pair, to the third shape we do **exactly the same**.

Example:

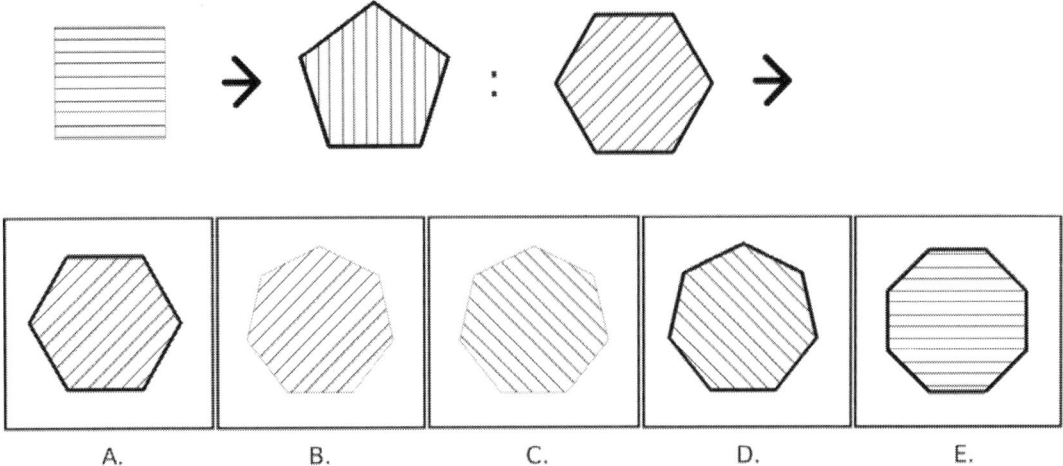

In the first pair:

The number of sides increases by one.  So in the second pair the number of sides must increase by one.  So it cannot be A or E.

In the first pair the shading rotates 90 degrees, so in the second pair, the shading must also rotate 90 degrees, so it cannot be B.

In the first pair, the outside line changes between thin and bold, so in the second pair the outside line must also go between thin and bold.  The outside line is bold so the second figure's line must be thin.  So it cannot be D.

Therefore, the answer is C.

EXERCISE 19:

1.

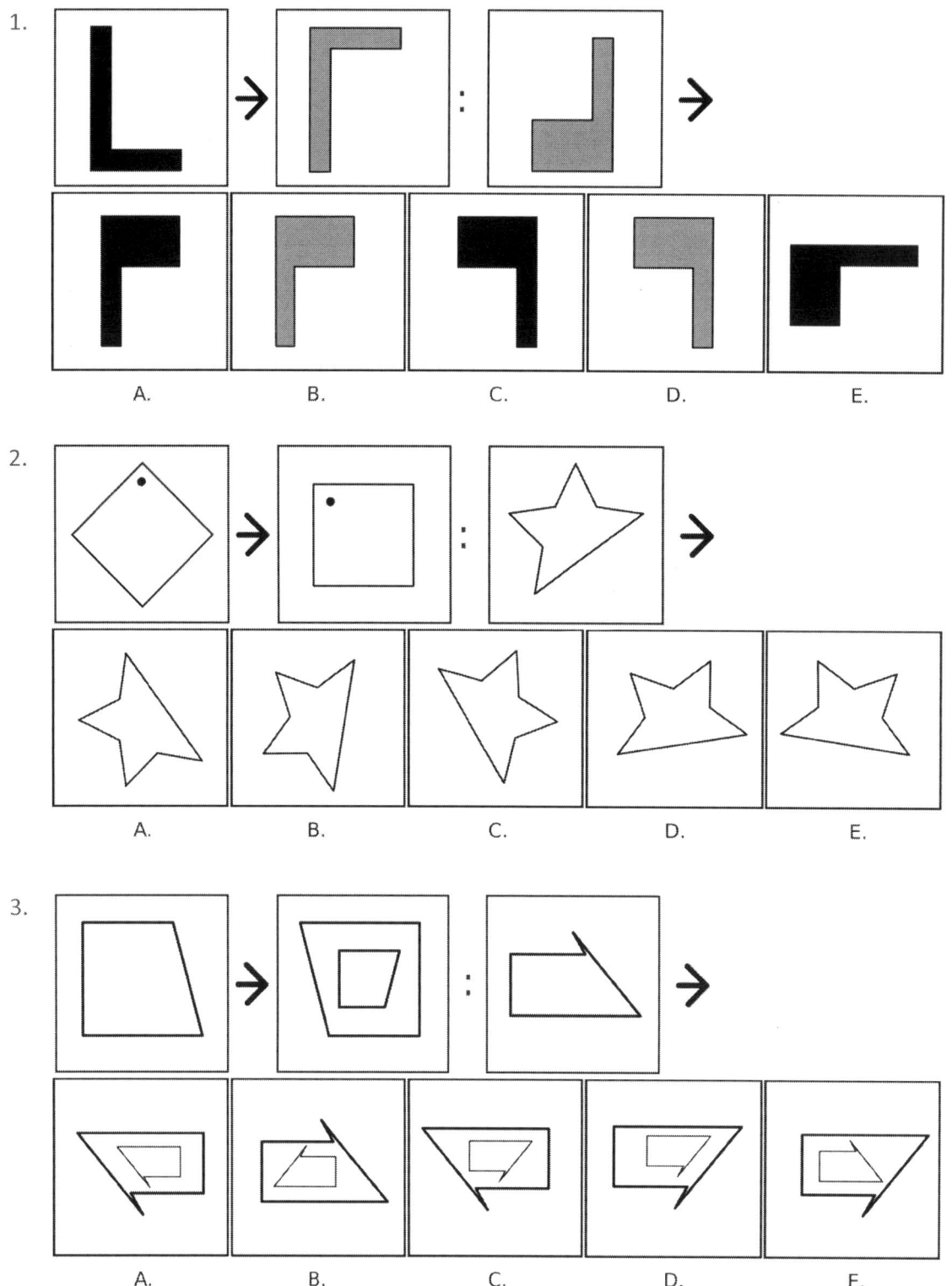

2.

3.

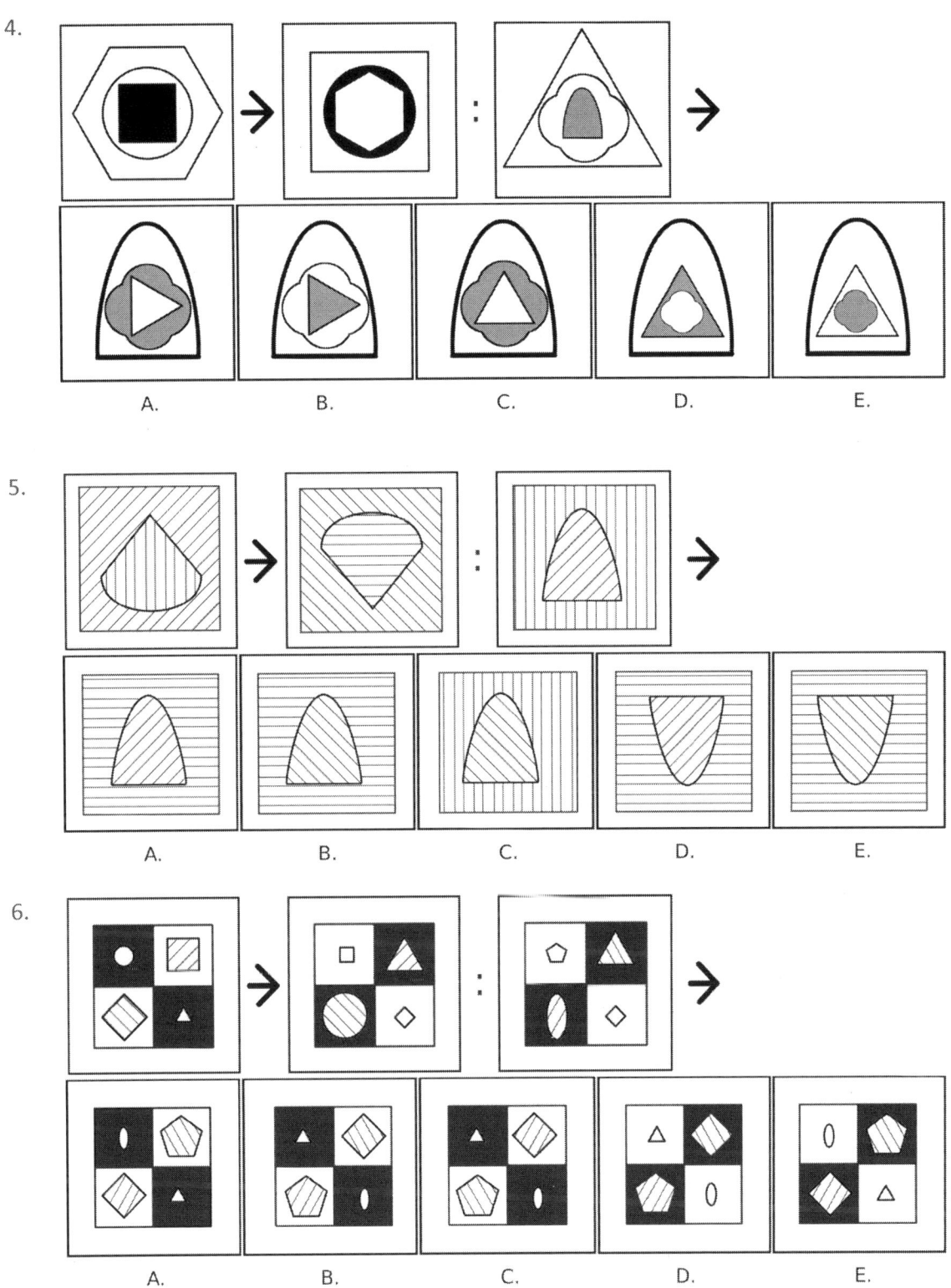

7.

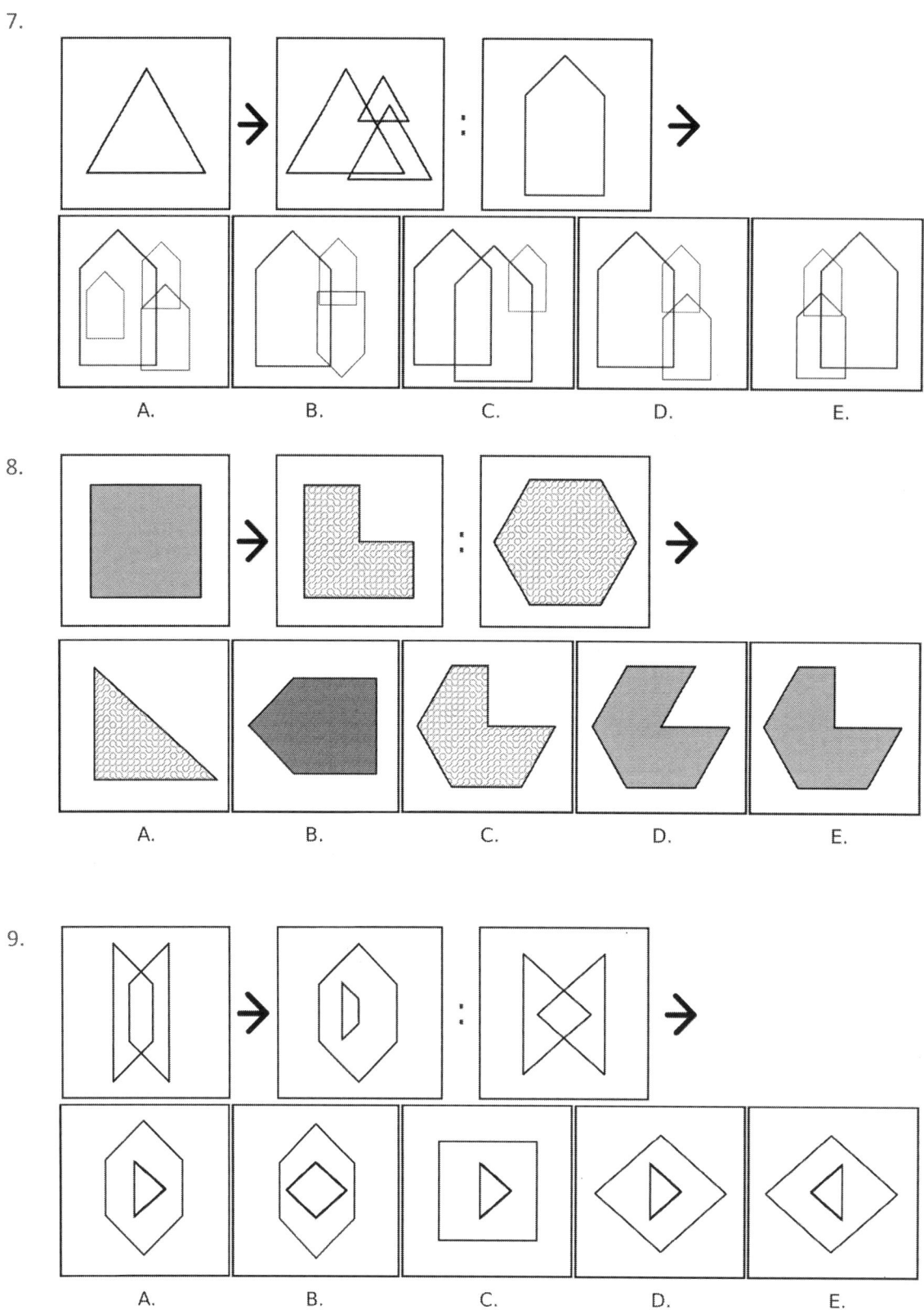

A.      B.      C.      D.      E.

8.

A.      B.      C.      D.      E.

9.

A.      B.      C.      D.      E.

10.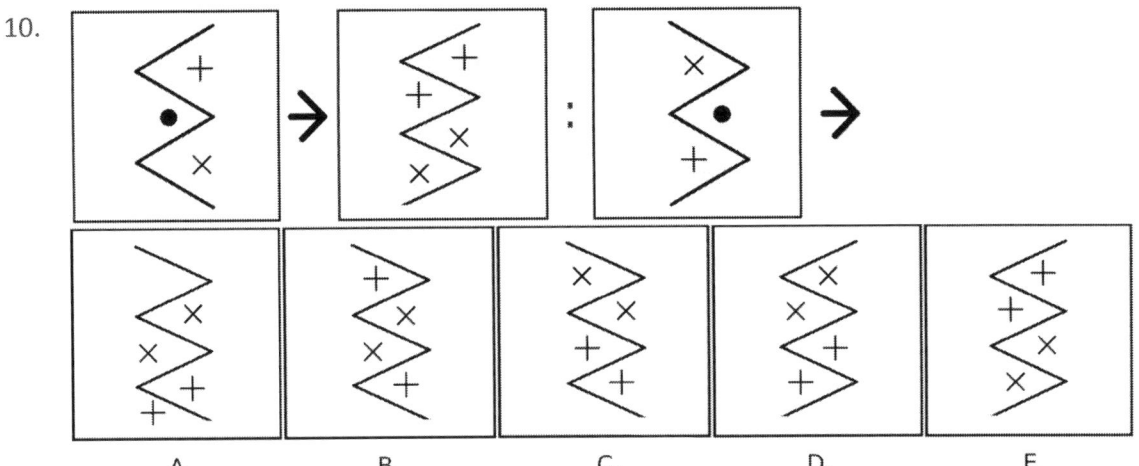

A.     B.     C.     D.     E.

# CHAPTER 20: FOOTPRINTS

In footprint, or plan view questions, you need to work out the 2D space that a 3D shape takes up.

If you look down at the shape from above, anywhere there is a cube blocking the light to the bottom – there should be a square on the answer regardless of how high up the cube is.

Example

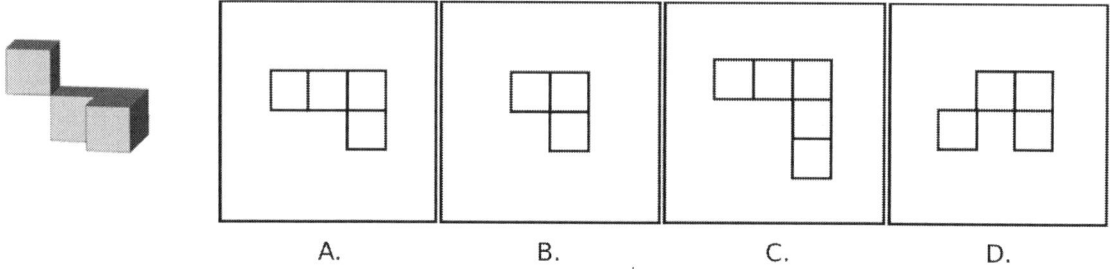

A.    B.    C.    D.

The answer we are looking for is A, as looking down from above, that is the squares that the shape uses (or the footprint that it casts).

## EXERCISE 20:

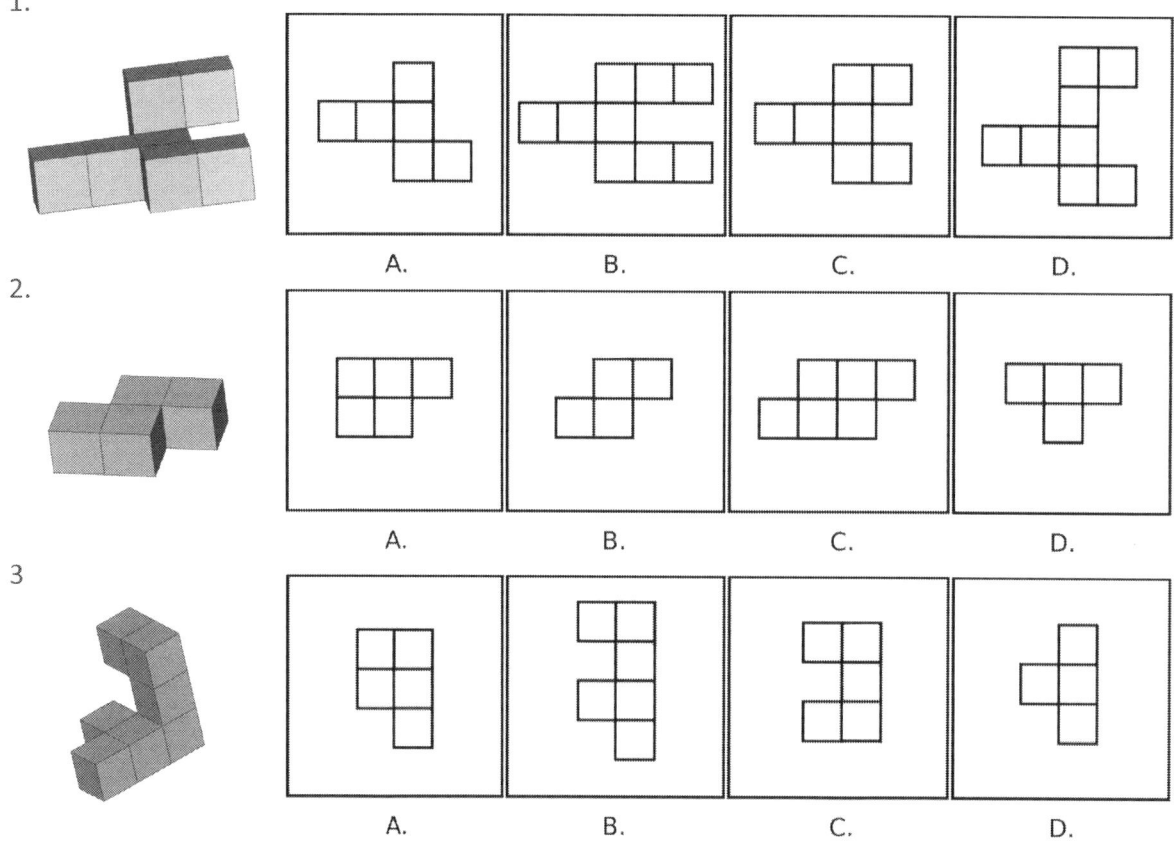

1.

A.    B.    C.    D.

2.

A.    B.    C.    D.

3

A.    B.    C.    D.

4.

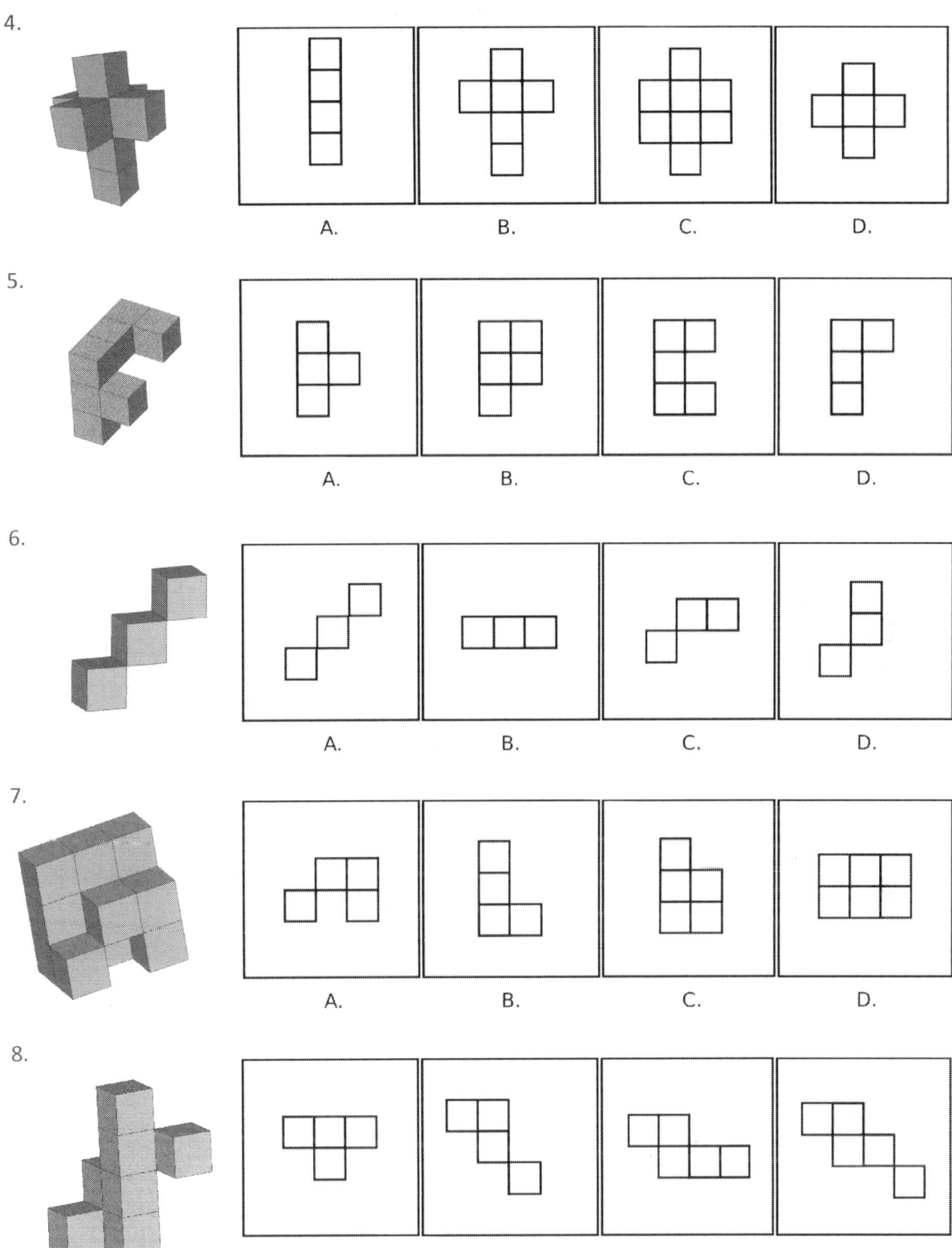

A.  B.  C.  D.

5.

A.  B.  C.  D.

6.

A.  B.  C.  D.

7.

A.  B.  C.  D.

8.

A.  B.  C.  D.

9.

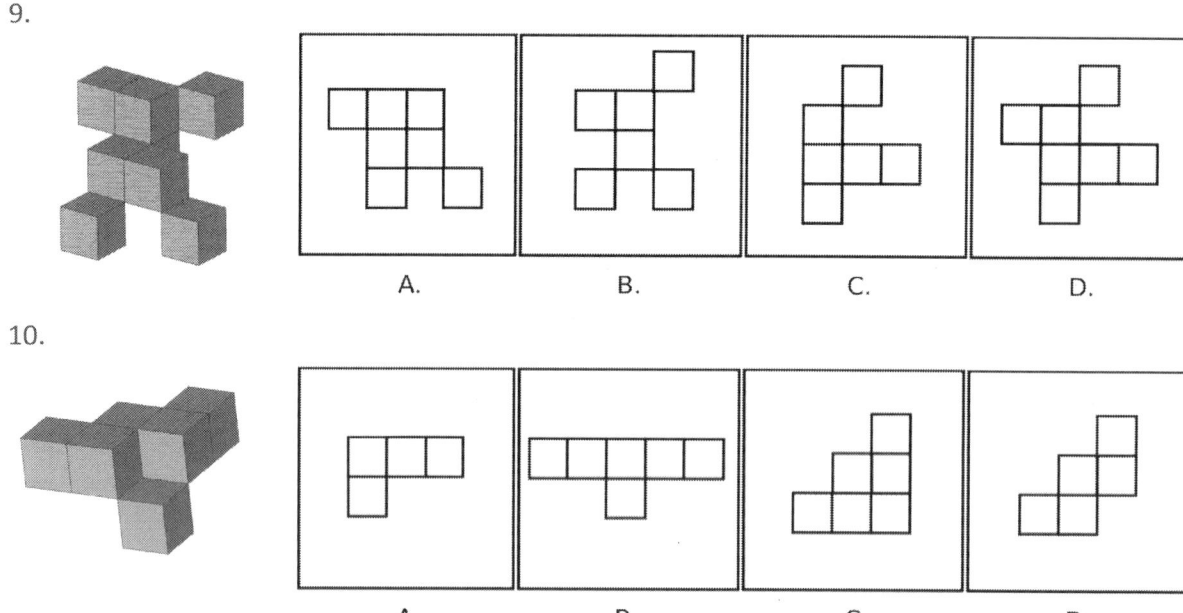

A.　　　　B.　　　　C.　　　　D.

10.

A.　　　　B.　　　　C.　　　　D.

# CHAPTER 21: PLAN AND ELEVATION VIEWS

## PLAN AND ELEVATION VIEWS OF SHAPES

When 2D drawings are made of a 3D shape:

- o The view from the top is called the plan.
- o The views from the front and the sides are called the elevations.

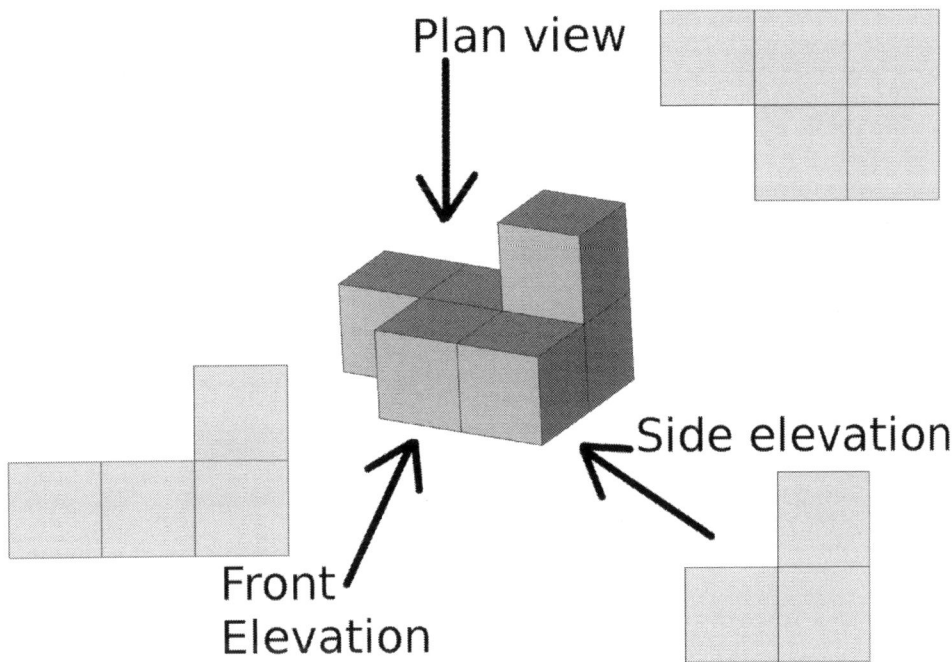

Often if there is a sudden change in height this is represented by a straight line.

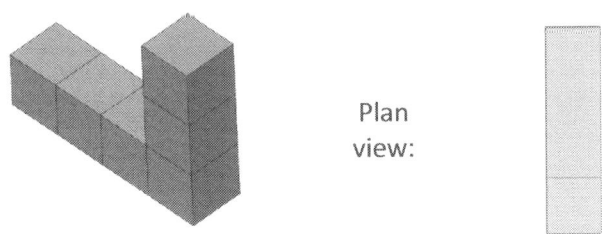

If a side is slanted, then it takes up less space in the 2D (plan or elevation)

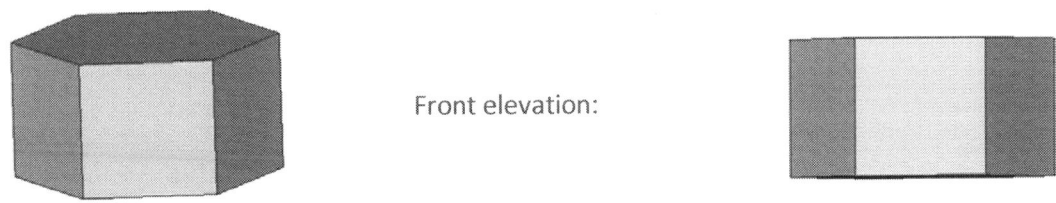

In the 11plus there are two possible question types on plans and elevations:

1. Choose the 2D drawing that is a depiction of the 3D shape shown.
2. Choose the 2D drawing that is **NOT** of the 3d shape shown.

Example:

Which of the plans below is not a correct view of the 3D shape on the left?

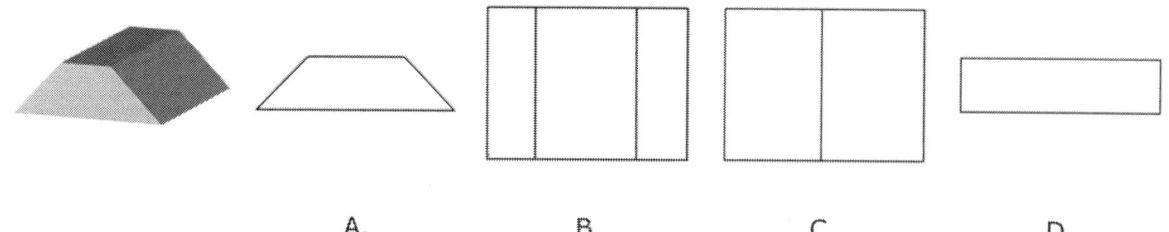

A.
B.
C.
D.

A.  Is the front elevation.
B.  Is the plan view (from top).
C.  D is the side view.

So the answer is C.

## EXERCISE 21
Which of these is not a correct view of the shape on the left?

1.

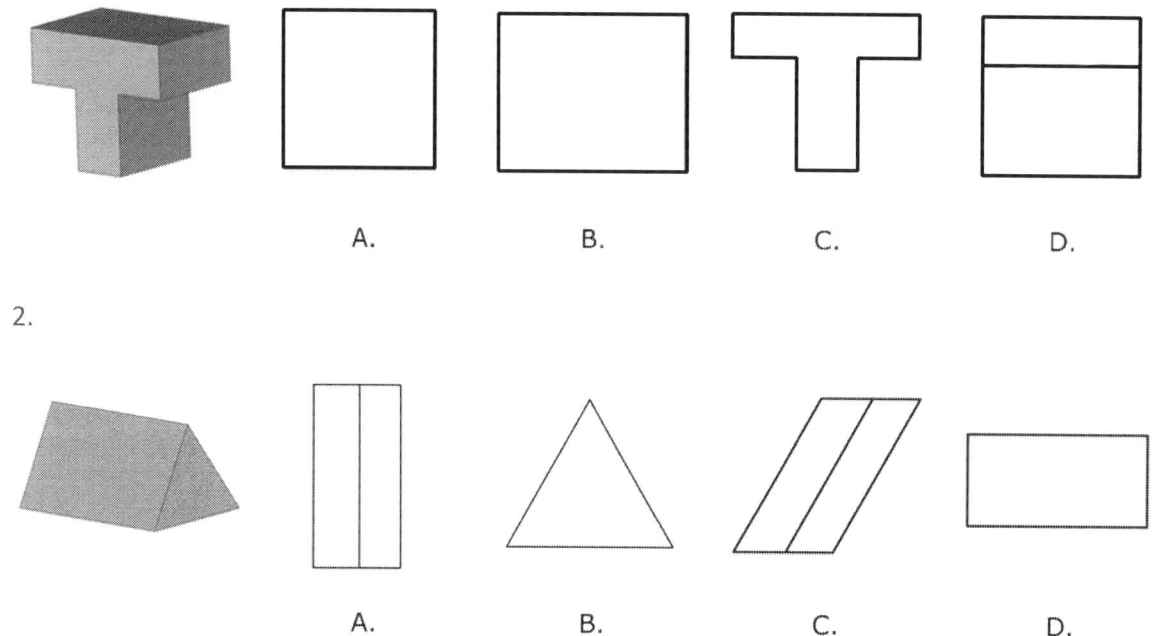

A.
B.
C.
D.

2.

A.
B.
C.
D.

3.

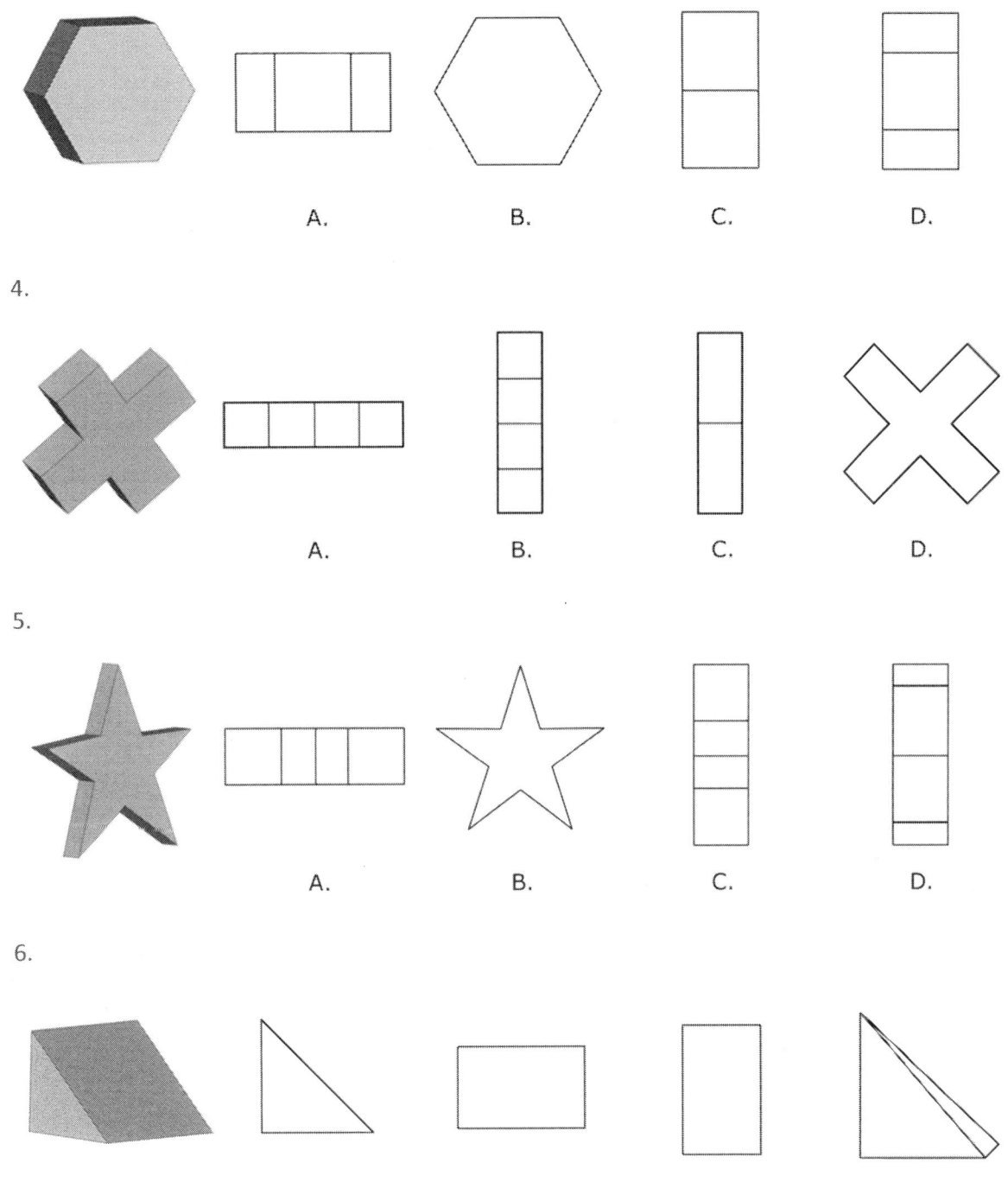

A.       B.       C.       D.

4.

A.       B.       C.       D.

5.

A.       B.       C.       D.

6.

A.       B.       C.       D.

Which of these is a correct view of the shape to the left?

7.

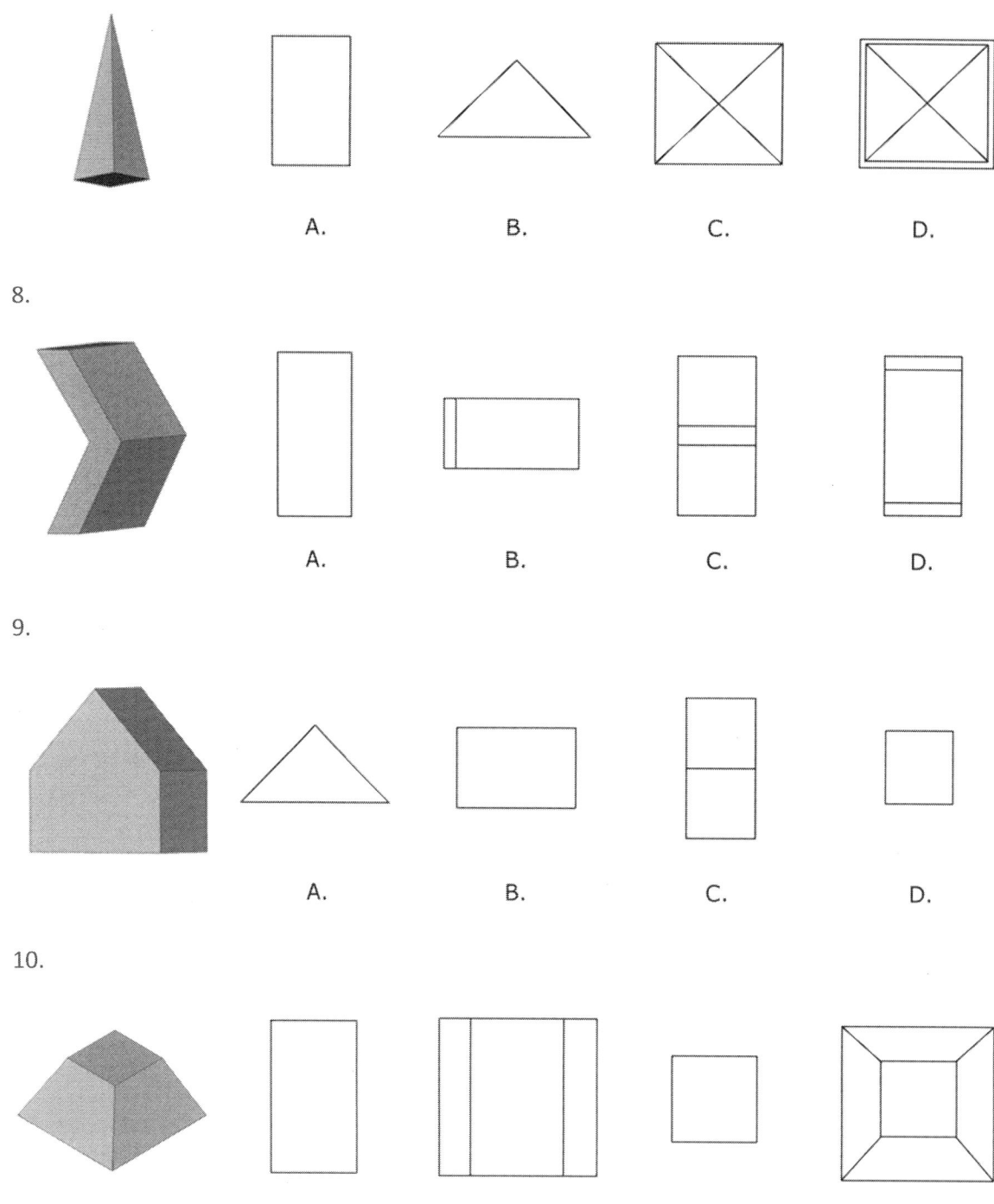

        A.        B.        C.        D.

8.

        A.        B.        C.        D.

9.

        A.        B.        C.        D.

10.

        A.        B.        C.        D.

# CHAPTER 22: 3D ROTATION

A 3D rotation can be rotated in many more directions than a 2D rotation.

To do problems involving a 3D rotation, first find a distinctive part of the shape and find which other shapes contain this section.

If looking at this shape, you might notice that there is a line of three small cubes connected to a line of four small cubes. Any shapes without this combination can then be eliminated.

Then you might notice than nothing else is attached to that line of three cubes, so any shape with something attached to them can be eliminated.

Continue to look at individual sections and how they relate to one another, until you have the answer.

Example: Which shape on the right is a rotation of the test shape?

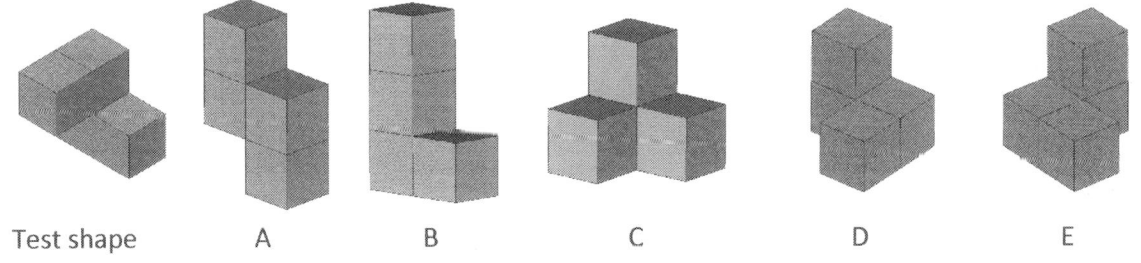

| Test shape | A | B | C | D | E |

The test shape has two lines of two cubes. So cannot be B or C.
The two lines are at right angles to each other. So cannot be A. This leaves D and E.

Now that we have the same basic shape we need to look at the rotation. In most questions you do not need to do this.

If the test shape is "pushed backwards" so that the two cubes that are on top stand up; then the two upright cubes are on the left with the two horizontal cubes at the front.
In D the two upright cubes are on the right, so it cannot be D.
The answer is E.

## EXERCISE 22:
Choose the shape that is a rotation of the shape on the left

1.

2.

3

4.

5.

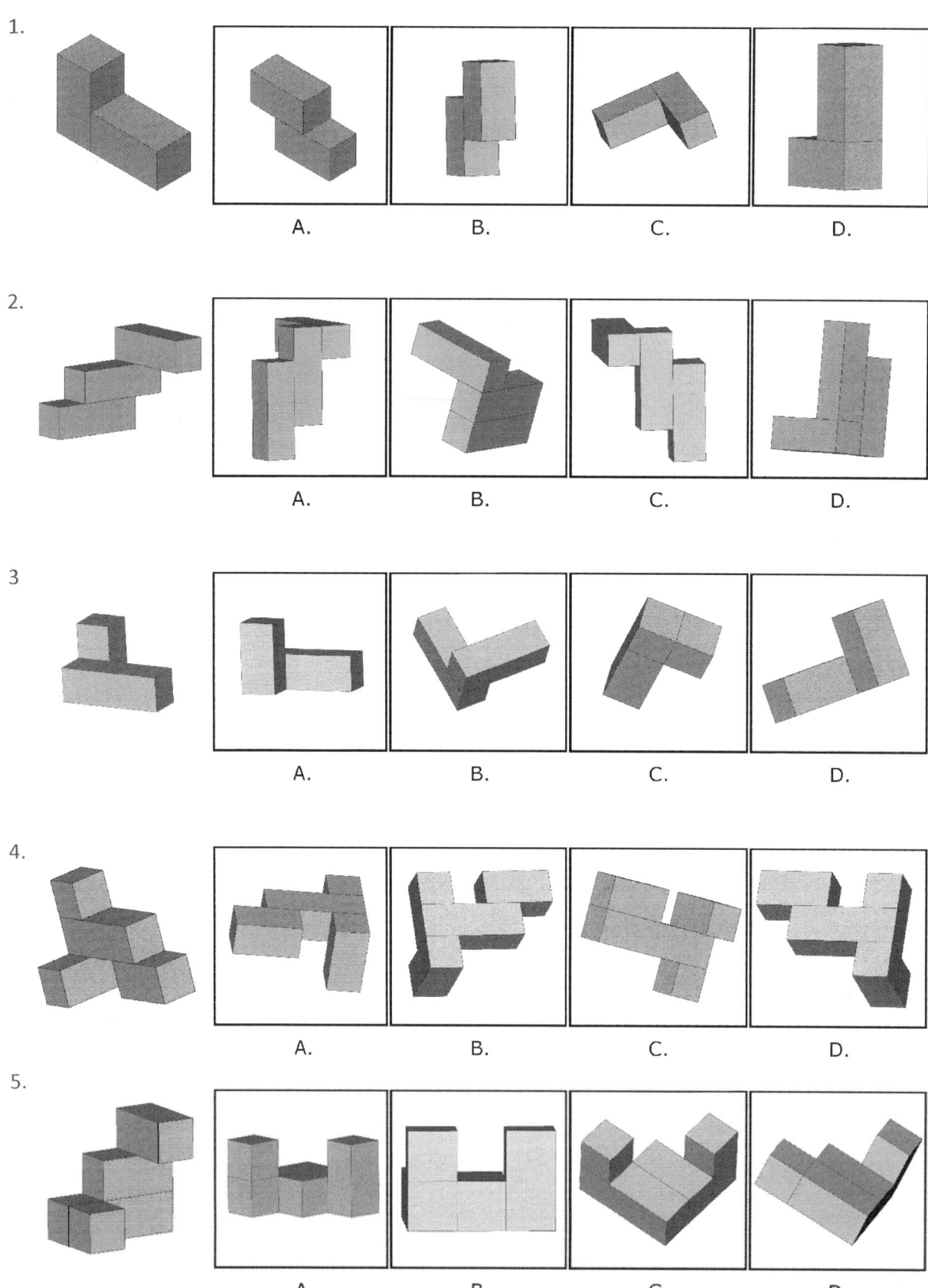

A.     B.     C.     D.

Match the five shapes below, labelled A-E with their correct rotations in questions 6-10.

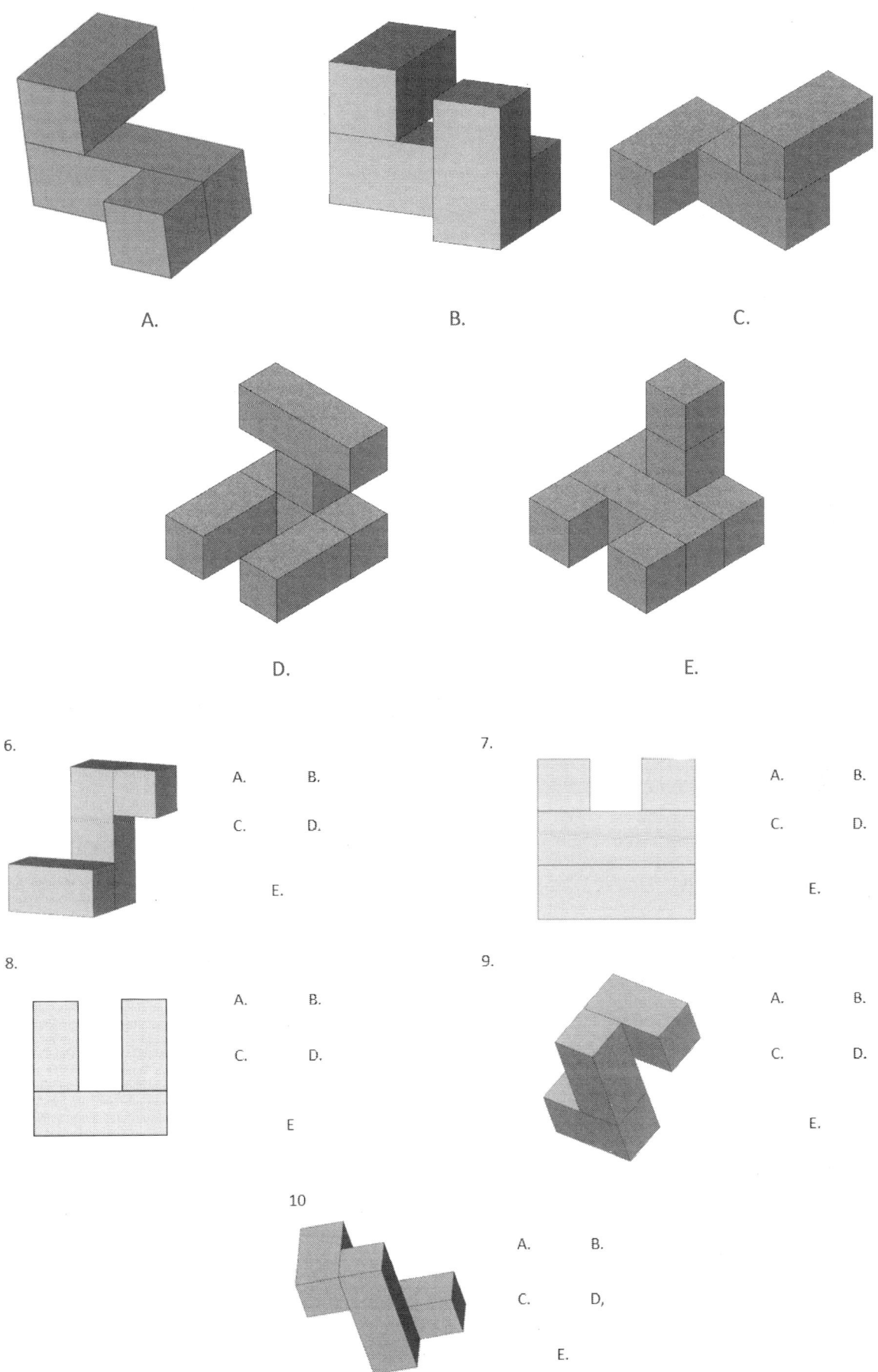

A.

B.

C.

D.

E.

6.

A.　　B.

C.　　D.

E.

7.

A.　　B.

C.　　D.

E.

8.

A.　　B.

C.　　D.

E

9.

A.　　B.

C.　　D.

E.

10

A.　　B.

C.　　D,

E.

# CHAPTER 23: BUILDING 3D SHAPES (COMPOSITE SHAPES)

In this question type you need to work out which group of blocks can be put together to make the required shape. There should not be any empty spaces hidden by other shapes. To answer these questions, use elimination.

Firstly, work out a type of block that must be used. Eliminate any option that does not have that block shape.

Secondly, eliminate any of the options that have shapes that cannot be used.

Example:

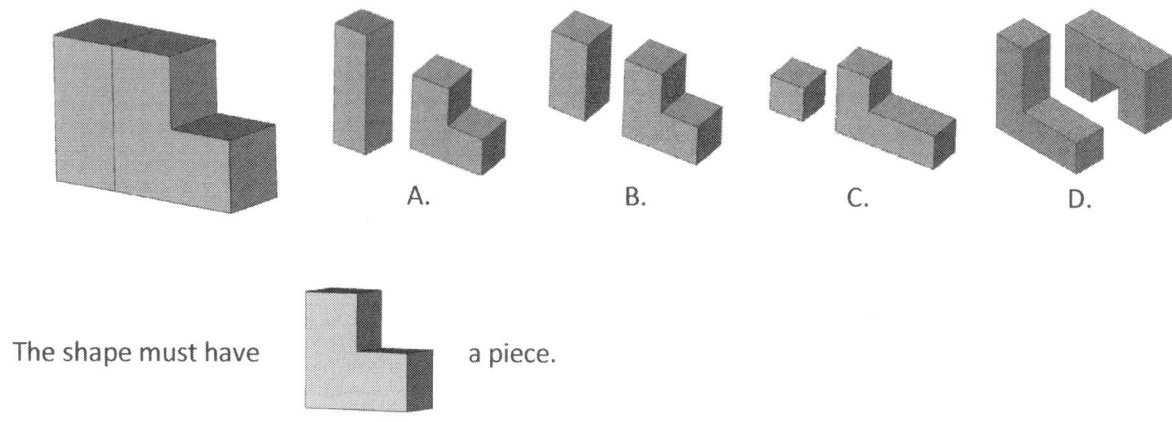

A.          B.          C.          D.

The shape must have                    a piece.

 Therefore it cannot be C. It cannot have a piece longer than two individual squares, so it cannot be A, C, or D.

Therefore we are left with B as the only answer.

All the blocks are based on a 1 x 1 cube. Blocks can slot into spaces made by other blocks. Each block has a width of a 1 x 1 cube.

Example:

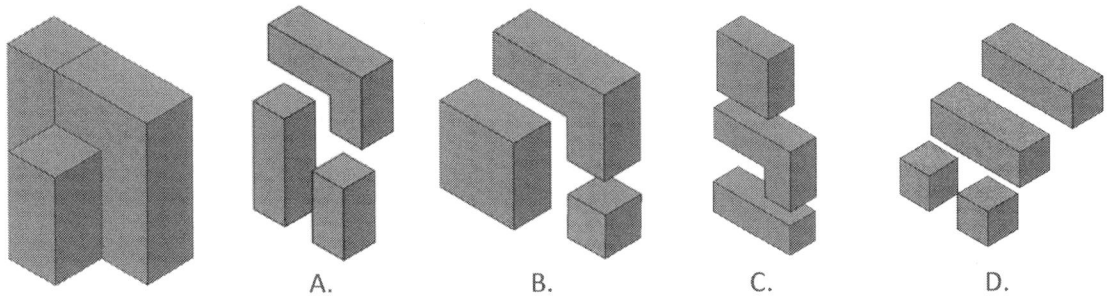

The answer is C as the two taller pieces fit together making a space. The third piece rotates 90°and slots in. Half the shape fits inside the space while half sticks out.


## EXERCISE 23:

1.

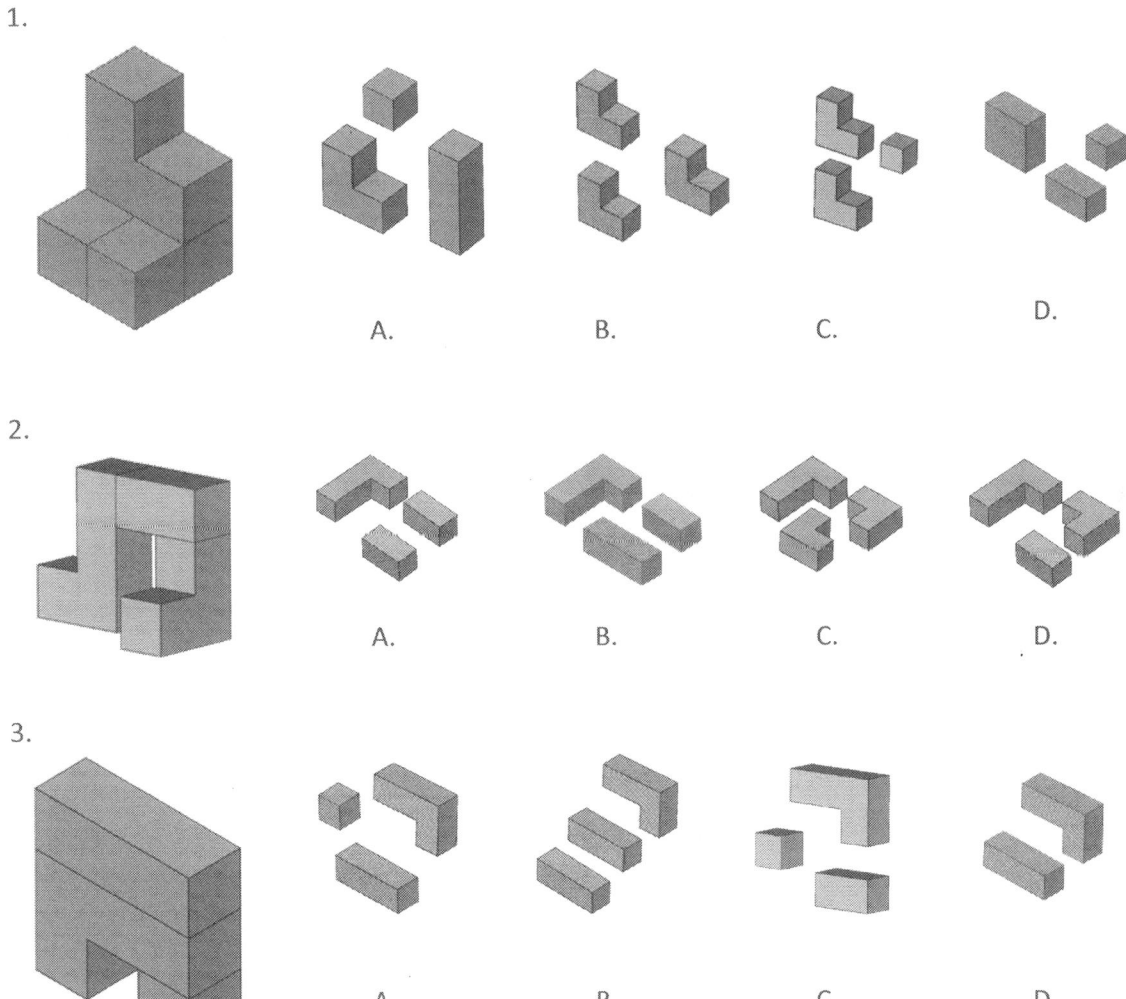

A.                    B.                    C.                    D.

2.

A.                    B.                    C.                    D.

3.

A.                    B.                    C.                    D.

4.

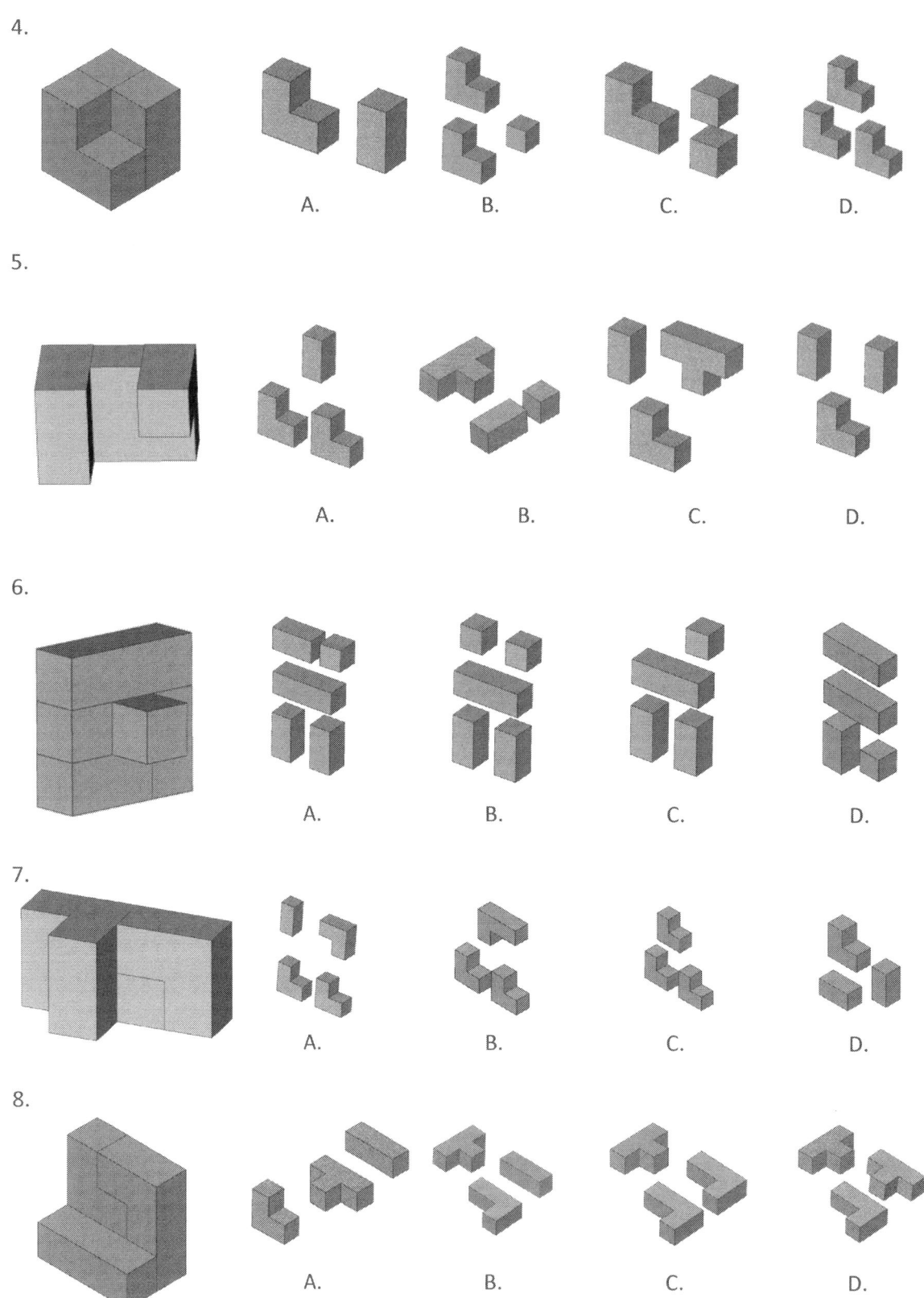

5.

6.

7.

8.

A.    B.    C.    D.

94

9.

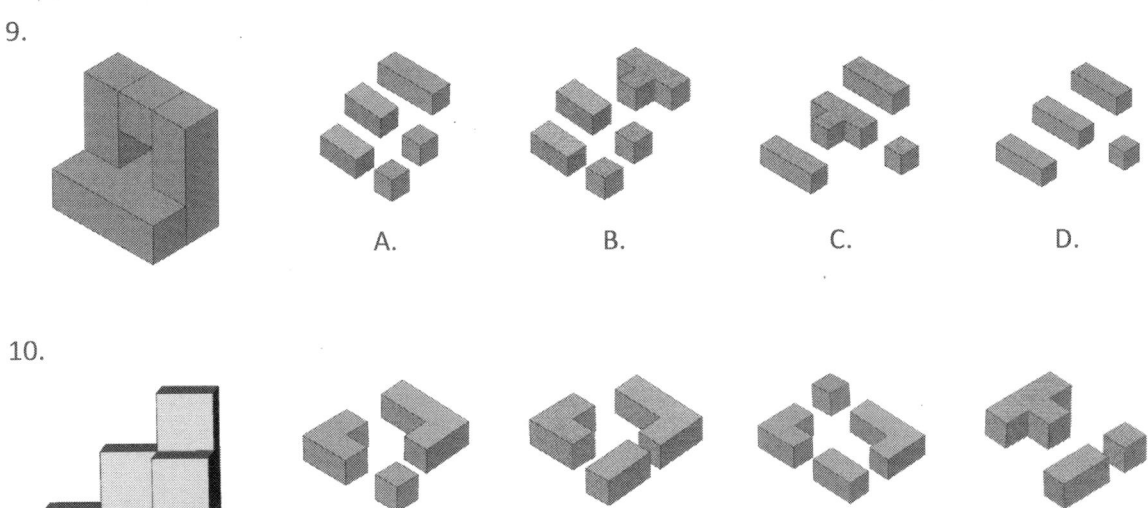

A.   B.   C.   D.

10.

A.   B.   C.   D.

95

# CHAPTER 24: NVR NETS

A net is a pattern that can be cut and folded to make a 3D shape. Alternatively, a net can be thought of as the 3D shape opened out flat. There may be several nets for a 3D shape.

To work out which net matches a 3D shape:

- The sides of the shape must be the same as the shapes in the net.
- There must be the same number of sides in the shape as the net.
- Look at where each side connects.

Example: Which net can be folded to make the shape on the left?

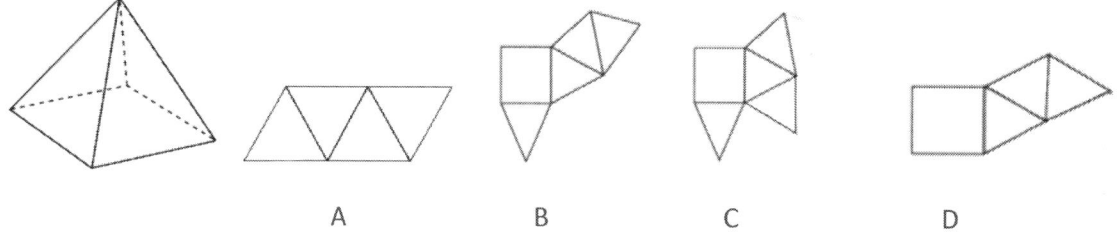

|   A   |   B   |   C   |   D   |

Answer: The shape must contain a square and triangles. So it cannot be A, as there's no square. There must be four triangles. So it cannot be D.

Each triangle must have a side that can join with a separate side of the square, so it cannot be C. Therefore the answer is B.

The same concepts are used for questions which give a net from which the shape needs to be determined. The shapes in the net must be the same as the faces of the 3D shape.

A very common shape used in the 11 plus is the cube. There are eleven different nets that will make a cube.

Any net with four squares in a row and one square either side:

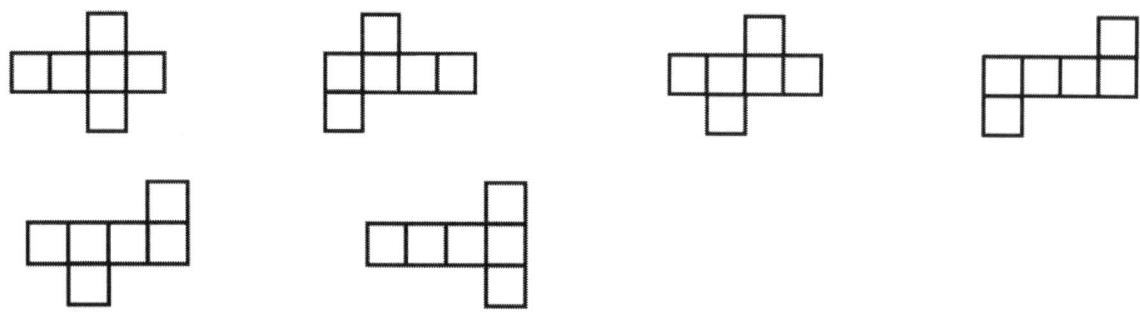

Any net with three squares in a row, with two on one side and one on the other, provided that the row of two squares are staggered and not blunt. The single square can be in any position on the other side of the three squares.

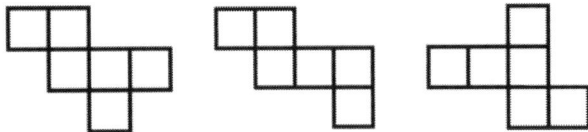

A net of three rows of two squares or two rows of three squares, provided that each row overlaps by only one square.

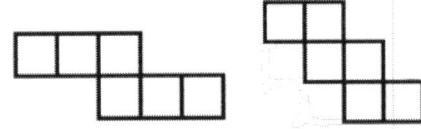

Any net that has four squares that make a larger square will **not** make a 3D shape.

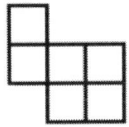

## EXERCISE 24:
Which option is the net of the shape on the left?

1.

2.

3.

4.

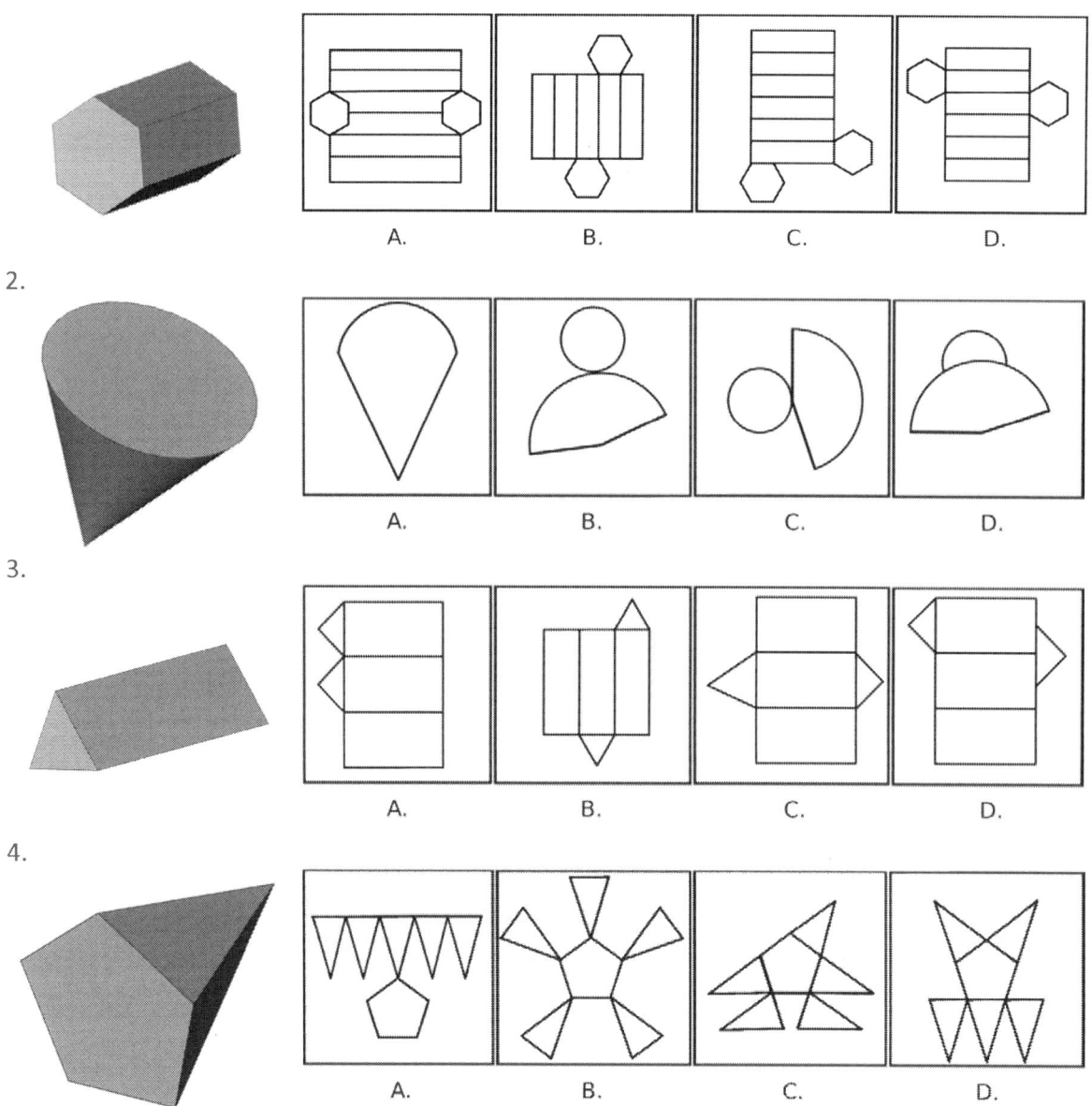

A.   B.   C.   D.

A.   B.   C.   D.

A.   B.   C.   D.

A.   B.   C.   D.

5.

 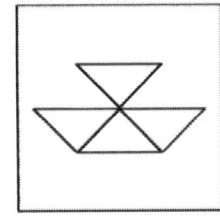 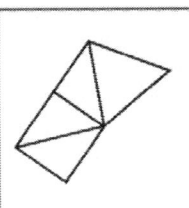 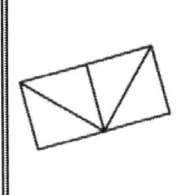 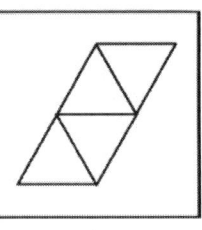

A.        B.        C.        D.

Which of the following is a net of a cube?

6.

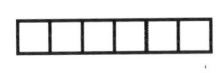 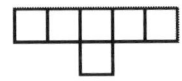 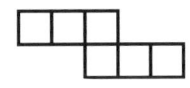 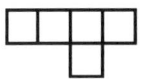

A.        B.        C.        D.

7

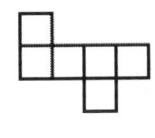 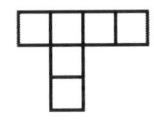 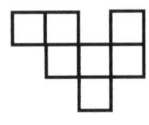 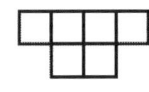

A.        B.        C.        D.

8.

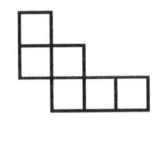 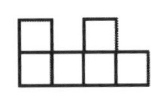 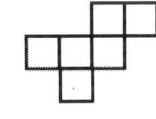 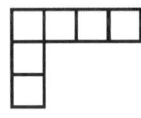

A.        B.        C.        D.

A cube has two shapes drawn on two of its edges.  The cube and net are shown below.

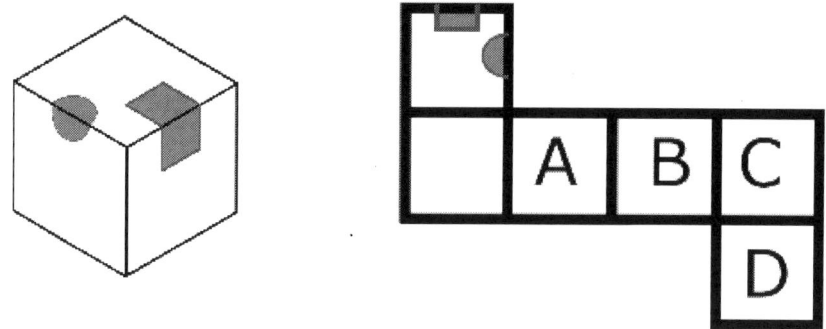

9.  Which side will the other half of the rectangle be on?  _____

10.  Which side will the other half of the circle be on?  _____

# CHAPTER 25: CUBES (OPPOSING SIDES)

A recent addition to the NVR question types are questions that ask students to identify the opposite sides of a cube net. The question could ask, if a particular side is the base, which is the top.

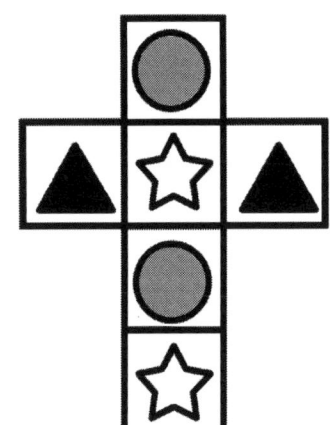

If the cube net has four squares in a row, then alternate squares are opposite, and the square either side are also opposite. In the net, the sides shown with the same symbol are opposite.

The two squares with the triangles can be anywhere along the length of the net, and will still be opposite.

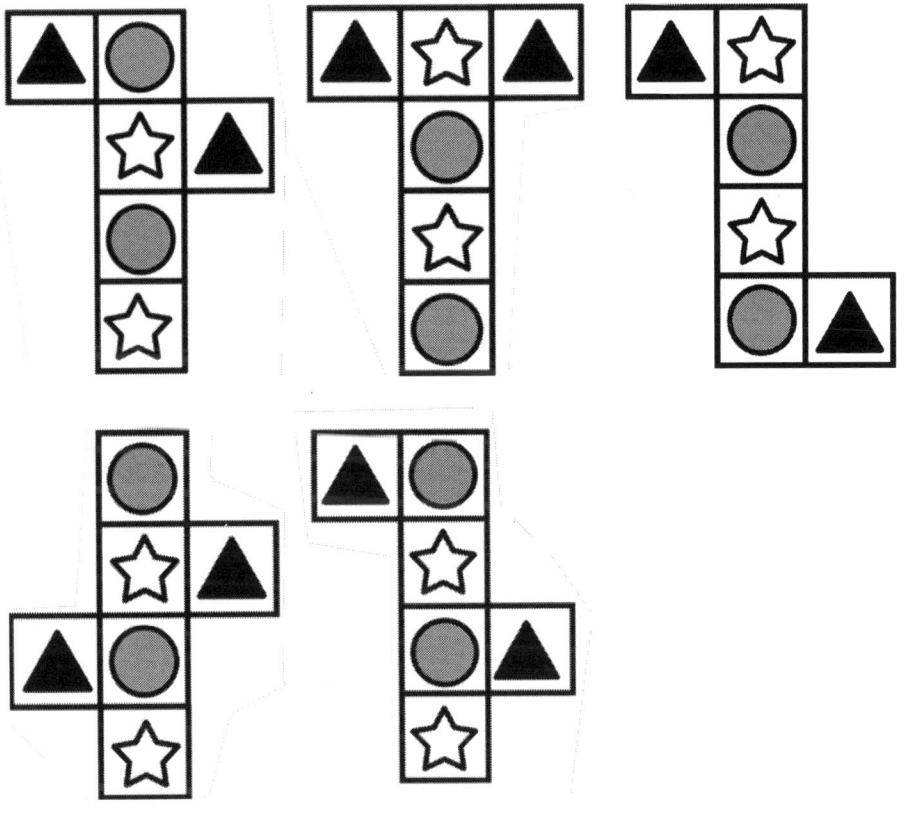

If there are two or three squares in a row, then the squares touching either side are opposite. When there is a row of three, the squares at each end are opposite.

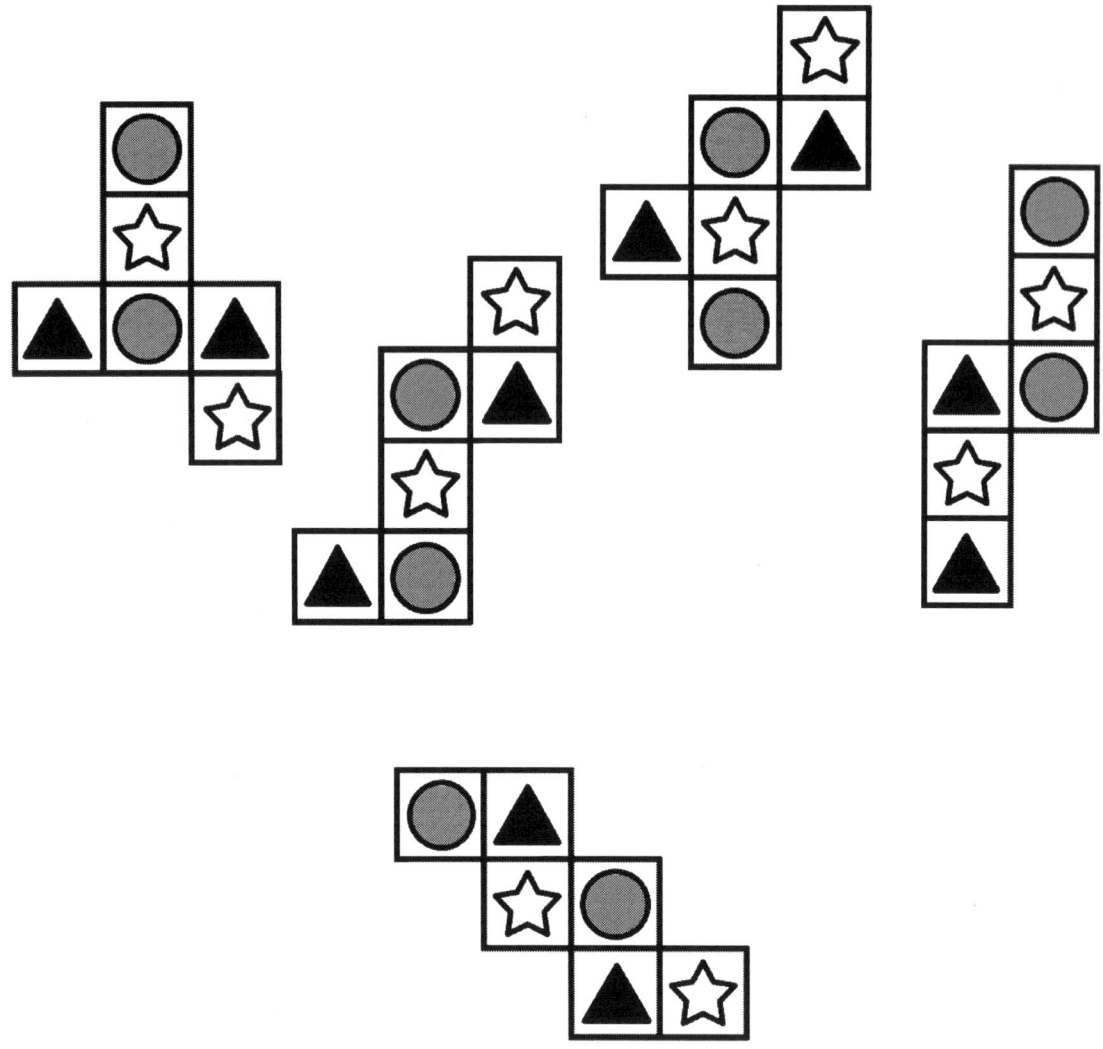

So, in conclusion, in any line of two, three or four squares, the squares that touch them on either side will be on opposite sides of the cube. The squares must meet along the side of the square (not just at the corners). If there is a row of three or four squares then: alternate squares along that row are on opposite sides of the cube.

EXERCISE 25:

Which side is opposite to the side containing the star?  Write your answers at the bottom of the
page.

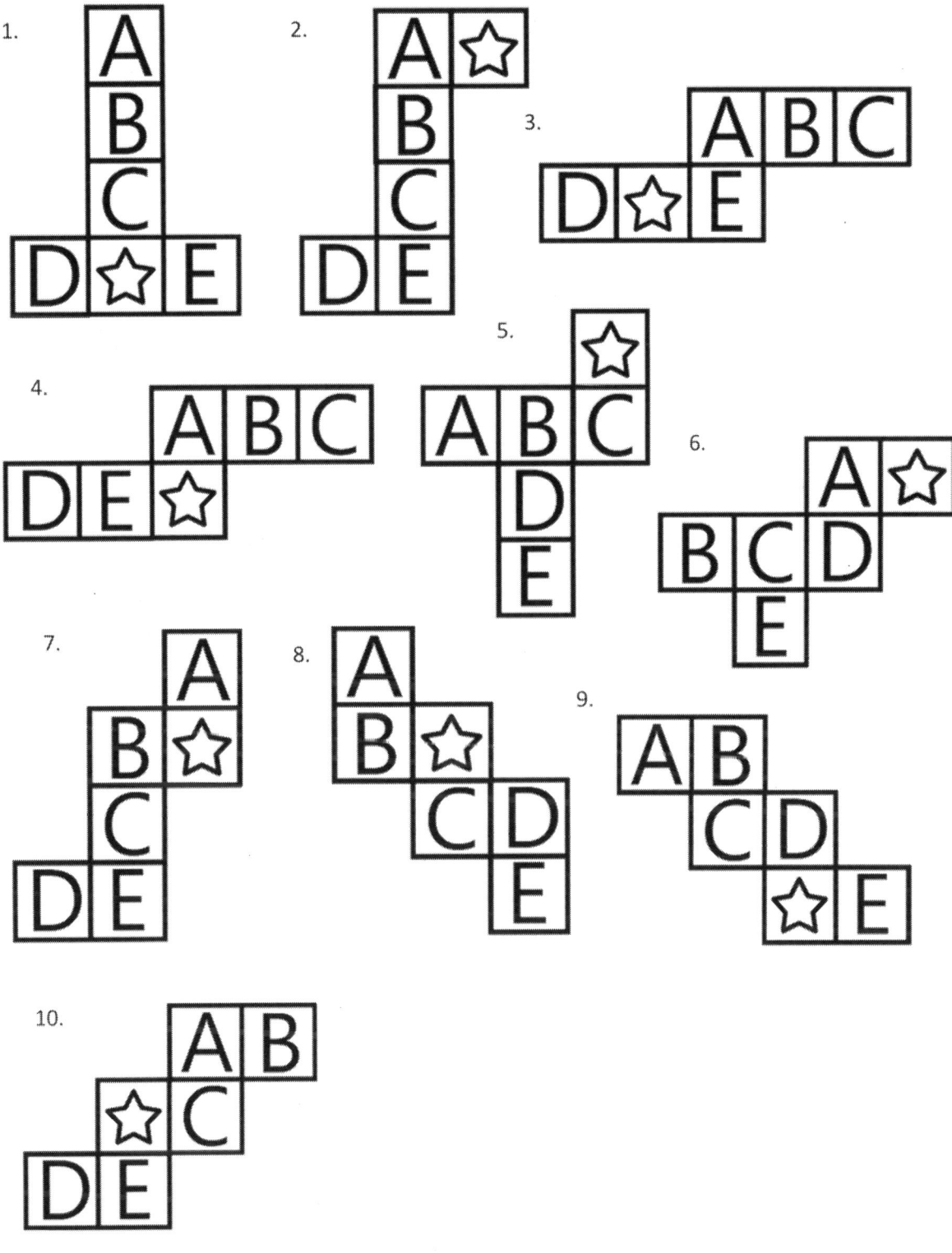

Answers:

1.____  2. _____  3. _____  4. _____  5. _____  6. _____  7. _____  8. _____  9. _____  10. _____

# CHAPTER 26: NVR NETS TO CUBES

A common 3D NVR or special reasoning exam question is matching nets to cubes. In this question type a net is given and you need to determine which cube can be made from the net.

To do this, look at each of the following in turn:

- Opposite sides
- Direction of symbols
- Order of sides

## Opposite sides

In the 3D view of the cube opposite sides cannot be seen. In the net, the sides shown here, with the same symbol are 'opposites,' so symbols on these sides cannot be seen on the same cube.

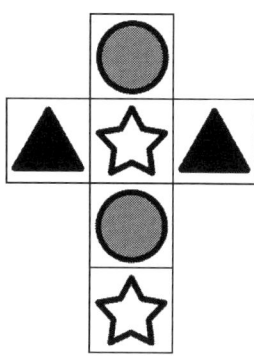

## Direction of symbols

Look at the symbols that have direction and where they are pointing to.

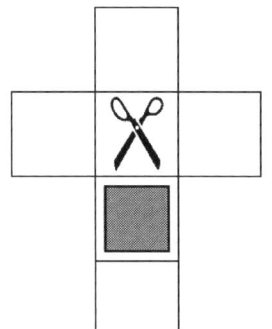

In the net shown, the blades of the scissors point to the square, so any cube where either:

- The blades point to a different shape, or
- The square is by a different part of the scissors, such as the handles or the sides can be eliminated.

## Order of sides

To do this, write around the top square, which shapes are around it. Then all of the shapes around the side can be rotated the same number of places clockwise or anticlockwise.

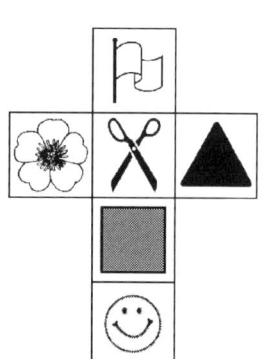

If the cube, has a smiley face at the top, then I can work out the sides and write them around the smiley face:

Now, if there is a cube with scissors at the front, I know that the flower must be to the left and the black triangle to the right.

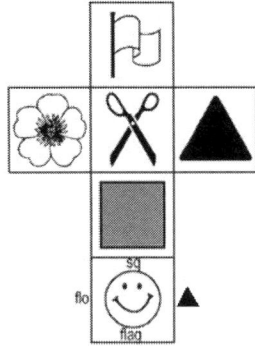

If a different shape is at the front, I can rotate all the sides in either direction.

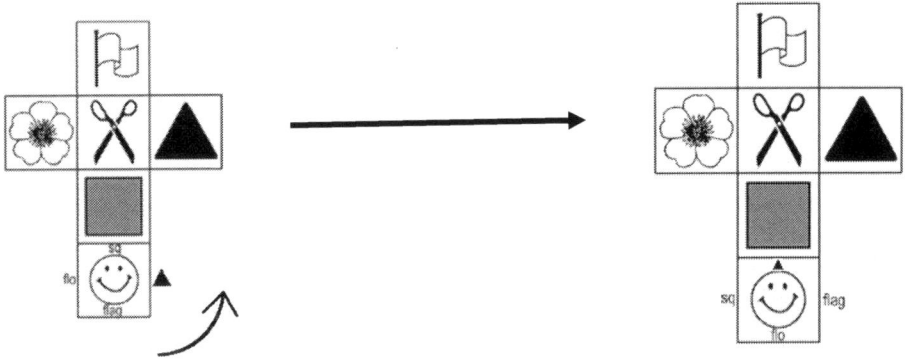

Rotating symbols

Sometimes it is useful to know that when a side moves one place around the net, the symbol rotates 90°.

If two sides meet at the corner of a net, then the two closest sides will be next to each other upon the 3D cube.

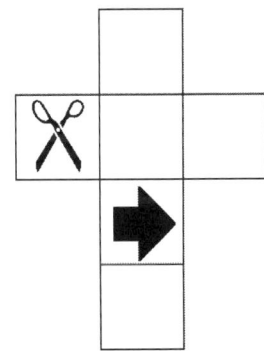

The sides with the scissors and arrow meet at a corner as shown.  Therefore the blades of the scissors will point to the back of the arrow.  As we can see in the resulting cube.

This tip is extremely useful in answering these types of questions.

Example: Which cube does this net represent?

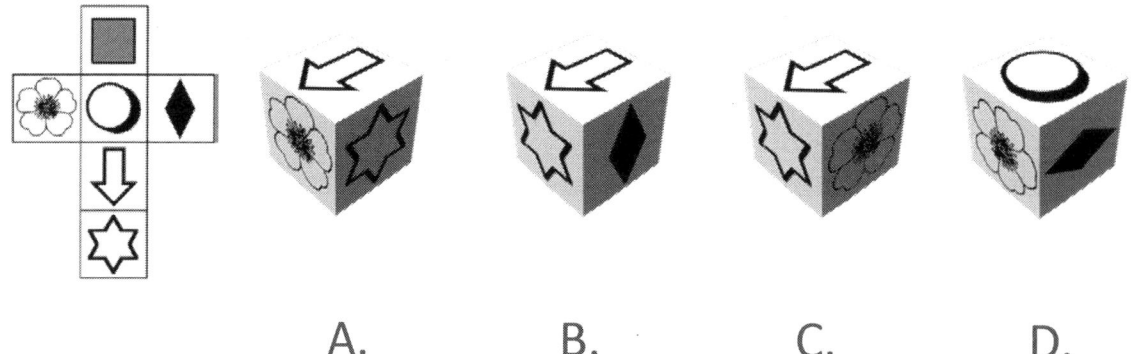

Answer:

The flower and diamond are opposite, so it cannot be D.
The arrow is pointing to the star, so it cannot be A.
Writing the shapes around the arrow, the flower is to the left of the star, so it cannot be C.
Therefore the answer is B.

## EXERCISE 26

Which cubes can be made from the following nets?

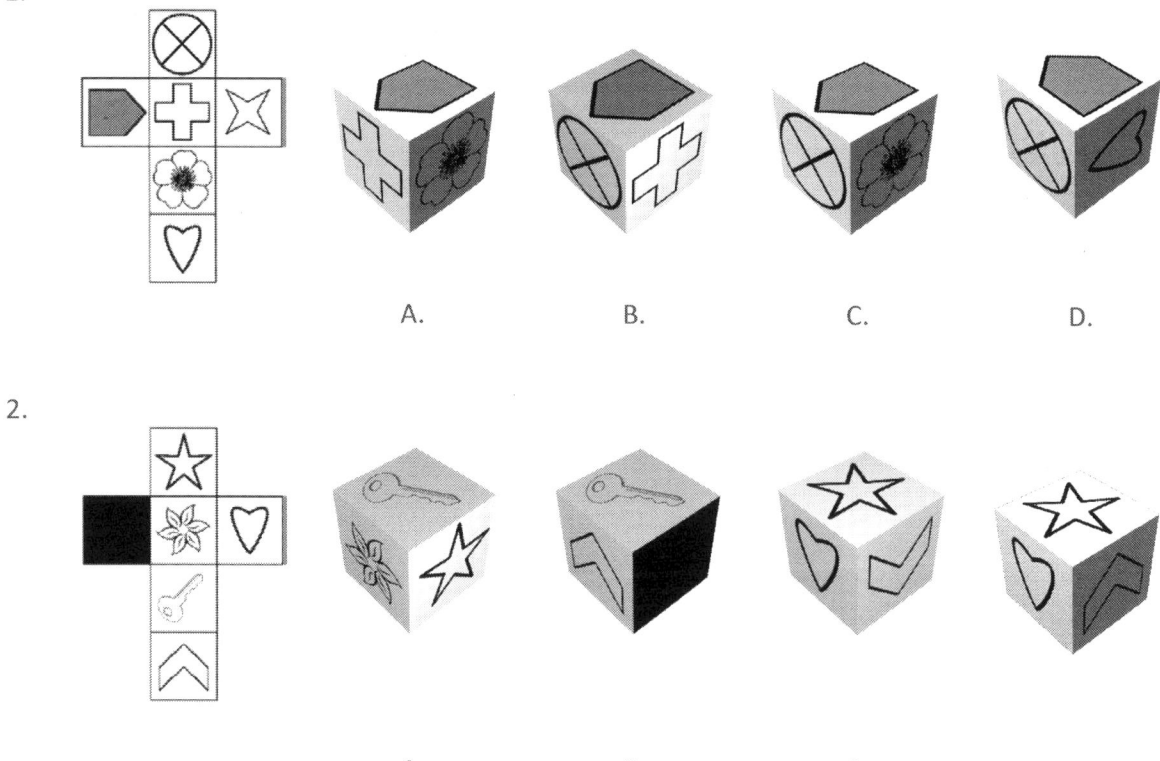

3.

                                    A.            B.            C.            D.

4.

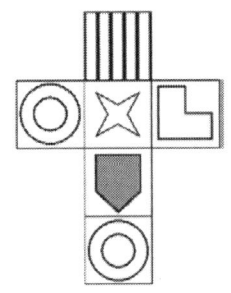  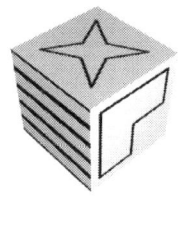  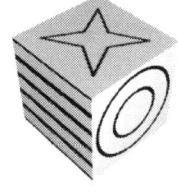    

                                    A.            B.            C.            D.

5.

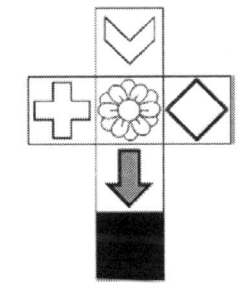        

                                    A.            B.            C.            D.

6.

    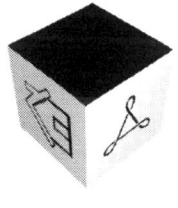    

                                    A.            B.            C.            D.

7.

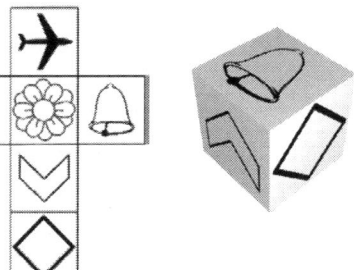  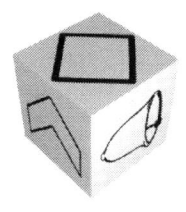 

A.        B.        C.        D.

8.

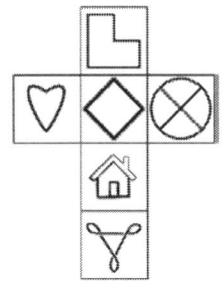 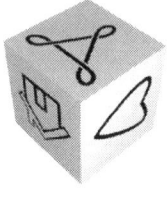   

A.        B.        C.        D.

9.

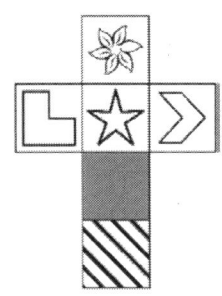    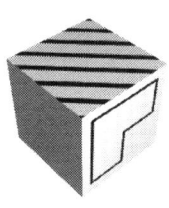

A.        B.        C.        D.

10.

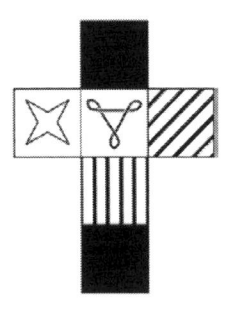 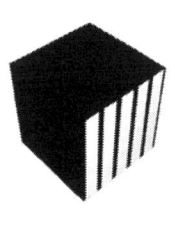 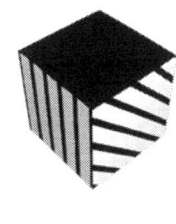  

A.        B.        C.        D.

# CHAPTER 27: NETS TO CUBES (NON-STANDARD)

Besides using the standard cube net, the alternative cube nets can be used.

While this makes it a little harder, the process is exactly the same as working out questions that use the standard net.  To do this, look at each of the following in turn:

- Opposite sides
- Direction of symbols
- Order of sides

Example:

Which cube does this net represent?

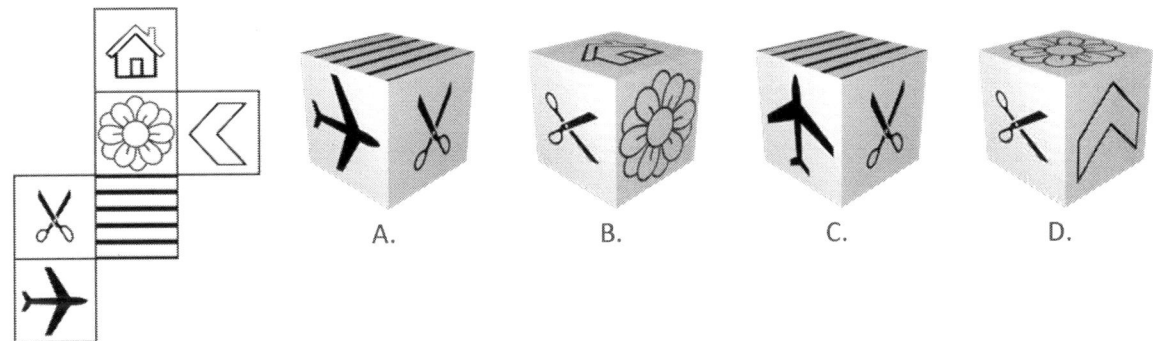

A.        B.        C.        D.

Answer:

The scissors and the chevron are opposite, so it cannot be D.
The side of the plane is beside the scissors (not the front) so it cannot be A
Writing the shapes around the side containing parallel lines, the scissors are to the left of the plane, so it cannot be C.
Therefore the answer is B.

EXERCISE 27:

Which cube do the following nets represent?

1.

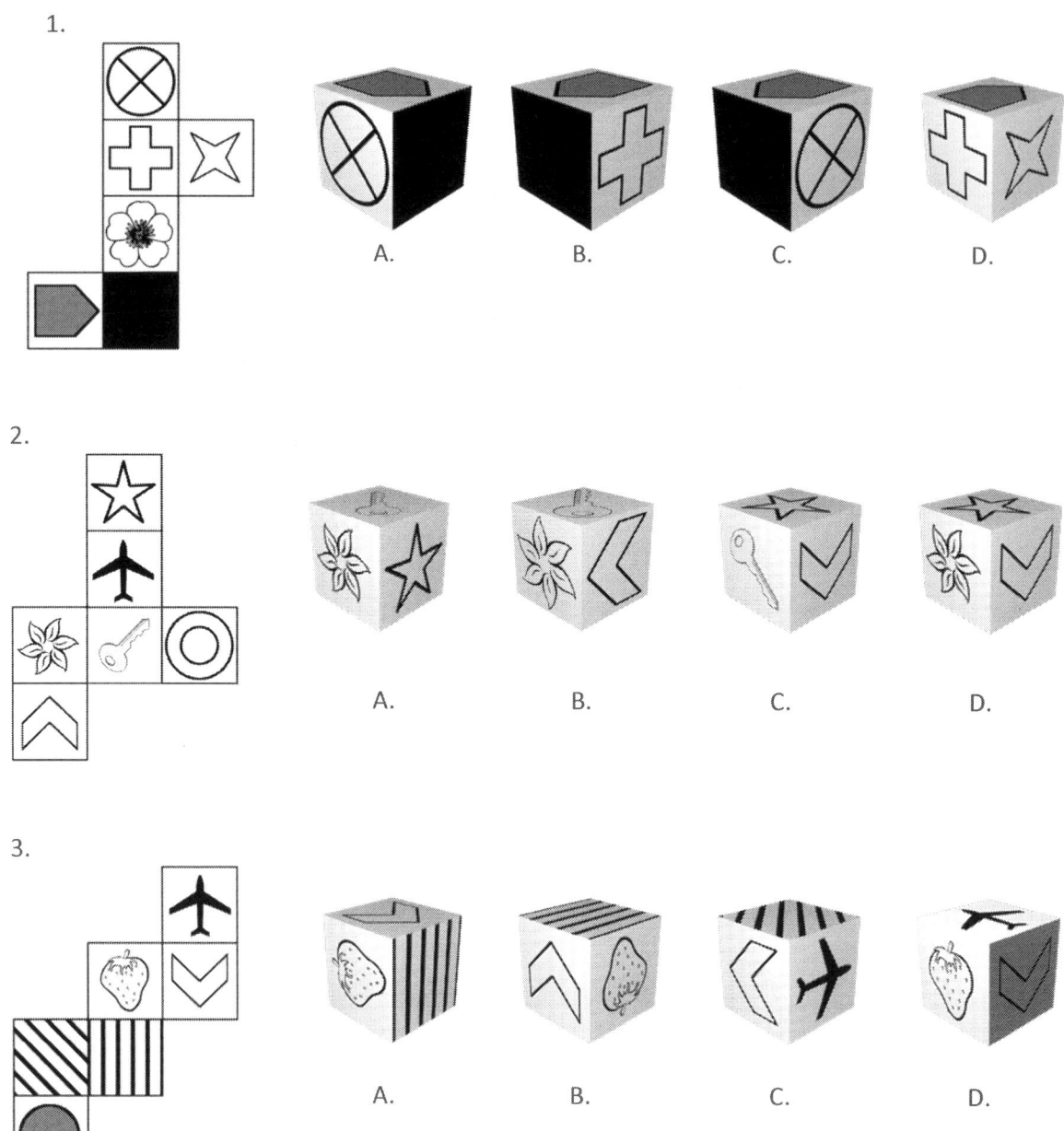

2.

3.

4.

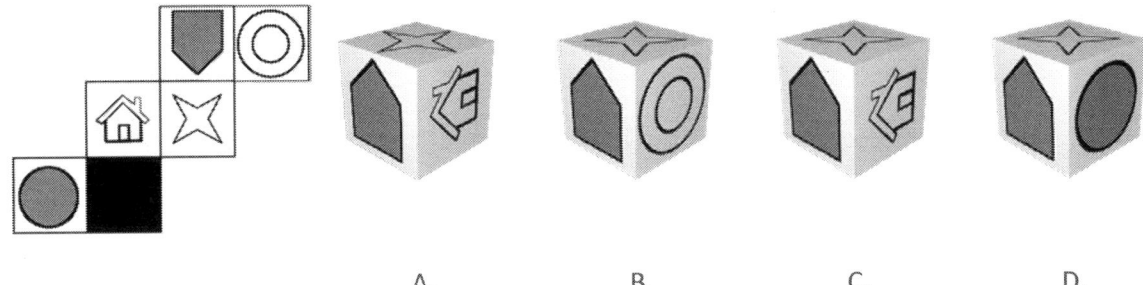

A.           B.           C.           D.

5.

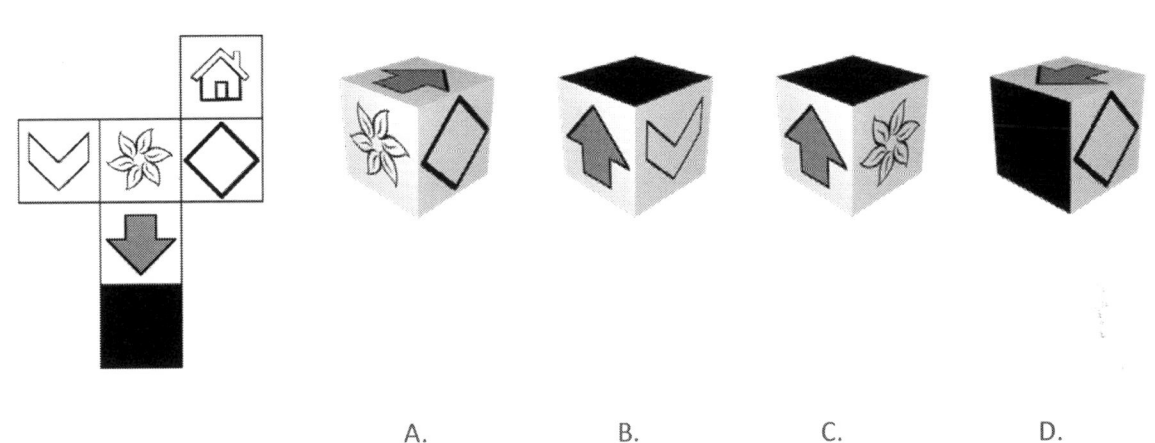

A.           B.           C.           D.

6.

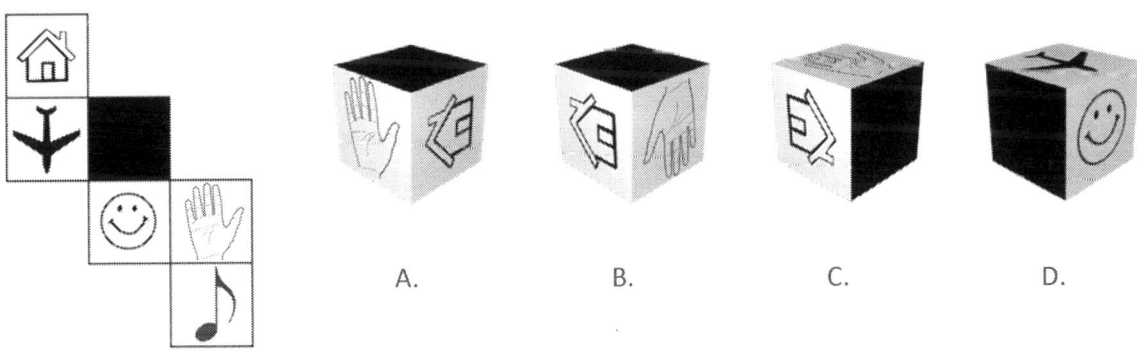

A.           B.           C.           D.

7.

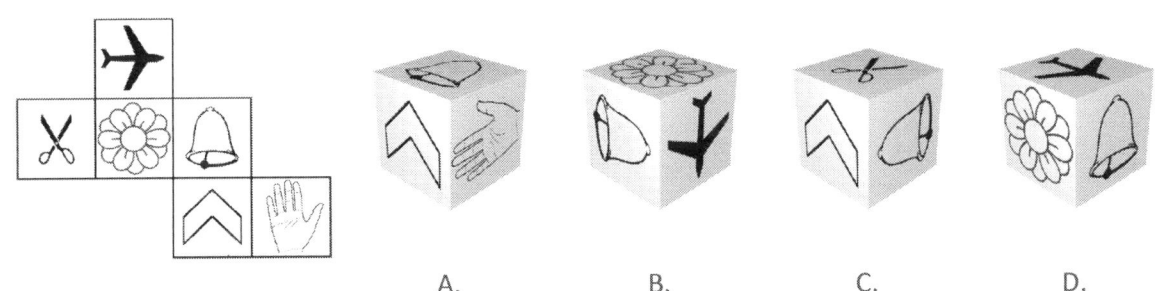

A.           B.           C.           D.

8.

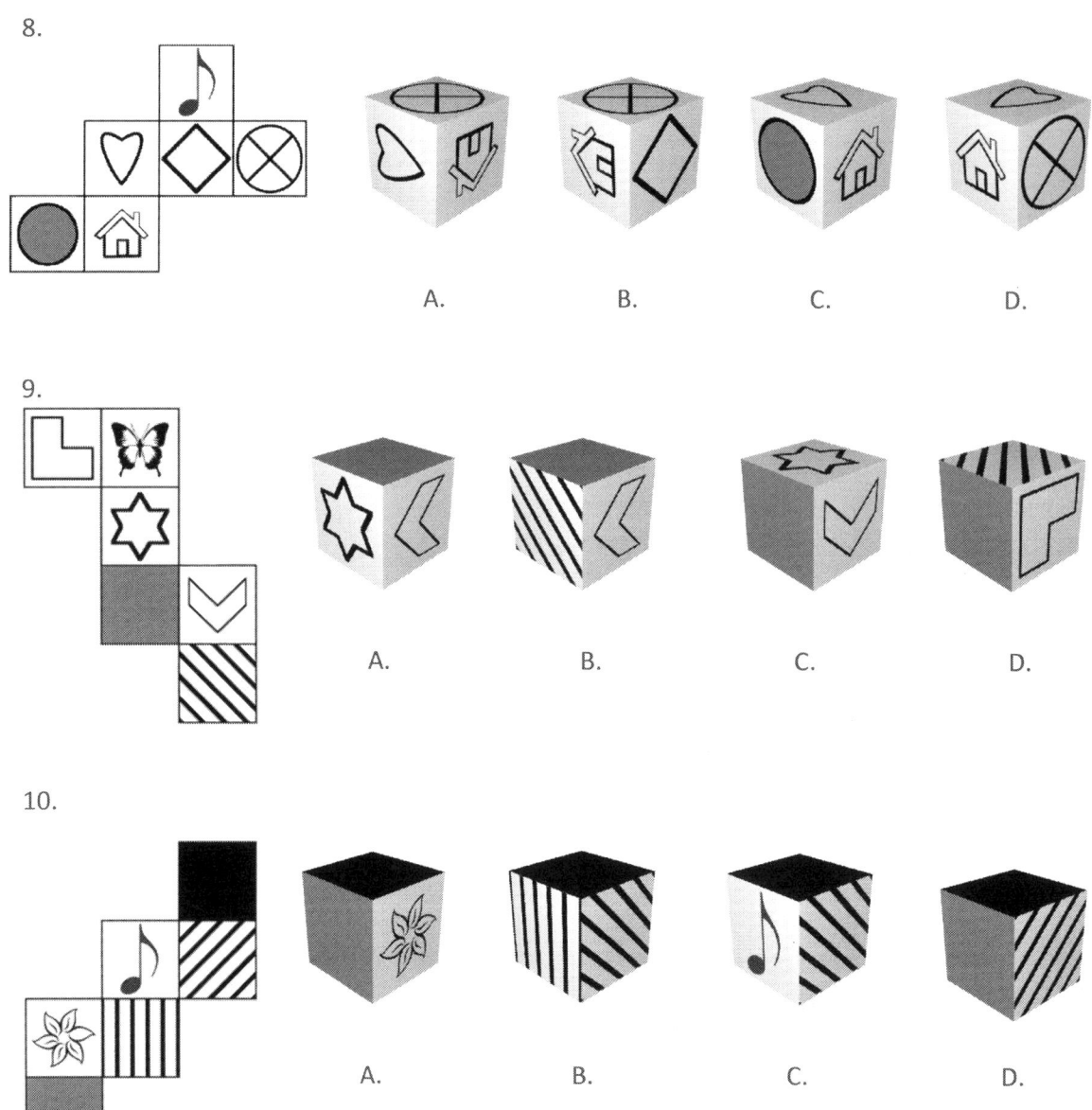

A.

B.

C.

D.

9.

A.

B.

C.

D.

10.

A.

B.

C.

D.

# CHAPTER 28: CUBES TO NETS

In this type of question you are given a cube and you need to choose which net that cube could be made from.

These questions are done in exactly the same way as when working out which cube is made from a net.

To do this, look at each of the following in turn:

- Opposite sides – the sides visible on the cube cannot be opposites on the net.
- Direction of symbols
- Order of sides.

Example

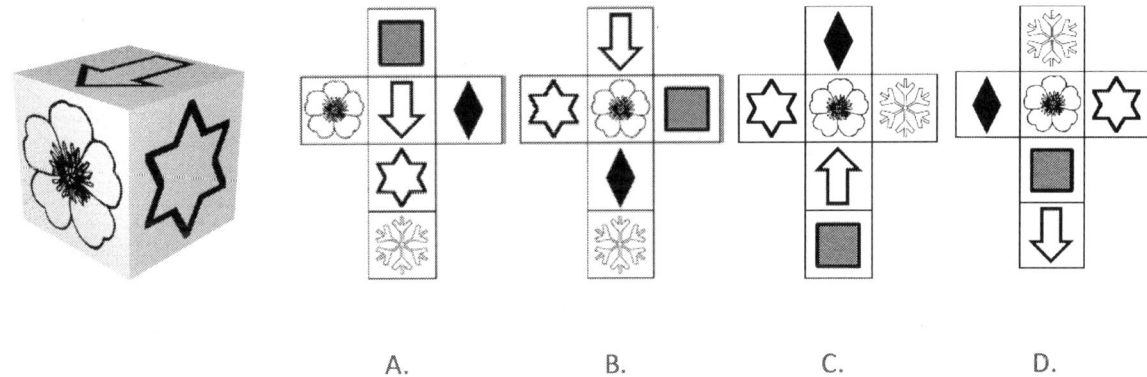

A.          B.          C.          D.

Answer

The arrow and flower are both visible on the cube, so it cannot be D (where they are opposites).

The arrow points to the flower, so it cannot be A.

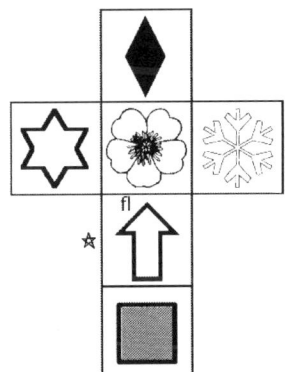

The arrow is at the top, so write the sides around the arrow. This time, I only need to include the positions of the other two shapes visible on the cube.

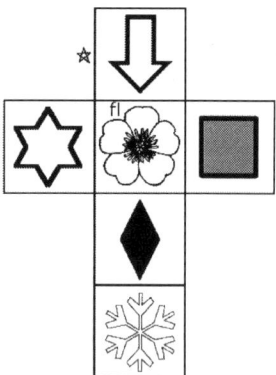

The star is to the left of the flower, so it can't be B.

*If there is time*, check C. Again, as the arrow is on top write the positions of the other visible shapes around the arrow.

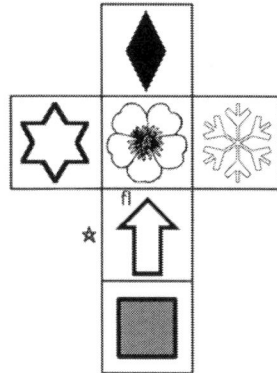

Now rotate the flower and star around one position anticlockwise, so that they are at the front.

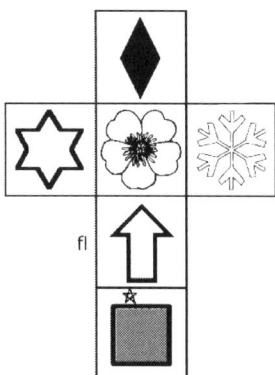

This is the same as the cube, so the answer is C.

EXERCISE 28:

1.

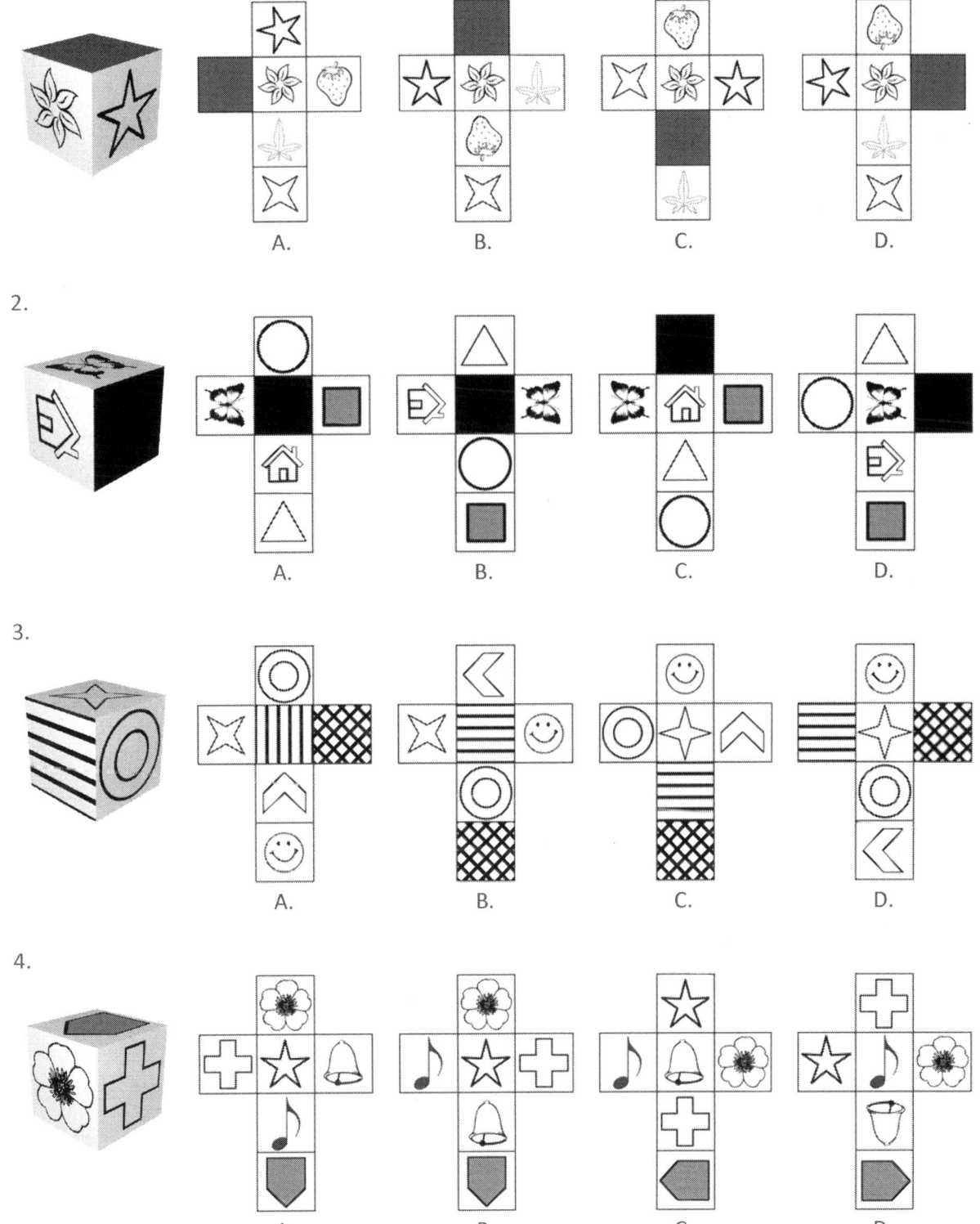

A.　　　B.　　　C.　　　D.

2.

A.　　　B.　　　C.　　　D.

3.

A.　　　B.　　　C.　　　D.

4.

A.　　　B.　　　C.　　　D.

5.

A.      B.      C.      D.

6.

A.      B.      C.      D.

7.

A.      B.      C.      D.

8.

A.      B.      C.      D.

9.

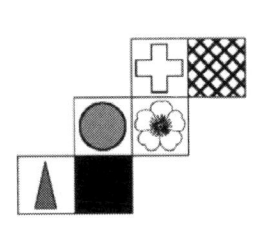   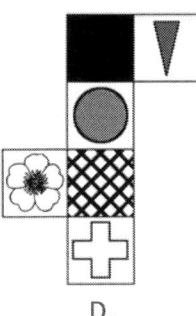

       A.               B.               C.               D.

10.

 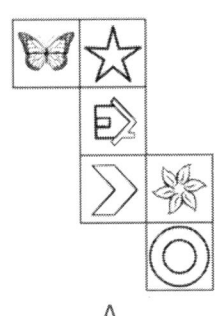 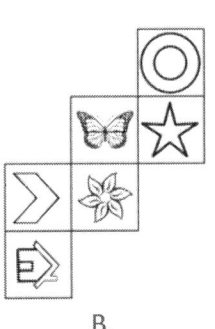  

       A.               B.               C.               D.

# CHAPTER 29: CUBES TO CUBES

In this type of question a number of images of the same cube are given. You need to identify the cube which is the same cube as this set of images.

For these questions, it is useful to know that if the cube is turned over so that the opposite side is on top, then the shapes around the side are in the reverse order.

To solve these problems:

> Look at the symbols and have a look at where they are pointing to. Remember to take notice of the detail in shapes, such as the side of the house which the chimney is on. Sometimes opposites can be worked out and used.
> Look at the order of the faces.

Example

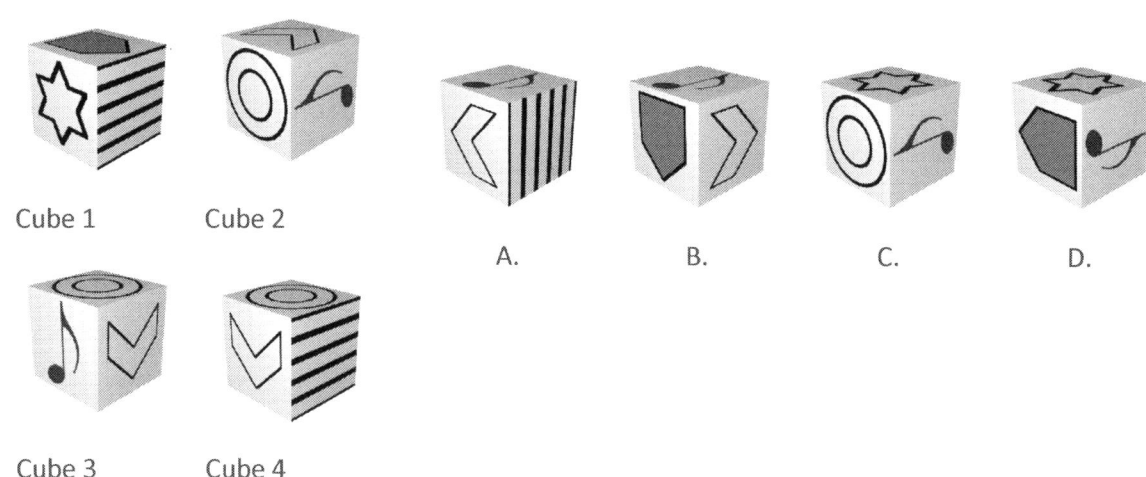

Cube 1    Cube 2

A.    B.    C.    D.

Cube 3    Cube 4

Answer

> Looking at cubes 3 and 4, the note is on the left of the chevron and the lines are on the right of the chevron. Therefore, the note and lines must be opposite. So, it cannot be A.
> Looking at cube 2 (or 3), the chevron is pointing in the same direction as the bottom of the note. So it cannot be B.
> Looking at cube 2, when the circles and note are on the side of the cube, and the chevron is at the top, then the circles are to the left of the note. Therefore, if the cube is turned over, so that the star is on top, the note should be to the left of the circles. So it cannot be C.

So the answer is D.

EXERCISE 29:
Which cube to the right is the same cube as the examples shown?

1.

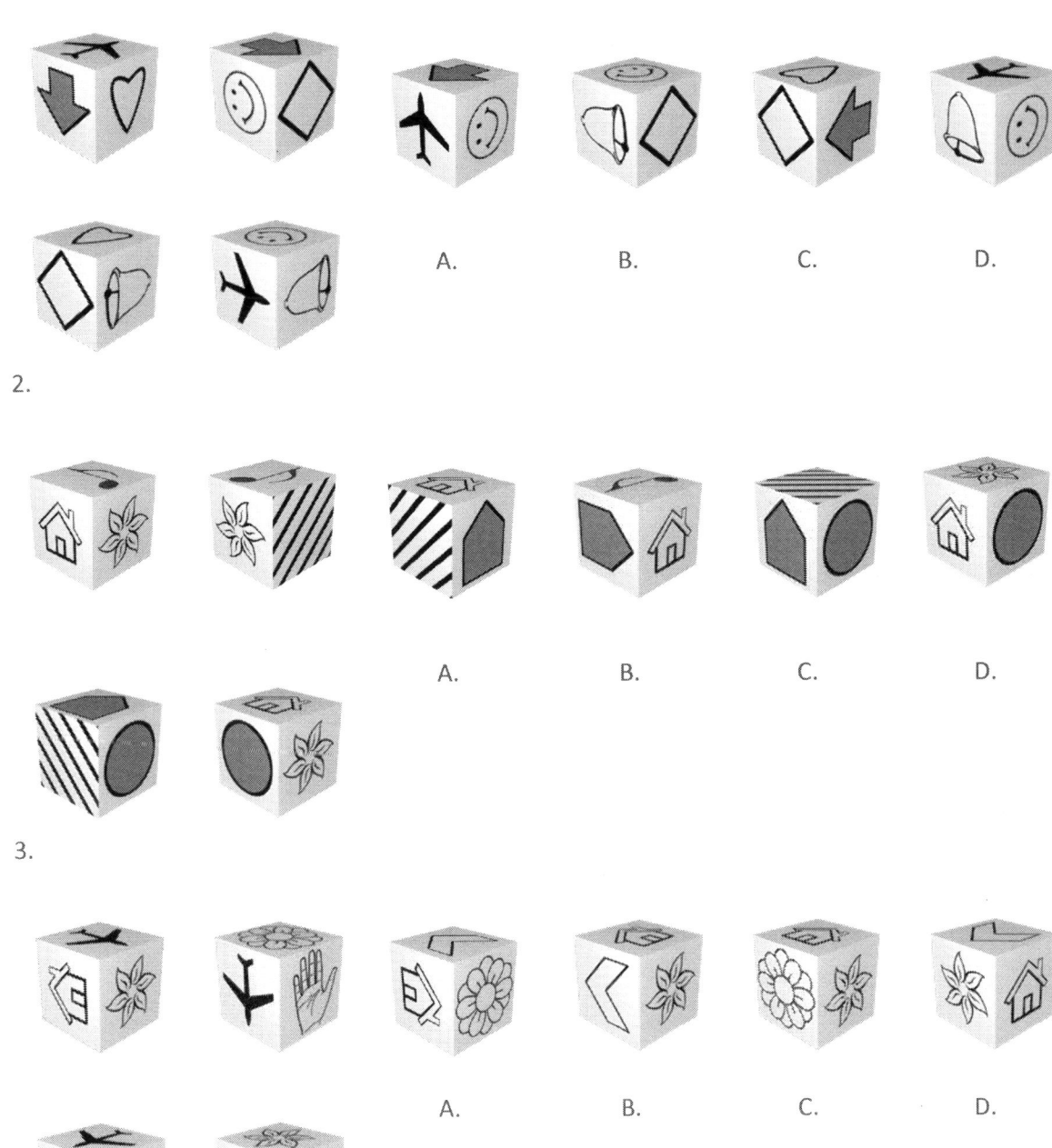

A.          B.          C.          D.

2.

A.          B.          C.          D.

3.

A.          B.          C.          D.

4.

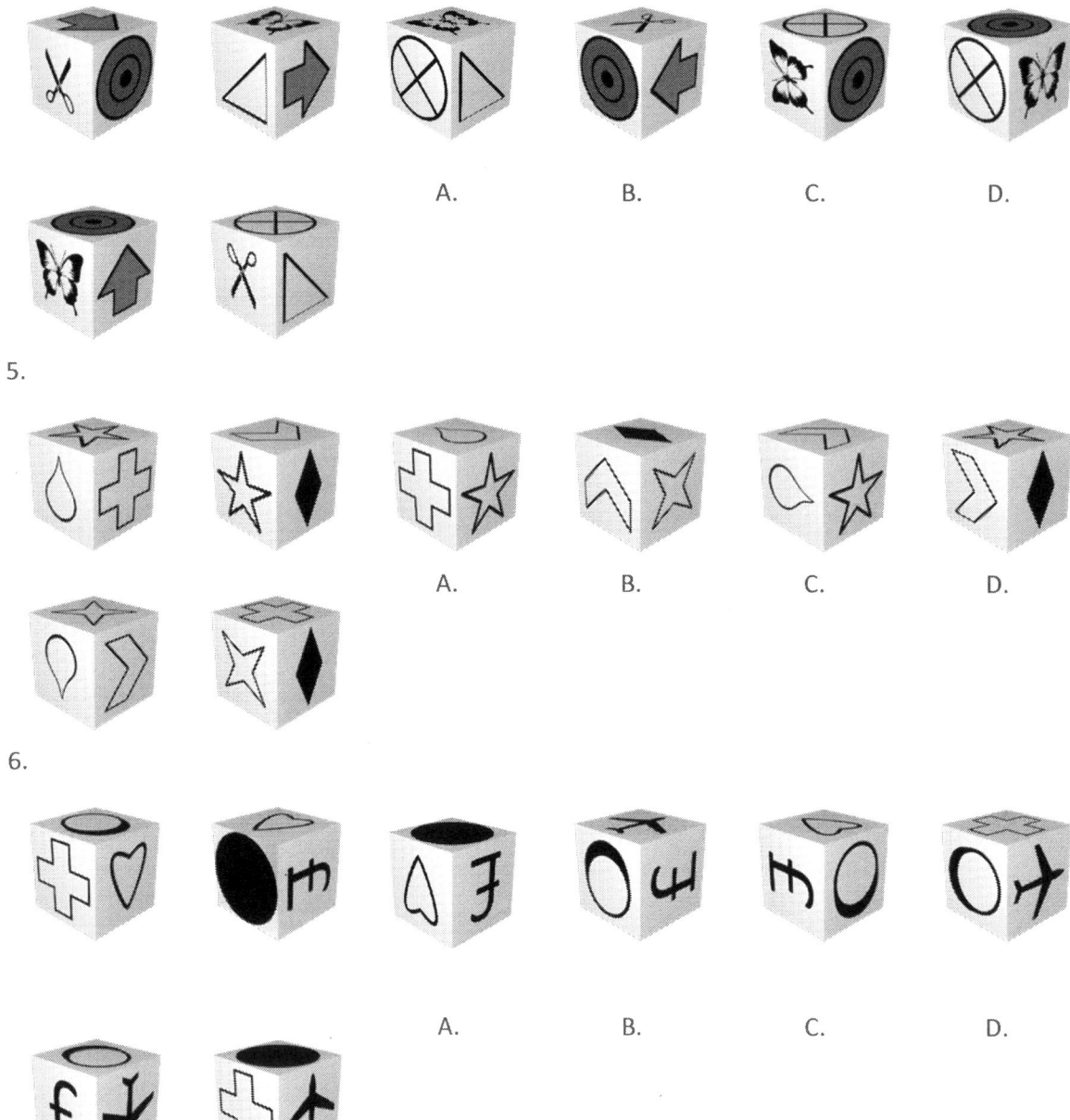

A.　　　B.　　　C.　　　D.

5.

A.　　　B.　　　C.　　　D.

6.

A.　　　B.　　　C.　　　D.

120

7.

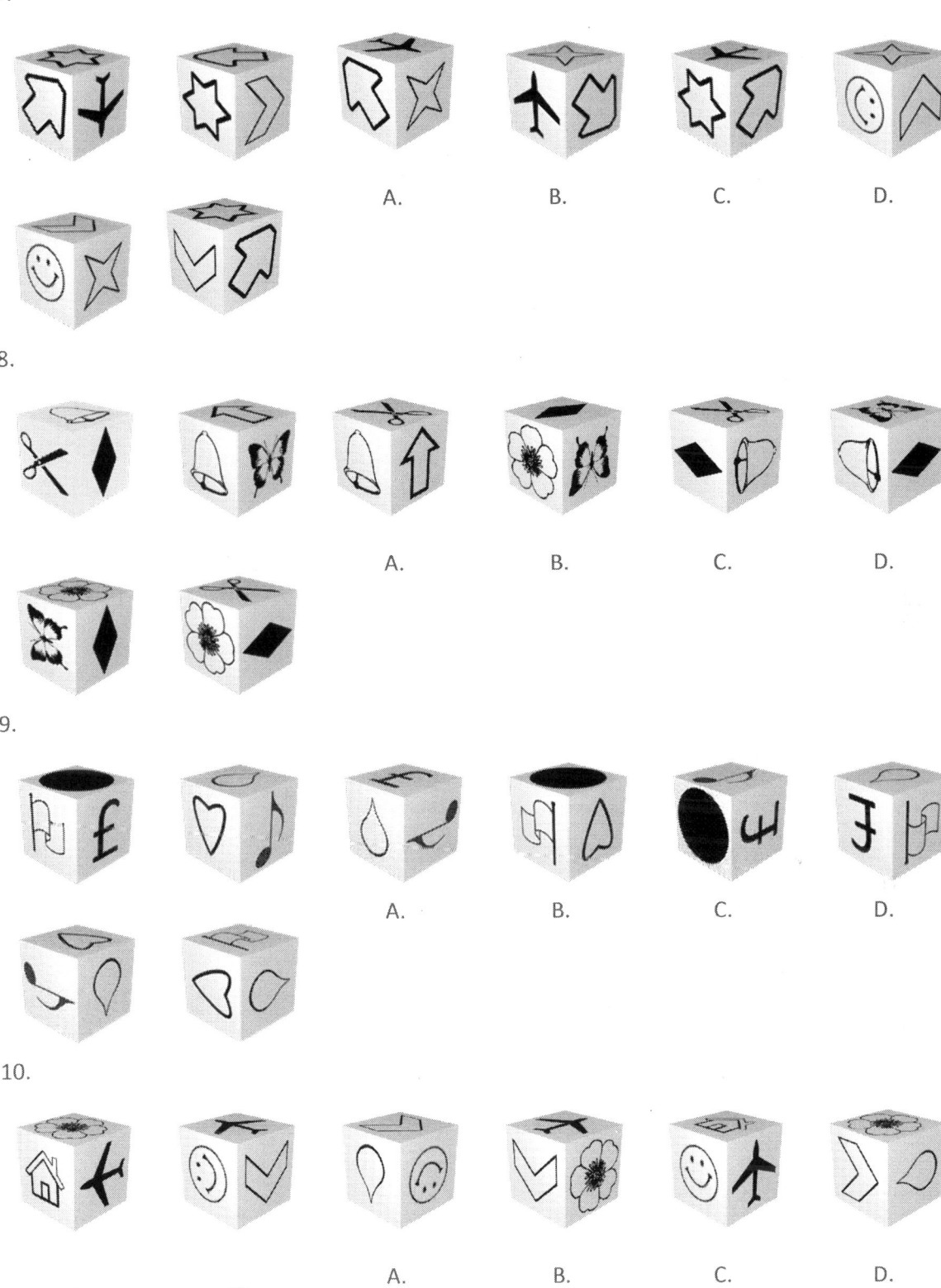

8.

9.

10.

# CHAPTER 30: CUBES TO CUBES (ANALOGIES).

In this type of question a cube is rotated, then a second cube is given.  The second cube must be rotated in **exactly the same way** as the first cube.

To do these questions you need to know that, when a cube is rotated, the four sides along the line of rotation stay in the same direction, while the shapes on the other two sides rotate by 90°for each turn.  They will rotate in the same direction as the cube is moved.  Also, the symbols will remain in the same position relative to each other, that is shapes will continue to point to the same parts of other shapes.  Assume that every side has a different shape on it.

When turned in the direction of the arrows:

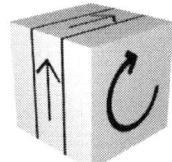

The shapes on the sides with the straight arrows will stay in the same direction. The side with the clock-wise arrow, the shapes will rotate 90°.

Example:

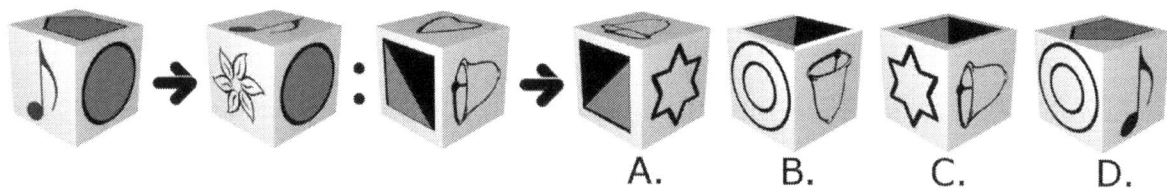

## Answer

Start by looking at the first pair.  The note has moved from the front to the top.  The irregular pentagon has moved to the back of the cube.  So this is the line of rotation and the note has stayed in the same orientation.  The right hand side of the cube will therefore rotate 90°.  This must be the case, even though with a symmetrical shape we cannot see this.

Looking at the second pair:

> In the first pair, the left side shape went to the top, so in the second pair the two-coloured square must go onto the top.  So it cannot be A.
> In the first pair the top shape is not shown on the second cube, so it cannot be D.
> The side on the right, must rotate 90°, therefore, it cannot be C.

So the answer must be B.

# EXERCISE 30

1.

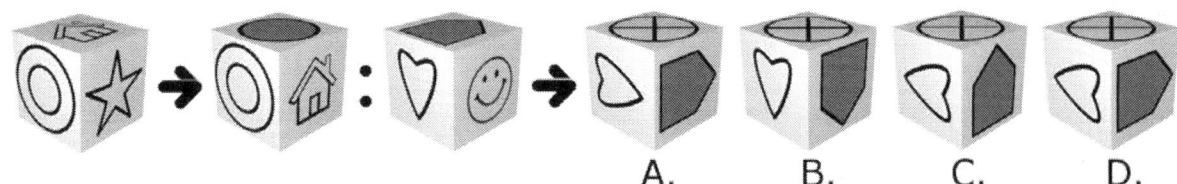

A.    B.    C.    D.

2.

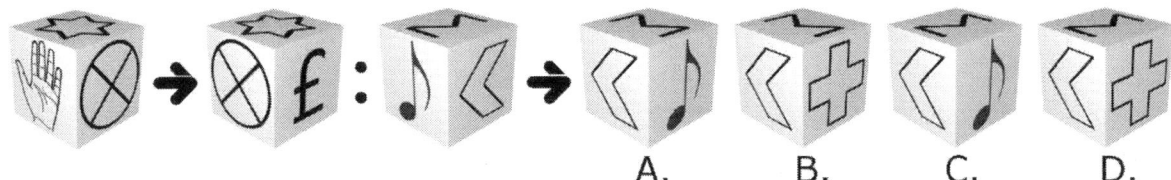

A.    B.    C.    D.

3.

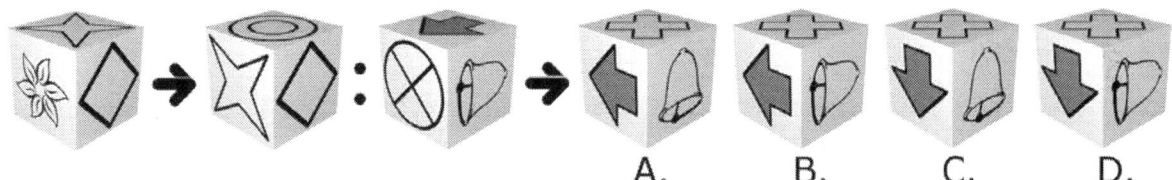

A.    B.    C.    D.

4.

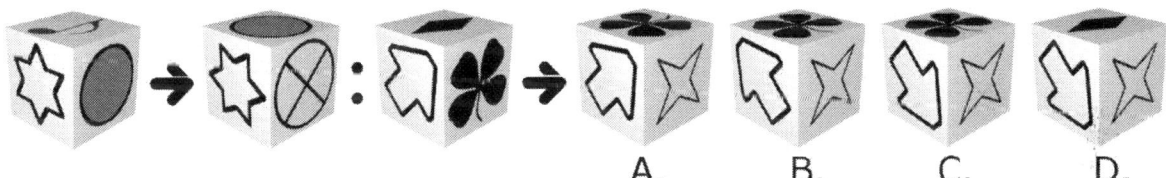

A.    B.    C.    D.

5.

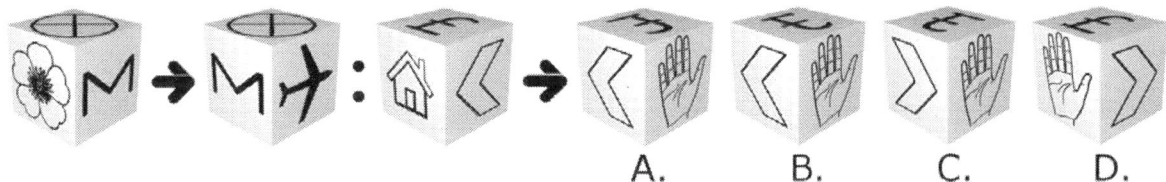

A.    B.    C.    D.

**6.**

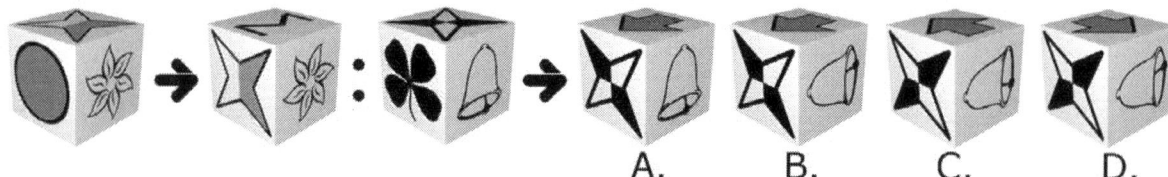

A.    B.    C.    D.

**7.**

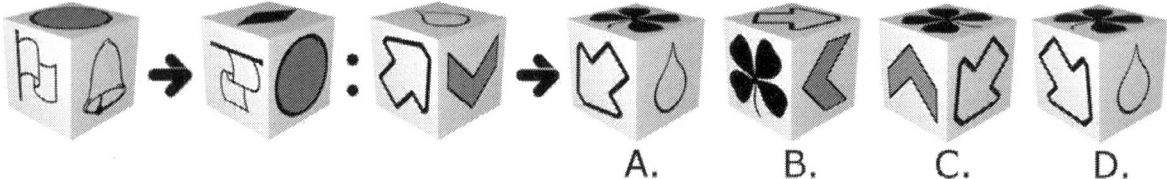

A.    B.    C.    D.

**8.**

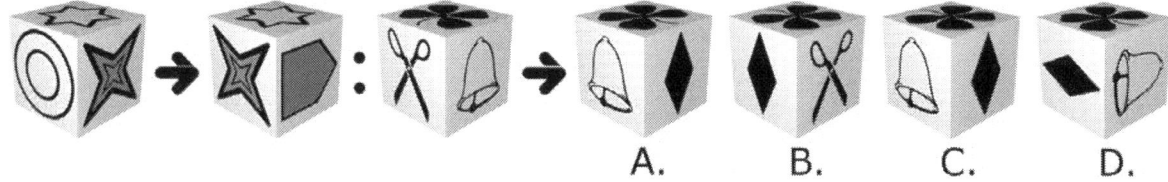

A.    B.    C.    D.

**9.**

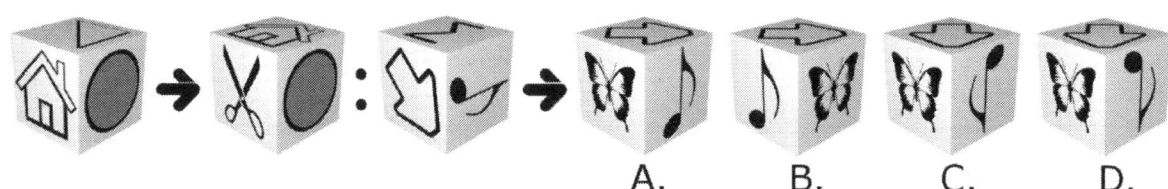

A.    B.    C.    D.

**10.**

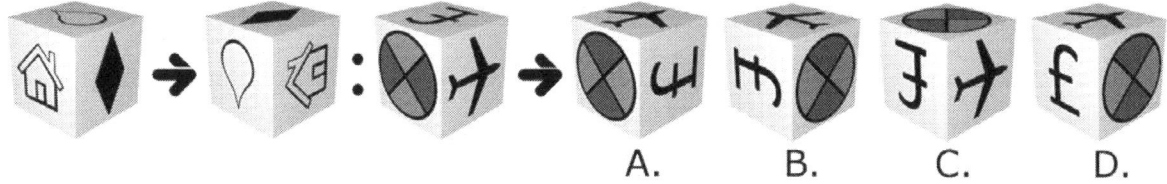

A.    B.    C.    D.

# NOTES

"Any fool can know. The point is to understand."
— **Albert Einstein**

Printed in Great Britain
by Amazon

55255700R00072